# Treating PTSD

*Treating PTSD* presents a comprehensive, compassion-focused cognitive behavioral therapy (CBT) approach that provides therapists with the evidence-based information they need to understand trauma's effects on the mind and body as well as the phases of healing. Chapters offer discussion, practical tools, and interventions that therapists can use with clients suffering from post-traumatic stress disorder (PTSD) to reduce feelings of distress and increase their sense of safety. Readers are introduced to the metaphor of "the valley of the shadow of death" to explain the experience of PTSD; they're also shown how to identify the work they'll need to do as therapists to accompany clients on their healing journey. Two new compassion-focused CBT interventions for trauma processing are also introduced.

**Shirley Porter, MEd, RSW, CCC,** is a registered psychotherapist who has been providing trauma counseling for more than 25 years. She currently works in the counseling department at Fanshawe College and is an adjunct clinical professor at Western University, both in London, Ontario, Canada.

# Treating PTSD
## A Compassion-Focused CBT Approach

**Shirley Porter**

Routledge
Taylor & Francis Group

NEW YORK AND LONDON

First published 2018
by Routledge
711 Third Avenue, New York, NY 10017

and by Routledge
2 Park Square, Milton Park, Abingdon, Oxon, OX14 4RN

*Routledge is an imprint of the Taylor & Francis Group, an informa business*

*Library of Congress Cataloging-in-Publication Data*
Names: Porter, Shirley, 1966– author.
Title: Treating PTSD : a compassion-focused CBT
    approach / Shirley Porter.
Description: New York : Routledge, 2018. | Includes
    bibliographical references and index.
Identifiers: LCCN 2018000124 | ISBN 9781138303324
    (hbk : alk. paper) | ISBN 9781138303331 (pbk : alk. paper) |
    ISBN 9781315123066 (ebk)
Subjects: MESH: Stress Disorders, Post-Traumatic—therapy |
    Cognitive Therapy—methods | Empathy
Classification: LCC RC552.P67 | NLM WM 172.5 |
    DDC 616.85/21—dc23
LC record available at https://lccn.loc.gov/2018000124

ISBN: 978-1-138-30332-4 (hbk)
ISBN: 978-1-138-30333-1 (pbk)
ISBN: 978-1-315-12306-6 (ebk)


Typeset in Galliard
by Apex CoVantage, LLC

# Contents

# Acknowledgments

When I approached Routledge, my intention was *not* to write a second book on PTSD, but rather to find a publisher to pick up my recently released book for PTSD, *Surviving the Valley: Trauma and Beyond*, since the original university press publisher had closed up shop and signed all rights over to me. No one was more surprised than me, when Anna Moore, Senior Editor at Routledge, asked if I would instead be interested in writing a book for therapists, and I found myself responding that I would be interested. Thus, I would like to begin by thanking Anna Moore for suggesting this project and giving me the opportunity to write with Routledge. Thank you also to Nina Guttapalle, Senior Editorial Assistant at Routledge, who answered my questions, polished my work, and guided me through the editorial process.

I would like to acknowledge and thank my clients, who during the past 25 years, have taught me so much and inspired me with their courage, resilience, wisdom, and perseverance. It is through our work together that I became aware of the presence of the Warrior Spirit in each of us, and the need to retrieve and embrace the fragmented parts of the self in order to heal. Thank you, most of all, for allowing me the honor of walking beside you during parts of your healing journey. What a tremendous privilege that has been and continues to be.

Thank you to my grad students who have challenged me to be a better teacher, supervisor, and clinician with your questions, curiosity, and appreciation of the theoretical and practical aspects of therapy. Because of you I have been challenged to break down and verbalize the how and whys of what I do as a clinician, which has required me to more deeply examine my practice, and to learn how to explain it in ways that are meaningful to my "audience", whether that audience is clients, grad students, the community, or my colleagues. Thanks for this. Your enthusiasm and motivation to learn always makes my heart smile.

Thank you to my coworkers and colleagues at Fanshawe College—many of whom are my dearest friends. The only reason we are able to do the difficult work we do, is because of the incredible team that we have. You are a source of support, guidance, caring, and compassion. How grateful I am for the blessing each of you is. A special thanks goes out to my colleague and friend, Dr. Catherine Miller, who was once again kind enough to proof this manuscript prior to submission.

Thank you to the members of my Bookless Book Club. You are my "tribe" and my people. You are an important part of my self-care plan. You are a treasured source of joy and friendship in my life—you provide much needed balance.

And finally, I offer my heartfelt thanks to my family. Brian, Marcus, and Aleisha—your love and support mean the world to me. Thanks for your understanding and for picking up the slack while I spent my summer vacation and many weekends, working on this manuscript. You continue to be the greatest blessing of all. I love you to *all the moons*—and back.

# Preface

When I began doing trauma counseling, more than 25 years ago, I hoped to become an "expert" in the field. To me that meant that by this time in my career I would have *the answers* and be totally confident in my work. I realize now that this was naïve. I certainly do not have *all*, or even *most*, of the answers. I've realized instead, that answers lie within individuals, and instead of *providing* answers, my role is to support my clients and to help facilitate discovery of their own truths. I've replaced the desire for certainty, with a commitment to ongoing curiosity and learning. Each day, I learn something new—whether it is through my work with clients, teaching or supervising students, talking with colleagues, or participating in professional development. There is much to learn in this field and I am grateful for the many teachers I've had along the way.

My journey in this field has brought me to a place where I have embraced what I will call a compassion-focused CBT approach to treating PTSD. This happened as a result of having observed in my clinical practice that compassion is essential in healing from trauma—compassion from the therapist as a foundation of the therapeutic alliance, and the development of self-compassion on the part of the client.

My theoretical background is eclectic. For me, that means I start with a client-centered basis. From there, over the years, I have incorporated a number of theoretical approaches and interventions in my work, including: Cognitive Behavioral Therapy (CBT), Brief Solution Focused Therapy, Eye Movement Desensitization and Reprocessing (EMDR), Dialectical Behavioral Therapy (DBT), Relational-Cultural Therapy (RCT), Imagery Rescripting and Reprocessing Therapy (IRRT), and Motivational Interviewing (MI). The reason that I have studied and incorporated aspects of so many different approaches into my practice is because during the course of my career, I have come to believe that one theoretical approach to treating PTSD will not be *the* answer for *all* clients. Furthermore, I truly believe that in doing trauma work with our clients, the onus is on us to be flexible and adaptable so that we fit the individual needs of our clients, rather than expecting our clients to fit our preferred approaches.

Initially, I found working with PTSD to be confusing and a bit messy. The complexity of it was something I couldn't totally get my mind around. I realized that if I was feeling overwhelmed in trying to understand PTSD, then likely my clients were too. Trauma occurs in situations where a person is often fearful and not in control, and thus, healing cannot occur in a similar context. I needed to find ways to demystify the experience of trauma, PTSD, and the healing process—to make it easier to understand—to make the complex, understandable. This I needed to do so that my clients could be informed and willing collaborators in a transparent therapeutic process. My clients responded positively to the use of practical examples and metaphors, which I will share with you. Also, having found that for some of my clients, EMDR and traditional CBT were not a fit, I felt compelled to dig deeper and piece together another intervention for trauma processing, which would better fit their needs. Hence, I developed a Compassion-Focused CBT (CFCBT) intervention that combines components of CBT, EMDR, and body awareness, with an emphasis on mobilizing clients' inherent wisdom and resiliency. This approach has met with much success among my clients. My intention is to share it with you in the hopes that you too will find it to be a helpful intervention to add to your toolkit.

My intention in writing this book is to provide practical information to inform your understanding of trauma and how to operationalize this information in the counseling process. It has been my experience that while many counselors, both new and experienced, understand the theory of trauma treatment, they want to know what it actually looks like in terms of the intricacies of working with clients and to have access to tools that they can use to make the counseling process more accessible to their clients. This is what I hope to offer.

To further clarify my context, I will share with you that not only has PTSD been a professional interest of mine. It is also an incredibly personal one. Over the years, I have sat in "both chairs", as therapist and as client. As a result of childhood trauma, I have had to deal with the impact of activated PTSD symptoms at different points in my life. Every therapeutic tool and intervention I offer, I have considered extensively from both chairs—and my own clinical and personal experiences definitely inform my understanding and approach to trauma.

# Introduction

Trauma work is atrocity work.

—Sandra Butler (1992)

As a new therapist in the early 1990s, I had the opportunity to hear feminist activist and author, Sandra Butler speak on the topic of childhood sexual abuse and abuse against women. The statement above is one that I have never forgotten. It helped to prepare me for what I was going to face in this work. It reminded me that as therapist, I had to go in equipped and strong, in order to be able to bear witness, and to provide a setting and therapeutic relationship that could contain my clients' reactions (and my own) to the horrors they had survived. At first it was intimidating and sometimes downright frightening for me as a therapist. After many years of doing this work, however, I have learned how to prepare my clients and myself for this journey through the valley of the shadow of death, where for PTSD survivors, experienced historical atrocities continue to live within a context of timelessness.

Trauma work is, at its core, atrocity work. In this work, we will sometimes bear witness to horrors we could never have imagined even in our worst nightmares. It is in the details of these stories where our clients' deepest wounds were inflicted. Our clients have been changed by their experiences. We too will be changed by bearing witness. Traumatic stories invariably involve tremendous loss at different levels. They are stories of vulnerability, powerlessness, and despair. Some are stories of the cruelty and betrayal by others. Some are about accidents or choices made that had unintended consequences. And still others are about the cold reality of cause and effect. At the base of these stories, however, often hidden from direct sight, lay a tremendous resiliency, strength, and warrior spirit. It is within this inconspicuous base where our clients will find the courage and strength required for their healing journey. As therapists, it is this resiliency that we need to continue to keep our eyes on as we journey with clients through their version of the valley of the shadow of death. It is this focus that will prevent us, both clients and therapists, from being consumed by the despair that permeates parts of this valley.

## The Valley of the Shadow of Death

You might recognize the term "the valley of the shadow of death" from a religious text. It is part of the 23rd Psalm, which begins with the words, "The lord is my shepherd" . . . I want to take a moment to be clear that use of the valley of the shadow of death metaphor does not require any religious or spiritual leaning on your part or on the part of your clients. This metaphor was chosen because of its power and fit when it comes to describing the experience of PTSD and phases of the healing journey.

The valley of the shadow of death is a dark and desolate place. It exists in the shadow of actual or symbolic deaths. The valley becomes the primary residence of those with active PTSD. It is a place of felt isolation and timelessness. The darkness plays tricks with one's senses and causes fragmented sensory and affective reliving of the most painful experiences of one's life—in a seemingly endless loop. It can make one forget that light exists at all. Hope is elusive. The disorientation and despair that prevail can cause even the strongest person to forget who they are and to doubt their sanity. There are no marked pathways out of the valley—each survivor will have to forge their own.

In my first book, *Surviving the Valley: Trauma and Beyond* (Porter, 2016), I used this metaphor to explain PTSD and the phases of healing to survivors of trauma, their loved ones, and the professionals who support them. In the context of this book, I will use it to explain our experiences as therapists as we, ourselves, prepare to enter the valley to be with our clients, help them to assess injuries, gather supports, prepare for the climb, and accompany them on their journey to safety.

## Introduction to the Concept of the Warrior Spirit

When one experiences PTSD, trauma memories are fragmented into different sensory pieces because the whole is too much for the mind and body to process in its entirety. High levels of neuro-hormones released during the traumatic experience can inhibit and impair different areas of brain function. Just as the sensations and remembrances of trauma are fragmented when PTSD occurs, so too is the sense of self.

Trauma work is about reclaiming, accepting, and even embracing the parts of the self that were injured during trauma—those parts that often, in desperation, one tries to cut off or abandon, because they were associated with unbearable physical, emotional, and/or spiritual pain. Remembering all of the details of the trauma is not necessary, but we do need to bring home the injured parts of the self, in order for healing to occur.

I have found that the Warrior Spirit is a powerful metaphor that can be used to identify, name, reframe, and mobilize trauma survivors' resiliency in the service of healing. It can shift clients' views and experiences of the self—from a sense of powerlessness, ineffectiveness, and despair—to one of power, strength, resiliency, and hope. (For those who don't find this terminology a fit, it can be referred to instead as the "wise, strong, and compassionate part of the self"). The Warrior Spirit is the inherent strength and wisdom that resides in each of us. PTSD can cause one to forget or overlook this truth. It is this Warrior Spirit that will sustain our clients with the courage, strength, wisdom, and determination needed to find their way out of the valley and into wholeness.

Rothschild (2000) has noted that dual awareness is a prerequisite for trauma processing. The Warrior Spirit provides a name and concrete persona for the part of the self that will be engaging in dual awareness during trauma processing, in order to monitor and ensure safety, and braking as necessary. The Warrior Spirit is not just our higher self and not just our rational mind. It is a combination of our fiercest and most courageous survival instincts, our inherent body wisdom, and our rational and emotional minds, which is able to create an integrated narrative of all the experiences of our life— including trauma. It is from this internal locus of tremendous strength and wisdom that fragmented parts of the self can be reclaimed and reconnected, and healing can occur.

In order to assist clients with connecting to the Warrior Spirit within them, I will typically ask if they recall that part of them that quietly observes in those moments when they are struggling with overwhelming distress and/or flashbacks. The Warrior Spirit might make observations such as, "I'm really losing it here", or the like. Most of my clients can relate to this. It is then that I explain dual awareness, and how we need to help them to become more aware of and connected to this calm, internal strength within them, that can help anchor them in the present and knows how to comfort them, if they allow it.

A warrior has many roles—not only in battle, but also in times of peace. Warriors have a keen survival instinct. They prepare and equip themselves for upcoming challenges. They have deep, sometimes incomprehensible, reservoirs of strength. They are willing to traverse those shadow places where atrocities have occurred. Even in the face of fear, they persist. In times of peace, when the battle is over, they gather up the innocents, and ensure they are cared for. They rebuild, repair, and strengthen. They are guardians of peace, safety, and freedom.

Within the valley of the shadow of death, the Warrior Spirit seeks out the parts of the self that were left behind during trauma—those parts that were sacrificed, hidden, or abandoned because their pain and weight were too much to bear at the time. Within each flashback we find one of those sacrificed parts of the self.

The Warrior Spirit's courage and strength are combined with profound gentleness and compassion. To help our clients to heal and experience the wholeness of the self, we need to support them as they collect the sacrificed parts of the self and restore them back into their bodies and minds. This is the role of the Warrior Spirit. Whether it is returning to the terrified and sobbing 8-year-old self who had just witnessed the abuse of a sibling, the 23-year-old shocked and horrified soldier-self who witnessed an IED kill his best friends, or the 35-year-old frightened and despairing father-self who has witnessed the death of his family in a car accident—the Warrior Spirit is willing to expend the effort to find these parts of the self, embrace them with compassion, and welcome them back into wholeness. The Warrior Spirit, through connection with the survival, emotional, and conscious rational parts of the brain, is able to retrieve and accompany the abandoned parts of the self to the safety of the present moment—forever removed from continued reliving of the trauma.

It is important that our clients understand that distancing from parts of the self, in order to survive, should not be judged in a negative way. It is often an unfortunate necessity of survival. It was this adaptability and ingenuity that allowed them to survive. And rather than the shame and frustration that are sometimes attached to these abandoned parts of the self, they deserve our appreciation and respect. Sometimes the sacrificed parts of the self feel a need for forgiveness, and if so, the Warrior can provide it in an unconditional and loving way.

I remind clients that it is their Warrior Spirit that allowed them to survive the atrocities they have lived through—reminding them of this incredible part of themselves that they've likely forgotten in the fog of trauma. I also reassure them that their Warrior Spirit will be there to guide them, comfort them, and give them strength in their journey out of the valley. Thus far, I've had only had a few clients for whom the concept of a Warrior Spirit isn't a fit. Generally, I have found that even the most traumatized and symptomatic clients have embraced it and appeared to find renewed hope and a change in perspective regarding how they saw themselves.

Anna[1] had a history of severe and prolonged childhood trauma (i.e., physical, emotional, sexual abuse). She struggled with self-injury and addictions. She was chronically suicidal and had attempted suicide on several occasions. During the first few times we met, she barely spoke above a whisper and would never look me in the eyes. I recall one of the first times she looked at me when I was speaking with her. It was after she had confided in me about some of her childhood trauma experiences, and I spoke to her about the courage, strength, and wisdom of her Warrior Spirit. I remember how she looked in my eyes searchingly, as she thought about what I was saying. For the first time, I saw hope in her eyes, and a light. This concept did not make her life immediately better, but I noticed that when she spoke about her struggles in subsequent sessions, she talked about getting through them by leaning into her Warrior Spirit. She also said that through her Warrior Spirit she was able to promise herself that she would keep fighting to heal.

## Therapist Preparation

As therapists who choose to do trauma work, we need to be appropriately prepared and equipped before embarking on the journey into the valley. A client-centered approach is necessary to provide the context in which client safety and a strong therapeutic alliance can be developed. However, much more is needed. Therapists who do this work require a clear understanding of how trauma affects the mind and body, and the ability to communicate this information to our clients in ways that they can understand—recognizing that in the throes of traumatic stress reactions, memory and attention can be significantly compromised. Thus, the information we provide must be brief, easy-to-understand, and presented in a manner that is meaningful to our clients. We also need to have developed the knowledge and clinical skills specific to trauma work. Trauma work is fundamentally different from the other types of counseling work we do. The clinical knowledge and skills that we use in helping clients with more generic psychosocial issues in their lives will not be sufficient, nor would they provide the level of safety necessary. Therefore, before embarking on this journey, we must be adequately equipped in terms of trauma-specific therapeutic training and skill development.

We need to be mindful that trauma work can be life-threatening work for our clients. The valley can be steep and the climb, treacherous for some. This is because the despair and levels of distress that may be activated can, at their worst, push clients toward thoughts of suicide. Clients need to know what to expect. The have a right to know that this work can be very hard on them physically, emotionally, and cognitively. It is our job to assist them in becoming appropriately equipped for this journey—with effective tools, skills, supports, and resources, prior to embarking. This needs to be done *before* we actually start the climb, i.e., the work of trauma processing. Additionally, in order to ensure clients are active and willing participants in the therapeutic relationship and process, all aspects of our work together must be transparent and consented to by the client. Informed consent is imperative. Some clients will decide to stop at a safe plateau, i.e., the distress reduction and stabilization phase, and if this is the case, we need to respect their decision. Trauma work cannot be successful if clients are coerced or pressured against their will. A major component of the experience of trauma involves powerlessness and lack of control/choice. Thus, pressing someone to keep climbing and to revisit trauma under such circumstances, when they don't have the energy, strength, or will to do so, is likely to lead to retraumatization.

Therapist self-care in doing this work is also mandatory. The work can feel toxic on some days. We thus need to develop ongoing strategies and supports to maintain our well-being as well as protect ourselves, and to heal when we are injured by some of the atrocities to which we bear witness.

In summary, prior to starting to work with clients in the valley, we need to:

- Be educated as to how traumatic events can affect the mind and body, during and after trauma (including in cases of complex trauma) in order to understand how individuals can arrive in the valley and what it is like to find oneself there;
- Operationalize those trauma-informed and culturally-sensitive values and considerations, that we as therapists can espouse in our practice, to support a strong and respectful therapeutic alliance;

- Know what types of injuries our clients may have sustained, and have access to the tools and resources to appropriately assess and address them;
- Be able to assist our clients in developing resources, tools, and supports that they can use to manage distress;
- Have developed the knowledge and skills necessary to provide evidence-based trauma-processing interventions;
- Be able to communicate all of the above information to our clients in easy to understand language so that they will be informed, voluntary collaborators in a transparent and respectful therapeutic process; and
- Actively maintain our own self-care and tend to any injuries we might sustain, as we guide and support our clients' journeys through the valley of the shadow of death.

In the next several chapters, I will attempt to convey to you what I have learned in each of these areas in my work with youth and adult clients. It's taken me many years to gather the understanding and tools that I will share with you. My hope is that in sharing this information, you will be saved some time, and will find that you too are more effective in doing this work.

## Note

1 The client's name has been changed and identifying information excluded.

# Part I

# Therapist Preparation for Trauma Work

# 1   A Brief History of Our Understanding of Trauma

> In traumatic neurosis the operative cause of the illness is not the trifling physi-cal injury but the affect of fright—the psychical trauma. . . . Any experience which calls up distressing affects—such as those of fright, anxiety, shame or physical pain—may act as a trauma of this kind.
>
> —Breuer and Freud (1957, pp. 5–6)

In the above quote, Breuer and Freud provide one of the earliest definitions of potentially traumatic events, and how such highly distressing emotional events can cause *injury to the mind*, which can result in what we now know of as PTSD. This proposed explanation for the source of traumatic stress reactions, forms the basis of our understanding today. In the century since it was proposed, evidence has mounted to support and expand our understand-ing of the characteristics of events that are more likely to result in traumatic stress reactions among survivors, as well as how different areas of the mind are affected when a person is suffering from PTSD.

Prior to entering the valley, we need to get our historical bearings. It can be helpful to have an understanding as to how the concept of trauma and treatment interventions have evolved over the past century. Thus, what I would like to do is provide an overview of some of the key developments of our understanding in this area and to point out how individuals suffering from severe traumatic stress reactions were perceived and, consequently, responded to, by professionals at different points in history. It will become apparent that in the not so distant past, trauma survivors were regularly subjected to stigma, minimization, accusations of deception and weak moral character, and in some cases, brutal and cruel retraumatizing interventions used by the medical community. While we might be tempted to look down on past professional responses to trauma, we would be wise not to fool ourselves into believing that we have somehow overcome the stigma, minimization, denial, and tendency to blame the victim that continue to be rampant in many parts of society today. We will also review the current prevalence rates of trauma among civilian, first responder, and military populations, to remind us that people from all walks of life end up in the valley, though for some the risk is increased.

## Studies of Hysteria

In the late 1800s, Charcot, a French neurologist, was renowned for his lectures and demonstrations at the famous Salpêtrière Hospital where he worked and taught. During the course of his career, he worked with individuals suffering from "hysteria" (which would later be renamed post-traumatic stress disorder), and he was one of the first to describe typical symptomology. He focused on reporting physical symptoms, which included such things as: "special seizures", vomiting, partial blindness, paralyses, pain, and sensory impairment (Charcot, 1889). He believed that cases of hysteria were very rare, and in fact it was more likely that physicians would encounter women who were faking their symptoms. (It was believed that hysteria occurred predominantly in women since its cause was thought to be related to the ovaries). His perception of patients presenting with these symptoms is clear within this quote: "one finds himself sometimes admiring the amazing craft, sagacity, and perseverance, which women, under the influence of this great neurosis, will put in play for the purpose of deception—especially when a physician is to be the victim" (p. 230). The emphasis at this point in time appeared to be on noting minute details regarding symptoms and ensuring, through extensive surveillance, that patients were not faking their symptoms in order to gain attention. Charcot treated hysteria using hypnosis.

Around the same time, Breuer and Freud also noted their observations of the symptoms described previously. Additionally, they introduced the concept of dissociation, as related to "abnormal states of consciousness" (Breuer & Freud, 1957). They were among the first to recognize that, for many of their patients, a traumatic event in childhood was connected to persistent symptoms. Breuer and Freud also had a more positive perception of their patients: "among hysterics may be found people of the clearest intellect, strongest will, greatest character and highest critical power" (Breuer & Freud, 1957, p. 13). They proposed that hysterical symptoms would disappear once patients were able to describe in words their experiences and accompanying affect. Thus, psychoanalysis as a treatment for hysteria, often in conjunction with hypnosis, came into being.

Freud attempted to trace the specific source of trauma among several cases of adult hysteria. He identified the common denominator as being a history of childhood sexual abuse, sexual assault, and/or incest. He presented his findings in a paper called, *The Aetiology of Hysteria*, which was originally published in 1896 (Freud, 1962). A short time later, however, he retracted and revised his theory, reattributing the underlying cause of hysteria to fictional "phantasies" of repressed sexual desires rather than actual childhood sexual abuse experiences (Freud, 1954). Thus, although Freud had initially listened to and believed his clients' accounts of childhood sexual trauma, at some point he made a decision not only to disbelieve them, but also to turn their narratives of abuse back on them, and in effect blamed his patients' repressed desires for being the source of their illness.

In a series of lectures at Harvard, Janet (1920) provided a more comprehensive overview of the physiological, emotional, cognitive, and behavioral symptoms of hysteria. These included: amnesia; reenactment of disturbing or feared events during sleep; dissociation; memory, problem-solving, and concentration impairments; constriction of scope of conscious awareness; emotional indifference and depression; and somatic complaints. He recognized that external sensory experiences that were somehow related to a past "dreaded" experience could elicit symptoms, even after years without symptoms. He viewed physical symptoms as a representation and acting out of painful emotion. Janet attributed his patients' susceptibility to these symptoms as an indicator of moral weakness and psychological instability. Like his mentor, Charcot, Janet also utilized hypnosis as a primary means of treating hysteria.

## From Shell-Shock and Combat Exhaustion to PTSD

The next time a spotlight was placed on what we now know of as PTSD was during World War I (WWI). Early in this war, physicians noticed a growing number of psychological casualties. In an effort to explain the source of these injuries, Captain Charles S. Myers, who as medical doctor treated injured soldiers using hypnosis, described three cases in great detail. He traced the origins of the symptoms to the effects of "shell shock":

> these cases . . . appear to constitute a definite class among others arising from the effects of shell shock. The shells in question appear to have burst with considerable noise, scattering much dust. . . . It is therefore difficult to understand why hearing should be practically unaffected, and the dissociated "complex" be confined to the senses of sight, smell, and taste (and to memory). The close relation of these cases to those of "hysteria" appears fairly certain.
>
> (Myers, 1915, p. 320)

In England and France during WWI, the attitudes and treatment of soldiers suffering from shell shock varied greatly depending on the ideologies of treating physicians. The primary goal, however, was always to get these soldiers back to the front lines as soon as possible. Some were treated with hypnosis and "suggestive therapy" in an environment of quiet and rest. Others were treated much more aggressively using electricity with "firm psychotherapy" (Bogousslavsky & Tatu, 2013). What follows is part of an account by Dr. Yealland, a physician in London, England, of his treatment of a soldier, a veteran of many battles, who was suffering from mutism:

> Many attempts have been made to cure him. He has been strapped down in a chair for twenty minutes at a time, when strong electricity was applied to his neck and throat; lighted cigarette ends had been applied

to the tip of his tongue and "hot plates" had been placed at the back of his mouth. Hypnotism had been tried. But all these methods proved to be unsuccessful in restoring his voice. . . .

In the evening he was taken to the electrical room, the blinds drawn, the lights turned out, and the doors leading into the room were locked and the keys removed. The only light perceptible was that from the resistance bulbs of the battery. Placing the pad electrode on the lumbar spines and attaching the long pharyngeal electrode, I said to him, "You will not leave this room until you are talking as well as you ever did: no, not before." The mouth was kept open by means of a tongue depressor; a strong faradic current was applied to the posterior wall of the pharynx, and with this stimulus he jumped backwards, detaching the wires from the battery. "Remember, you must behave as becomes the hero I expect you to be", I said.

(Yealland, 1918, pp. 6–8)

It should be noted that during WWI, the British Army did not accept the concept of shell shock as a defense for desertion (Babington, 1997). Sympathy and compassion were often non-existent, while suspicion of cowardice and malingering was prevalent. Consequently, 346 British and Commonwealth soldiers were executed for alleged cowardice or desertion, many of whom were likely suffering from traumatic stress injuries (Crocq & Crocq, 2000).

American psychiatrist, Thomas W. Salmon, visited British hospitals, prior to the U.S. entering WWI. His intention was to gain an understanding of shell shock and how it was being treated, so that he could better prepare the U.S. military medical response to these psychological casualties. During his visit he noted that soldiers diagnosed with war neurosis were generally stigmatized within the military and society, and if they did not recover within a short period of time, were certified as "insane" and sent off to their local asylum (Salmon, 1917). He indicated that he didn't agree with this, and contrasted it with his own experience at home, "in most states our state hospitals enjoy a reputation which would no more stigmatize insane soldiers than it does their sisters and daughters when they require treatment" (Salmon, 1917, p. 16). As a result of his observations in Britain, he developed a comprehensive and detailed plan for treating American soldiers. Additionally, he suggested that the military immediately: allocate resources for the care of soldiers who would suffer from shell shock; implement intensive screening to prevent those more likely to develop nervous disorders from enlisting in the Army; and observe soldiers during their training to identify those more vulnerable to mental and nervous disorders. He emphasized that treatment must be available immediately at the front lines, and only if this was unsuccessful should soldiers be evacuated to the psychiatric hospitals located on military bases. Dr. Salmon's recommendations for treatment, which focused on proximity, immediacy, and expectancy, came to be known by the acronym PIE (Jones & Wessely, 2003).

In summary, soldiers with acute stress reactions were treated immediately at the front lines, with the expectation that they would be returning back to their combat duties. Persuasive psychotherapy was utilized (Crocq & Crocq, 2000). Dr. Salmon's recommendations were accepted, and this led to a more understanding attitude toward those suffering from shell-shock, as evidenced by the fact that no American soldiers were executed for desertion, and by the development of a treatment approach which demonstrated an underlying belief that rest, safety, reassurance, and encouragement were vital components of the recovery process (Babington, 1997). This remained the first-line of treatment for soldiers suffering with acute stress reactions throughout WWI and the wars that followed.

In World War II (WWII), shell shock was more accurately renamed "combat exhaustion" (Swank & Marchand, 1946). Throughout this war, the American military used aggressive pre-screening measures to proactively weed out anyone who might be considered vulnerable to psychological injury in combat due to character and personality defects (Pols & Oak, 2007). They soon learned, however, that predicting who would suffer from psychological injuries, based on their current screening efforts, was not an exact science. During this war,

> more than 800,000 men were classified as 4-F (unfit for military service) due to psychiatric reasons . . . (and) America's armed forces lost an additional 504,000 men from the fighting effort due to psychiatric collapse.
> (Grossman, 2009, p. 43)

Following WWII, evidence emerged which demonstrated that psychological injuries in the field were not the result of character flaw or some sort of personal deficit, but were rather a predictable consequence that would affect the majority of soldiers who faced the atrocities of war for a prolonged period of time:

> Combat exhaustion may appear in as few as fifteen or twenty days or in as many as forty or fifty days. . . . One thing alone seems to be certain: Practically all infantry soldiers suffer from a neurotic reaction eventually if they are subjected to the stress of modern combat continuously and long enough . . . an occasional soldier seems capable of withstanding combat for an inordinate length of time . . . No personality type dominates this small "abnormal" group, but it is interesting that aggressive psychopathic personalities . . . stand out.
> (Swank & Marchand, 1946, pp. 243–244)

After WWII, the U.S. Department of Veteran's Affairs began building hospitals that were affiliated with medical schools in order to provide the best care to injured veterans. It was through these hospitals that WWII veterans suffering from PTSD began receiving psychotherapy (Pols & Oak, 2007).

In Vietnam, "(t)he prevalence of delayed and chronic PTSD, in spite of the careful prevention of psychiatric casualties . . . was a rude awakening" (Crocq & Crocq, 2000). It was due to the activism of Vietnam veterans that "posttraumatic stress disorder" was finally introduced into the DSM-III (APA, 1980).

One potential contributing factor for the increased prevalence of PTSD among Vietnam veterans as compared to those in WWI and WWII has to do with the firing rates. A mass interview of WWII veterans indicated that on average, no more than 15–25% of soldiers ever fired their weapons—which was attributed to the inherent mental block that human beings have to killing another person (Marshall, 1947). Through operant and classical conditioning techniques, which continue to be used today (Grossman, 2009), the firing rate in Vietnam reached 83% (Glenn, 1987). While a success for the military, this training appears to have contributed to the high rate of psychological injuries among these veterans. As one of my clients, a veteran who served as a sniper in combat zones within the Middle East once said to me, "They taught me how to kill, but they never taught me how to live with it." Other potential explanations for the increased prevalence of PTSD among this group of veterans include the lack of unit cohesion, in that most of these soldiers entered and left their time in combat as individuals rather than as groups, and that they were subjected to stigma and hostility upon their return to the U.S. (Pols & Oak, 2007).

Vietnam veterans suffering from PTSD have been treated using pharmacological interventions, as well as individual and group psychotherapeutic approaches (Pols & Oak, 2007). Currently, the U.S. Department of Veterans Affairs provides over 200 specialized treatment programs, as well as evidence-based psychotherapeutic care for veterans suffering from PTSD (e.g., Cognitive Processing Therapy, Prolonged Exposure Therapy) (U.S. Department of Veterans Affairs, 2017).

## Domestic and Sexual Violence

During the 1970s women's movement, the realities of domestic and sexual violence in the daily lives of women came to the fore, and with it, came the realization that the majority of individuals in the U.S. who were suffering from PTSD were not soldiers returning from war, but rather, women and children who lived lives of captivity within their own homes (Herman, 1992).

Prior to 1969, studies on rape were focused on protecting the accused. After that time, they began to more appropriately focus on how to protect and support rape survivors (Chappell, Geis, & Fogarty, 1974). Burgess and Holmstrom (1974) introduced the "Rape Trauma Syndrome". They defined Rape Trauma Syndrome as a two-phase reaction, with somatic, psychological, and behavioral components that occur in response to rape or attempted rape. The first phase is characterized by disorganization in a woman's life following the rape, which includes significant physical symptomology, and a dominant feeling of fear. There may be pain associated from the actual trauma of rape, as well as muscular tension, sleep disturbance, night terrors, headaches, gastrointestinal pain, and/or gynecological symptoms. The second phase is described as occurring a few weeks after the rape. During this phase the woman attempts to reorganize her life, but begins to experience intrusive symptoms such as phobias and nightmares.

These latter studies helped us to better understand the experience of rape as a significant form of trauma, which often results in rape-related PTSD symptoms—i.e., flashbacks, hypervigilance, nightmares, psychic numbing, constricted behavior due to fear, social withdrawal, sleep disturbance, memory and concentration issues, as well as active avoidance of reminders of the rape—that can sometimes last for years (Burgess, 1983).

It was also during the 1970s and 1980s that research into domestic violence and childhood abuse proliferated. That which had been unspoken and kept in the shadows began to be talked about and explored. As a result we learned about the staggering prevalence and impacts of these types of traumas. In terms of the scope of domestic violence in the U.S., the National Violence Against Women Survey estimates the prevalence of intimate partner victimization to be almost 25% for women and 8% for men (Tjaden & Thoennes, 2006). A review of the research on domestic violence indicated that 31% to 84% of women who were victims of domestic violence reported symptoms of PTSD (Jones, Hughes, & Unterstaller, 2001). This is comparable to the rates of PTSD among first responders and among soldiers returning from combat in Vietnam. (See following section on *Prevalence Rates of PTSD among Civilians, First Responders, and Combat Soldiers*).

As a result of the aforementioned studies on domestic and sexual violence, stigma for survivors of these types of trauma has lessened to the point that more are willing to talk about it and request counseling support. This is not to say that stigma no longer exists, since it still continues to be an obstacle to many individuals requesting support. However, client-centered and feminist-based individual counseling, group therapy, and crisis counseling services have been developed and implemented that are specific to the unique needs of these populations. It is through studies of these populations that we have begun to understand that there appears to be a constellation of unique symptoms among survivors of prolonged trauma, who live within a context of captivity. Out of these observations has come the concept of complex trauma (Herman, 1992), which will be discussed in detail in Chapter 4.

## Prevalence Rates of PTSD Among Civilians, First Responders, and Combat Soldiers

In a large-scale national survey of Americans, 61% of men and 51% of women reported having been exposed to at least one traumatic event in their lifetime (Kessler, Sonnega, Bromet, Hughes, & Nelson, 1995). Using results from the National Comorbidity Survey—Replication, it was determined that 40%

of Americans reported exposure to at least one potentially traumatic event by the age of 13 (Koenen, Roberts, Stone, & Dunn, 2010). Thus, exposure to trauma would appear to occur most commonly in childhood. The good news is that most people do *not* go on to develop PTSD. Among those who develop acute traumatic stress reactions immediately following a traumatic experience, the vast majority recover from their symptoms within a few weeks. For the civilian population, the rate of experiencing PTSD is estimated at between 6–8%, with women found having a higher incidence, of up to 12%, compared to 5% for men (Kessler et al., 1995; Kessler, Berglund, Demler, Jin, Merikangas, & Walters, 2005; Pietrzak, Goldstein, Southwick, & Grant, 2011; Resnick, Kilpatrick, Dansky, Saunders, & Best, 1993).

As might be expected, emergency responders experience even higher rates of PTSD. Studies have found that within the police, firefighter, and paramedic populations, reported rates of PTSD range from 20% to 35% (Corneil, Beaton, Murphy, Johnson, & Pike, 1999; Darensburg, Andrew, Hartley, Burchfiel, Fekedulegn, & Violanti, 2006; Robinson, Sigman, & Wilson, 1997; Sterud, Ekeberg, & Hem, 2006).

The lifetime PTSD rates for veterans have been found to vary depending on the specific conflict, ranging from 12% for the Gulf War (Kang, Natelson, Mahan, Lee, & Murphy, 2003), to 18% for those who served in Iraq/ Afghanistan (Hoge, Riviere, Wilk, Herrell, & Weathers, 2014), and as high as 31% among Vietnam veterans (Kulka et al., 1990).

## Allowing History to Inform Our Understanding of the Valley and Our Work

The valley of the shadow of death has existed for centuries. As we have come to understand from the brief history of trauma outlined in the preceding pages, PTSD is not new. It's just that it has taken us a few hundred years to come to a more accurate and compassionate understanding of how one ends up in this valley, and how to best support people who end up there. While the evidence exists that acute stress disorder and PTSD are not the result of moral weakness or deficits in character, we are all aware of systems and individuals (often in positions of power) who would insinuate, or directly suggest, otherwise. We still have a lot of work to do in terms of educating institutions and individuals, as well as advocating for those who have been traumatized and are at risk of being further retraumatized by the uneducated or willfully ignorant.

## A Few Observations About the Concept of "Mental Illness"

Before we start this journey, I feel the need to share one of my concerns with you about the concept of "mental illness", which I believe contributes to misunderstanding and the continued stigma of people who suffer from these disorders, including individuals with Post-traumatic Stress Disorder (PTSD). Please read the following definitions below, and take note of what is missing.

*Mental illness refers to a wide range of mental health conditions—disorders that affect your mood, thinking and behavior.*

—*Mayo Clinic*

*Mental illnesses are health conditions involving changes in thinking, emotion or behavior (or a combination of these). Mental illnesses are associated with distress and/or problems functioning in social, work or family activities.*
—*American Psychiatric Association*

When I asked my first year grad students, they saw it right away. What is missing in these definitions is a reference to the fact that these illnesses are physiologically based and also result in *severe and debilitating physical symptoms and impairments.* Not only do the illnesses that fall into this category cause changes in mood, behavior, thinking, and emotions, but they also result in physiological distress. I also object to the term "mental illness" since "mental" refers to the mind only and these illnesses are in fact—*of the mind and body.* I can't help wondering if this misnomer and these lacking definitions contribute to the stigma that people suffering from depression, anxiety, PTSD, etc., continue to face. There is still an unfortunately large segment of our society, from all walks of life, who believe that these illnesses are all in "one's mind", and something people should be able to "get over". This perception adds an unnecessary burden to those who are already coping with so much. Given that Major Depressive Disorder (MDD) and anxiety disorders often occur concurrently with PTSD, this burden can be multiplied for individuals with more than one diagnosis. Consequently, it is important for us to educate our clients and others regarding the reality of these illnesses.

When I describe the experience of severe depression to individuals who don't understand its physical manifestations, I compare it to feeling like one has influenza—minus the congestion and cough. The limbs are heavy and achy. The body and mind are exhausted. Getting out of bed to take a shower can take monumental effort. At least with the flu, one can be fairly certain that symptoms will subside in a week or two. However, with depression, these symptoms can last for months or years. It is no wonder that despair can creep in. Without the understanding of those around them, persons suffering from depression might end up being angry with themselves and, along with others, add to their burden of suffering with unnecessary judgment and shame.

Likewise, anxiety has very physical symptoms, which are often misunderstood. When explaining the experience of an anxiety attack, I compare it to the reaction that a parent has when shopping with a small child, in that moment when they realize the child is no longer in sight. The body and mind together begin to panic. Attention narrows. The heart beats rapidly and breathing becomes shallow and quick. You might break into a sweat and experience chills. You might feel nauseous. Your body might begin to shake. Your mind is flooded with fears of the worst. You can't control the frightening imaginings of what might have happened to your child. As your body panics, your mind panics, which escalates the physical panic, which escalates the emotional panic. . . . Now imagine that your body reacts this way in situations that are part of your daily life, and where there is no apparent trigger. When an anxiety attack begins, you don't know how long your body will be in this state. How frightening that must be.

I was recently discussing the experience of Generalized Anxiety Disorder (GAD) with a client. He spoke about how it was impossible to stop the barrage of fears, and to think clearly. Through our discussion we came to the metaphor of GAD as being caught in a snowstorm in whiteout conditions. You can barely see a foot in front of your face. Fearful thoughts, like the snow in a whiteout, are blinding and disorienting. They are all you can see and the effort to get through them takes everything you have.

I would describe PTSD as being left without the essential buffers needed to filter and protect you from internal and external stimuli. Your body and mind respond in extreme ways that don't make sense within the present moment in time. Others might accuse you of over-reacting, or alternatively, of shutting down or zoning out. You can't control these responses. You relive the worst moments of your life in fragments—and yes, it is *reliving, not remembering*. Sometimes these fragments will be visual. Sometimes you will relive sounds, smells, tastes, or physical sensations. During reliving you might also feel intolerable levels of terror, panic, despair, guilt, or shame. Sometimes your body will experience pain related to the trauma, or related to an intense stress response—even though nothing threatening is happening externally at the present moment. Reliving doesn't stop when you try to sleep. Nightmares, insomnia, and night terrors threaten sleep. You are compelled to always be on your guard—to watch and listen, to stay tense and on the edge of your seat, as you assess everyone and everything for threat. Deep inside, you truly believe you can never be safe. To protect yourself from reliving, you start to constrict your world. There will be certain places, people, and/ or other things that you avoid. Avoidance takes a lot of energy as you seek to protect yourself from potential traumatic stress triggers.

These are the realities of those who find themselves in the valley of the shadow of death. Few understand this, and likely this is why stigma remains a problem. We need to find the words to describe that which, for many, has been unspeakable—and we need to speak these words in ways that not only our clients, but also in which society as a whole can relate.

# 2 Trauma Foundations

> Trauma results in a fundamental reorganization in the way the mind and body manage perceptions. It changes not only how we think and what we think about, but also our capacity to think.
>
> (van der Kolk, 2014, p. 21)

Trauma changes the way the body and mind process information. As a result, trauma-related thoughts, as well as sensory and affective experiences, continue to ambush our clients in the present moment. Hence as therapists, if we wish to be effective guides and therapeutic supports, we will need to understand what happens in the mind and body of individuals who find themselves in the valley. To this end, we require at least a basic understanding of the neurobiological basis of trauma and the concept of neuroplasticity, which forms the basis for our expectation of the possibility of healing from trauma. We will also need to be familiar with key diagnostic features of PTSD and Acute Stress Disorder, the additional reality of chronic pain for many of our clients, and the possibility of delayed onset PTSD. And finally, it is via a commitment to acquiring the knowledge and skills central to developing a trauma-informed and culturally sensitive therapeutic practice that we will be prepared to more respectfully, safely, and effectively work with our clients who find themselves in the valley.

## Overview of the Neurobiology of Trauma

During the past few decades, our understanding of the mechanisms of the brain that respond to stress in general, and more specifically, to traumatic stress, has increased tremendously thanks to Magnetic Resonance Imagery (MRI) technology. MRIs have been able to demonstrate differences in brain functioning between individuals suffering from PTSD compared to those who are not (Lanius, 2011; Lanius et al., 2001, 2003). A comprehensive explanation of how the mind and body are impacted by trauma can be found in van der Kolk's *The Body Keeps the Score* (2014). For our purposes, we will focus on three key areas of the brain and how they respond to traumatic stress—these being the amygdala, the hippocampus, and the prefrontal cortex.

Within the limbic system, which is responsible for survival, is the amygdala that operates as the early warning system in the brain. When a potential threat or danger is perceived through the senses, the amygdala responds immediately by activating the body's sympathetic nervous system. This happens before any considered assessment of the reality and degree of threat is made. When this system is activated, powerful stress hormones are released that increase heart rate, breathing rate, and blood pressure, in order to prepare the body to respond to the perceived threat through fight or flight actions (Bruner & Woll, 2011; van der Kolk, 1994). In addition, the amygdala is responsible for storing unconscious emotional memories (Bruner & Woll, 2011; Rothschild, 2000).

The meaning of an experience is processed by the hippocampus and prefrontal cortex, which are responsible for locating our experiences within the time and space contexts of our lives (Rothschild, 2000; van der Kolk, 2014). The hippocampus is essential for storing narrative memories, which are involved in the creation of long-term memory (Ashwell, 2012; Bruner & Woll, 2011). The prefrontal cortex is responsible for rationally assessing perceived threats, considering options, and making a response plan (Ledoux, 1996).

Although it appears that the high levels of stress hormones associated with traumatic events do not impact the functions of the amygdala, there is evidence that they may suppress the functions of the hippocampus and prefrontal cortex. As Ledoux (1996) explains:

> The hippocampal steroid receptors are part of a control system that helps regulate how much adrenal steroid hormone is released. . . . In the face of stress, the amygdala keeps saying "release" and the hippocampus keeps saying "slow down". Through multiple cycles through these loops the concentration of the stress hormones in the blood is delicately matched to the demands of the stressful situation. . . . If stress persists too long, the hippocampus begins to falter in its ability to control the release of stress hormones, and to perform its routine functions.
>
> (p. 240)

Thus, if the hippocampus cannot perform its functions, it is possible that no explicit conscious memory of the trauma will be formed. Additionally, when the functions of the prefrontal cortex are compromised, we are left unable to rationally assess the present moment and context, and instead are subject to operating in "survival mode" in accordance with the unconscious directions of the amygdala. It appears that as a result of the suppressed functions of these two important areas of the brain, some individuals, while having little or no conscious memory of traumatic events, continue to experience very powerful and disturbing unconscious emotional and sensory memories related to the trauma, which have a sense of being endless (Ledoux, 1996; Rothschild, 2000; van der Kolk, 2014). Moreover, research has demonstrated that trauma creates physiological changes that result in changes to how the brain's alarm system works and how it filters information (van der Kolk, 2014).

## Neuroplasticity and the Role of Trauma Therapy

One of the most exciting benefits of better understanding how the brain works, is that we have come to realize that the brain is not a rigid, fixed structure. Rather it is a living and adaptive part of us that continues to develop and respond to internal and external stimuli. For those whose minds have been hijacked by PTSD symptoms, this offers hope. Through trauma therapy, the brain can be "rewired" to adapt in ways that reduce or eliminate the impact of trauma symptoms (van der Kolk, 2014).

The therapeutic alliance can have an important transformational influence within the schemas and workings of the brain:

> Therapy is just another way of creating synaptic potentiation in brain pathways that control the amygdala . . . helping the cortex gain control over the amygdala.
>
> (Ledoux, 1996, p. 265)

> Attention to the therapeutic relationship will, with some clients, help to transform negative implicit memories of relationships by creating a new encoding of positive experiences of attachment.
>
> (Rothschild, 2000, p. 82)

Additionally, research utilizing MRI assessments of the brain has provided evidence to support the hypothesis that CBT changes the workings and structure of the brain, while improving clinical outcomes among individuals with PTSD (Levy-Gigi, Szabo, Kelemen, & Keri, 2013; Sheline et al., 2017).

## PTSD Symptoms and Diagnosis

Herman (1992) identifies three categories of PTSD symptoms: 1) hyper-arousal; 2) intrusion; and 3) constriction. Hyperarousal refers to a constant "wired" state of attention due to the ongoing expectation of threat and danger. Symptoms of this heightened state of alertness include overreactions to annoyances, an exaggerated startle response, sleep disturbances, and psychosomatic pain. Intrusive symptoms are those that cause the individual to relive the trauma again and again in the present, such as flashbacks and reliving nightmares. Constriction symptoms include avoidance, dissociation, numbing, depersonalization, and other alterations in consciousness.

Continuing to live in a state of hyperarousal, while enduring painful reliving of the trauma whenever reminders are present, can intensify conscious and unconscious efforts to restrict one's thoughts, feelings, and exposure to life which will potentially include reminders of the trauma and additional threats. Thus, the trauma survivor's world can become very small, both internally and externally, in an effort to protect and continue to survive.

Only psychologists, psychiatrists, or medical doctors with specialized training can make a diagnosis of PTSD. According to the DSM-5 (APA, 2013), several criteria must be met in order for a person to meet the diagnosis of PTSD. (I will summarize and simplify these criteria for the sake of providing an understanding, not a diagnosis). The individual must have experienced or witnessed, threatened or actual serious injury, sexual violence, or death—or have heard about these things happening to a loved one—or have experienced repeated exposure to the details of these types of events (as in the case of first responders or disaster workers). Additionally, the following symptoms must be present:

- *Intrusive Symptoms*—Recurrent reliving of the trauma;
- *Avoidant Symptoms*—Persistent avoidant behaviors regarding reminders of the trauma;
- *Negative Mood Symptoms*—Negative changes in thoughts and mood following the traumatic event;
- *Increased Arousal Symptoms;*
- The abovementioned symptoms have lasted more than 1 month;
- As a result of these symptoms, the individual is experiencing clinically significant levels of distress as well as impaired functioning in one or more areas of his/her life; and
- These symptoms are not due to the effects of substance use or any other medical cause.

It is of note that for those diagnosed with PTSD soon after their trauma experience, we can expect that 50% of these individuals will recover completely within 3 months (APA, 2013).

## Acute Stress Disorder

Acute Stress Disorder is comprised of a combination of the same types of intrusive, dissociative, avoidant, hyperarousal, and negative mood-related symptoms as are found in PTSD. Diagnosis requires the presence of at least nine symptoms within the categories of negative mood, dissociation, arousal, avoidance, and intrusion (DSM-5, APA, 2013). One of the major differences between Acute Stress Disorder and PTSD diagnostic criteria is the time frame involved. Whereas PTSD cannot be diagnosed unless symptoms persist for more than a month, Acute Stress Disorder symptoms occur soon after the trauma, have persisted for at least three days, and can last *up to* a month. After a month of symptom persistence, a person who is diagnosed with Acute Stress Disorder is likely to be given a new diagnosis of PTSD. For the majority of people, acute stress symptoms will peak in intensity during the first few weeks following the trauma and then diminish, eventually disappearing by the fourth week. The strategies for coping with Acute Stress Disorder are the same as those used for the stabilization and distress management phases of PTSD.

# Chronic Pain and PTSD

Physical distress has been included as part of the intrusive, recurrent symptomology that might occur as part of a PTSD diagnosis (APA, 2013). Increased somatization has also been proposed as a characteristic of individuals suffering from complex trauma (Herman, 1992). Thus, we need to consider the role of chronic pain in terms of the distress suffered by our clients with PTSD—both for individuals who have experienced trauma-related physical injury and those who have not.

Among patients suffering from injury-related chronic pain, up to 61% were found to also be experiencing moderate to severe PTSD (Ahman & Stalnacke, 2008; Stalnacke & Ostman, 2010). For these individuals, it is imperative that a multi-disciplinary approach be employed to address both of these conditions, as each can exacerbate the other.

In a review of the literature regarding somatic distress among individuals suffering with PTSD, Gupta (2013) noted increased rates of sleep disturbance, chronic pain syndromes, and gastrointestinal disorders. If you are already working with trauma survivors, this information will not be new to you. I have noticed, however, that my clients who suffer from somatic pain attributed to PTSD (rather than as a result of trauma-related injury) have often experienced their physical pain being minimized or going untreated by medical professionals. I am unsure what is at the root of this.

As therapists, it is important not to underestimate the physical pain that can be part of PTSD symptomology, and to advocate for medical intervention, if our clients feel they need it but are not being heard.

I would like to share some observations regarding two of my closest friends who have been dealing with active PTSD symptoms. We had been talking about the physical pain they were experiencing as part of the PTSD symptomology, and how difficult it can be to explain it to people, when it isn't the result of a known physical injury or illness. I mentioned that the McGill Pain Scale (Melzack, 1975; Katz & Melzack, 2011) is a respected scientific measure of pain, and wondered if it might be helpful to them. Both completed this measure on their own and were kind enough to share their results with me. They have also allowed me to discuss their results here. For comparison purposes, the average pain score for childbirth has a rating of approximately 34 on the McGill Pain Scale (Melzack, Taenzer, Feldman, & Kinch, 1981). One of my friends, who completed this scale on the basis of PTSD-related physical pain, had a score of 41, and the other had a score of 47. It was interesting to me to note that descriptors of their pain, which they both endorsed, included: heavy, exhausting, crushing, sickening, terrifying, and unbearable. While my sample of two is certainly not conclusive, it does show some promise that the McGill pain scale might be a helpful tool in understanding and communicating the PTSD-related somatic experiences of our clients. This tool might also be helpful in communicating this information to health professionals and for use in research with this population.

## Delayed Onset PTSD

Delayed onset PTSD, starting months or years after the original trauma(s) is not uncommon, and has been estimated, via a meta-analysis of prospective studies, to occur in 25% of cases with an onset of more than 6 months after the traumatic event (Smid, Mooren, van der Mast, Gersons, & Kleber, 2009). Another systematic review found that the rates of occurrence of delayed onset PTSD were 38% among military cases and 15% in civilian cases—with a range of onset between 9 months and 50 years—and all of the individual cases studied indicated potentially triggering events prior to onset (Andrews, Brewin, Philpott, & Stewart, 2007).

Repression of trauma memories is a common phenomenon, particularly in cases of childhood sexual abuse, combat exposure, or witnessing the murder or suicide of a family member (Goldsmith, Barlow, & Freyd, 2004; Scheflin & Brown, 1996), which can result in delayed onset PTSD. I've learned to be especially cautious in my approach when clients report what appear to be trauma-related symptoms, but cannot identify a trauma, and instead report having no memories whatsoever with respect to several years from their childhood. If there is no other reasonable cause for the memory loss, my thought is that if the mind has gone to the effort of repressing or not recording several years' worth of a person's life, there is the possibility that something very frightening was going on. I do not tell my client this because, in the first place I don't want to terrify them, and in the second place, I could be wrong. Although I might have suspicions, this isn't about satisfying my curiosity or trying to prove myself correct, but rather it is about going on the journey chosen by the client, whereby they choose the paths we go down, when we go down them, and how far. To do otherwise would be to undermine the client's inherent body-mind wisdom, and hence, their safety.

One of the most dramatic experiences of repressed memory I have witnessed was with Maria,[1] a client who came in to address low self-esteem concerns. In response to some negative messages she had internalized in a previous relationship, we decided to use EMDR. There were no indications of past trauma when I did the screening for EMDR. I was quite surprised, when a few days after the first EMDR session, Maria called me in tremendous distress. She was flooded with fragmented physical and emotional flashbacks. PTSD symptoms emerged in full-force. She became suicidal. We immediately went into stabilization and containment mode in our counseling. She was so dissociative that for months she could only recall an hour or so of what happened each day. She was in a definite state of crisis. It took months of stabilization work, as well as medical intervention, before fragmented memories started to surface. It was only then we became aware of the horrific physical abuse and sexual torture that she had survived in childhood.

## Concurrent Disorders

In a review of the literature on PTSD within the general population, Kessler (2006) examined the high rates of comorbidity with other psychiatric illnesses and noted:

> if we divide the sample of people with a history of PTSD into those with an active disorder and those in remission, we find that it is only those with active PTSD who have an elevated risk of secondary disorders. This means that the causal mechanism leading to the association between PTSD and the subsequent onset of other disorders is not due to some underlying vulnerability to PTSD, but rather to factors associated with PTSD itself. Although this finding does not prove that PTSD causes secondary disorders, it is consistent with the possibility that this is so.
>
> (p. 8)

To many clinicians in the field, this is not a new perspective but rather bolsters our own observations. If the emergence of these secondary psychiatric illnesses are, in fact, due to factors related to PTSD itself, helping our clients to identify effective, healthy tools to manage distress is a priority. This is not to say that other disorders always come after PTSD, but it is definitely something of which we, as clinicians, need to be mindful.

With this in mind, we need to be aware of the lifetime prevalence rates of concurrent disorders. Rates of concurrent PTSD and alcohol abuse/dependence have been found to be as high as 52% among men and 28% among women, while rates of concurrent PTSD and substance abuse/dependence were found to be 35% among men and 27% among women (Kessler et al., 1995; Pietrzak et al., 2011). Studies that have examined the comorbidity of eating disorders with PTSD have indicated prevalence rates of 26% for eating disorders in general (Swinbourne, Hunt, Abbott, Russell, St. Clare, & Touyz, 2012) and 37% for bulimia nervosa specifically (Dansky, Brewerton, Kilpatrick, & O'Neil, 1997). The lifetime prevalence rate of self-injurious (non-suicidal) behavior among adults in the U.S. has been found to be 6%. (Klonsky, 2011). This is lower than the lifetime prevalence rate of 13% to 23% for adolescents found in a review of the research regarding this population (Jacobson & Gould, 2007). Many of the risk factors associated with self-harming behavior overlap with symptoms and traumas associated with PTSD, including: dissociation; history of childhood sexual abuse or parental emotional neglect; avoidance/ numbing symptoms of PTSD; alexithymia; and childhood separation from caregiver (Jacobson & Gould, 2007; Klonsky, 2011; Weierich & Nock, 2008).

## Trauma-Informed Practice

If your experience is similar to mine, you will find initially that many clients who are suffering from PTSD-related symptoms have not yet connected the traumatic experience to their distress. Instead, their presenting issue when they come for counseling might be expressed as needing help coping with "stress". Some might present as being concerned that they might be suffering from anxiety or depression, and while this might be true, there might also be signs that something more is going on. We will not always know, from the outset, which of our clients are suffering from traumatic stress, but by taking a trauma-informed approach, we are more likely to notice the signs and respond effectively earlier on. Moreover, the steps we can take to operationalize trauma-sensitive practice will likely be perceived as supportive and respectful by all of our clients regardless of the issues they would like to address.

Trauma-informed practice refers to making a commitment to be educated about the complexities of trauma, how it might present, and effective trauma-focused treatments and resources. It further means we strive, in our practice, to ensure that we operate in ways that will not be triggering to our clients who are suffering from traumatic stress reactions. This typically entails efforts to reduce what may be perceived of as the inherent power differential in the therapeutic alliance, ensuring our clients are active and willing participants in the therapeutic process, respecting clients' choices as they decide upon the paths that will comprise their healing journey, and acknowledging and building upon our clients' inherent resiliency, strengths, and wisdom. Being trauma-informed in our practice has many practical space, interpersonal, theoretical, and professional implications for how we work.

In terms of the counseling environment, it is important that it feel safe to our clients. How I operationalize this is to set up my office in a calming and comfortable way, while paying attention to details. I have posted a "safe space" rainbow colored symbol in my office to let members of the LGBT community know that I am an ally. The artwork in my office is gentle, calming, and/or has supportive messages. The windows around my office door are opaque to protect client privacy (This was part of the planning when our office space was being built). I give my clients the choice of counseling chairs to sit in when they come into the office. On my bookshelf are various books about trauma, rape, depression, anxiety, etc., which I hope will let clients know that it is safe to talk about these often stigmatized subjects within these walls. Plants and flowers can be calming and welcoming. Some therapists include stones, shells, or water fountains as part of their office décor. Some use soft lighting or natural sunlight. Any effort you make to try to make your office more comfortable, calming, and welcoming to your clients is an opportunity to convey to your clients that they matter, and what they need matters. This is a message that some of our clients will not have heard before.

The interpersonal component is also understandably a priority in trauma-informed practice. This is a particularly sensitive area given that many of our clients will have been traumatized by significant interpersonal boundary violations. Ongoing therapist self-awareness and monitoring are essential. We need to be aware of how we are presenting to our clients. Many of our clients who have suffered through complex trauma will have become highly skilled at reading physical and emotional cues. They will quickly detect any incongruencies among our words, body language, and actions, and will likely shut down if this is detected. We need to be mindful of this. Genuineness is a must.

I recall an experience with a client, in which we had been doing some productive work in our first two sessions. During our third appointment, after five minutes this client informed me that she didn't want to speak to me anymore. I asked if I had done something to offend her. She told me that there was a look on my face that indicated I was upset with her. She said she felt like I wanted her to leave. I immediately realized that I had not been as effective as I thought at hiding the fact that at that moment I was experiencing severe back pain. Apparently, the pain was coming through my facial expression and was being misinterpreted as something entirely different. I acknowledged to her that I was dealing with pain and had not realized it was coming across in this way. I said I was sorry that the message she received from me nonverbally felt like I was upset with her. I asked her if, given this misunderstanding, she would be comfortable in us moving forward. She accepted my apology and agreed to continue with the session.

It is also important that we convey *genuine* caring and acceptance of our clients. Caring is a must in doing this work. It needs to be at the core of all of our interactions. Even in cases where our values differ from those of our clients, or we experience their personalities as difficult, there will always be at least a few client characteristics that we can genuinely admire, if we look for them. At the very least, our clients, by the nature of what they have survived, are strong and resilient. Their vulnerability and trust in sharing their stories with us is honoring and admirable. I've found that if I find myself starting to move into mentally judging a client in a negative way, I can immediately stop this by moving into a mindset of curiosity instead. This encourages me to wonder about and to try to understand my client's perspective. From this perspective, I am better able to connect with and accept my client in a non-judgmental way. This acceptance combined with unconditional positive regard, is especially important in our work with traumatized clients, many of whom are likely carrying around the additional burden of shame and might be feeling unacceptable and unlovable even to themselves.

Another part of trauma-informed practice is recognition of the need for clear, professional boundaries from the outset. This means having a discussion about expectations, roles, processes, and limits to confidentiality and contact outside of sessions. Our clients need to know that they can trust us to maintain personal boundaries—especially physical ones. New therapists might be tempted to place a hand on the arm of a distressed client in an attempt to try to comfort them. This should *never* happen with clients suffering from PTSD as it can trigger flashbacks, particularly in those who have survived physical and/or sexual abuse. The potential is there for our clients to interpret touch as a personal boundary violation. Such a perceived violation has the capacity to undermine the client's sense of safety and the entire therapeutic alliance. Furthermore, in the therapeutic relationship, it is imperative that the focus of counseling sessions remains on clients and their needs. As therapists we need to ensure we do not hijack these sessions, directly or indirectly, in the service of our own needs or goals. This will require continuous self-awareness on our part, as well as developing the resources and capacity to identify and address our own needs outside of session. Any self-disclosure on the part of therapists needs to be carefully thought out and assessed in terms of the motivations for sharing this information and the intended outcome of doing so.

In terms of trauma-sensitive clinical theory and practice, it is incumbent upon us, despite the busyness of our work and home lives, to keep up-to-date on evidence-based clinical approaches. This is vital in maintaining professional competencies. This means we need to engage in the continuous professional development regarding trauma-focused knowledge and skills. Through ongoing research, our understanding of trauma and effective means to address it is constantly expanding. It is incumbent upon us to keep current with this information. As we learn more about how trauma affects the mind and body, and effective approaches for client stabilization and trauma processing, we have the opportunity to become more effective practitioners. Incorporating a variety of strategies and interventions will likely be necessary to meet individual client needs.

## Note

1 The client's name has been changed and identifying information excluded.

# 3  Traumatic Stress Responses

We may, I think, tentatively venture to regard the common traumatic neurosis as a consequence of an extensive breach being made in the protective shield against stimuli.

(Freud, 2015, p. 25)

This is an insightful description regarding how trauma can cause injury to the mechanisms of the mind and body that would normally protect one against overwhelming emotional, cognitive, and physical events. In response to this "extensive breach", the mind and body go into survival mode, whereby responses are determined not by conscious choice, but by the most primitive parts of the brain in order to maximize chances for survival.

Thus, another preparation that we, as therapists, need to make prior to entering the valley is to be knowledgeable regarding the normal range of responses of individuals in the face of traumatic events, as well as how traumatic stress reactions might present following trauma. We require this knowledge in order to assist our clients to get their bearings in the valley. Some of our clients will be burdened by shame regarding the actions they did or did not take during the traumatic event. Education regarding how the brain chooses one's reactions in traumatic circumstances can help to lift this burden. Also, education that normalizes the traumatic stress reactions that our clients are experiencing can also be reassuring and ease a burden they may be carrying. Knowledge is an essential tool in the valley. It can clear the mind of confusion, fear, and unnecessary/unfair judgment and shame.

## Fight, Flight, Freeze, and Submit

*His father arrived home drunk and in a rage. One of the children had left their bicycle on the front yard instead of putting it away in the shed. Jenna, who was 7 years old was the "guilty party". She heard her father yelling and throwing things in the foyer. Tears streamed down her face. She was frozen and couldn't move. Jason, who was 10 years old, was shaking with fear and he ran out the back door and as far away from the house as he could get. Molly, his mother, walked into the foyer and tried to speak to her husband in a soothing tone. Her husband yelled at her to come to him. She did so, shuffling slowly, shaking, and staring at the floor. Michael knew what was coming next. He had just turned 16 years old and had seen this pattern play out for most of his life. His father raised his fist to strike Michael's mother, when Michael stepped in front of her and punched first. His father went down. Michael continued to punch and kick his father until he surrendered.*

The reactions of the children and mother in the above-described scenario exemplify some common responses that can occur during a traumatic incident. During a traumatic event the body responds *instinctively* to perceived threats in an attempt to increase chances for survival. Typical responses include flight, freezing, fighting (including conditioned responses), and submission. These responses are decided upon, without conscious consent, by the most primitive areas of the brain, which are responsible for survival. For our purposes we will refer to this as the "survival brain".

The *flight* response occurs when the survival brain judges that escape is the best option for survival, and is feasible given the circumstances. The increased adrenaline, which is part of the stress response, is used to mobilize the body to try to escape. The goal is to place physical distance between oneself and the perceived threat. In the moment, this was the instinctive response that Jason's mind chose for him, resulting in him fleeing out the back door and running as far away from the threat as he could get.

With the *fight* response, a person actively engages with or against the threat in an effort to protect themselves and/or others. In situations where a person fights, their survival brain has quickly assessed the situation and instinctively determined that this is the best and most feasible response to protect themselves and/or others. Michael had seen this pattern of violence play out many times throughout his life. In the past, he might have fled, or frozen, but for some reason, in this moment, his survival brain decided that he was going to fight. It may be that Michael has reached a point physically where his survival brain, in its assessment of options, has determined that he could actually pose a counter-threat to his father and protect his mother. It may be that his father has shown some physical weakness, which conveyed the message that Michael has an advantage. It may also be that Michael's mom, Molly, was beaten so badly last time that he fears she won't survive another beating—and that might have been enough to tip the balance. Whatever the reason, Michael was compelled to fight.

When fight or flight responses are perceived by the survival brain as not viable, the body resorts to disengagement in the form of *freezing* (Rothschild, 2000). Freezing is a response whereby the body and mind become immobilized, and this sometimes includes an inability to speak and/or amnesia following the event. This seems to be especially common in children who are abused, or witness abuse, and appears to be linked to the dissociation response. In freezing, the body and mind shut down to protect one from overwhelming terror. In this example, 7-year-old Jenna freezes in the face of a situation she feels she cannot escape or fight.

*Submission* is an often forgotten but frequent response to intraspecies conflict (Grossman, 2009). Thus, it can occur in situations in which other human beings are perpetrating the trauma. When it becomes apparent to the victim that fighting or fleeing is not an option, the individual might submit to the demands of the perpetrator who is viewed as more powerful, in order to try to appease him/her with the goal of protecting oneself and/or others. This response is not uncommon in domestic violence, sexual assault, robbery, or war-based traumas. In this example, Molly does what her abusive husband demands, and comes to him. This response might come as a result of her survival brain determining that this is the best way of potentially appeasing her husband's temper and protecting her children.

Also, though it doesn't fit with the above example, we need to remember that *conditioned responses* also fall into the *fight* category. This refers to those responses that have been overlearned to the point of becoming reflexive and is why police officers, fire fighters, paramedics, and soldiers engage in repetitive training in simulated settings. Operant and classical training methods are used in order to ensure that when confronted with traumatic situations and their survival brain takes over, they will revert to their training rather than freezing, fleeing, or submitting. Despite feelings of terror, powerlessness, and in the face of serious injury and/or death, these individuals will do what they have been trained to do. This is why police officers and soldiers will continue to fight in the face of overwhelming odds, often even after they have been seriously injured. It is why first responders continue to provide services in the face of horrific accidents, attacks, and natural disasters. The training that allows them to continue to function regardless of their own terror, horror, and feelings of helplessness, however, does not protect them from traumatic stress responses that might be a natural consequence of their experiences.

It is important to be aware that, given the survival brain is in control during trauma, clients might have engaged in behaviors that they would not have chosen had they been in a calm and rational state. This can cause a lot of distress for our clients, especially those who froze, ran, or submitted, because they (and possibly others) might judge them for their response. It is essential to reassure our clients that in such circumstances we do not get to consciously choose our responses in the moment, but rather the part of the brain dedicated to ensuring survival makes a decision based on the information it has available at the time. It might be helpful to point out that in fact their survival brain did its job effectively, given that they are sitting with us in the present moment.

## Normal Range of Traumatic Stress Reactions

Within hours and days of a traumatic event, is not unusual for individuals to experience a variety of traumatic stress reactions. Traumatic stress symptoms will vary from person to person. Not everyone experiences every symptom, and not every symptom is experienced in exactly the same way or with the same degree of intensity. These symptoms can cause a tremendous amount of distress and disruption in all aspects of a person's life, and can be intensified if a person doesn't realize these reactions are common and normal following trauma.

## Physical

Following trauma, if hyperarousal is maintained, the body will often express its distress through physical symptoms. Whatever a person's normal physical vulnerabilities to stress may be, trauma reactions tend to be noticed there first. For example, a person who tends to be vulnerable to headaches or gastrointestinal symptoms when stressed prior to the traumatic experience, will likely experience an increase in intensity and frequency of these symptoms following trauma. Other typical physiological trauma responses include: fatigue or exhaustion; body aches and pains; nausea and/or vomiting; sweating; breathing difficulties; muscle tremors; chills; and dizziness or weakness.

## Emotional

Emotional responses that follow trauma will often vacillate between overwhelming distress and intolerable numbness or emotional disconnection. Some of the more common intense emotional reactions include: agitation; anger/rage; irritability; sadness; despair; guilt; hopelessness; fear/terror; depression; grief; and shame.

## Cognitive

Trauma can overload one's ability to think clearly, rationally, and quickly. Common traumatic stress symptoms that may arise in the aftermath of trauma include: poor concentration and memory; amnesia about all or parts of the traumatic event(s); difficulty with decision making; poor problem solving; confusion; hypervigilance (constant scanning of surroundings for possible threats); nightmares and/or night terrors; and flashbacks (reliving sensory fragments of the traumatic experience).

## Behavioral

If the mind and body are on overload, behavioral changes can also result. Some commonly reported changes have been observed in: sleep patterns; appetite; appearance; alcohol consumption or substance use; risk-taking behavior (e.g., starting fights, impaired driving, promiscuous behavior including unprotected sex); and frequency of social interactions.

## Spiritual

Individuals who believe in God or a Higher Power sometimes experience a crisis of faith following trauma. This crisis may be temporary or prolonged and may include: feelings of betrayal, shame, and/or guilt; feeling abandoned; anger; despair; confusion and questioning; searching for meaning; a significant increase or decrease in time spent in prayer. Trauma can turn one's belief system upside down. It can change one's worldview and lead to an existential crisis.

## Dissociation and Flashbacks

Dissociation can occur not only during trauma, but also as either a temporary or ongoing traumatic symptom in the aftermath. Likewise, flashbacks might be a short-term or long-term symptom. Both of these types of symptoms appear to be connected to the inherent fragmentary nature of traumatic stress responses. Given that the parts of the brain responsible for the integration of sensations appear to be overwhelmed and impaired by the neurophysiological responses of the body to trauma, trauma survivors might struggle to recall a coherent narrative of the trauma. Instead, the trauma experience is often fragmented into so many "pieces"—smells, sights, sounds, emotions, physical sensations, and thoughts (van der Kolk & Fisler, 1995).

As mentioned previously, dissociation is a form of constriction. Individuals who were unable to fight or flee the traumatic event are left with few survival options, i.e., to freeze or submit in order to try to survive. Both of these forced options will sometimes include dissociation as part of the response. Dissociation allows one to split off from intolerable emotional and/or physical pain both during and after the trauma. Van der Kolk and Fisler (1995) explain it as follows:

> Dissociation refers to a compartmentalization of experience: elements of the experience are not integrated into a unitary whole, but are stored in memory as isolated fragments consisting of sensory perceptions or affective states . . . the word dissociation is currently used to describe four distinct, but interrelated phenomenon (1) the sensory and emotional fragmentation of experience . . . (2) depersonalization and derealization at the moment of the trauma . . . (3) ongoing depersonalization and "spacing out" in everyday life . . . and (4) containing the traumatic memories within distinct ego-states.
>
> (p. 510)

Hence, dissociation can present in several ways. It might involve the fragmentation of sensory and emotional trauma memories, and/or fragmentation within the sense of self. Some clients report having left their bodies and having viewed the traumatic event as though it was happening to someone else. Some of these clients may feel as though their emotions and physical sensations have been "switched off" indefinitely. Others will find that their attention and ability to stay present shuts down several times a day. For those who experienced extremely severe and prolonged abuse as children, dissociation may have taken the form of the development of separate identities as in the case of Dissociative Identity Disorder (DID), to compartmentalize the trauma and protect the most vulnerable parts of the self. If a dissociative response was used to survive trauma, it can be reactivated when survivors are confronted by internal or external reminders of the trauma.

Flashbacks can be a particularly painful symptom for PTSD survivors. Flashbacks are comprised of fragmentary sensory and affective trauma memories. Due to the impact of trauma on the brain, flashbacks are experienced as *reliving*, not *recalling*, (i.e., the reliving of trauma-related smell, sound, visual experiences, physical sensations, and/or intense emotions).

Via a study utilizing MRI brain scans, van der Kolk (2014) found that during flashbacks, the functioning of Broca's area is significantly decreased, and the entire left hemisphere of the brain can be deactivated. Broca's area allows us to put our feelings and thoughts into words. This can explain why, if our clients are triggered during counseling sessions, they might struggle to verbalize what they are experiencing. Furthermore, these scans demonstrate that when the left hemisphere of the brain is impacted, we lose the ability to sequence our experiences within a time frame, to understand cause and effect, and to plan for the future.

## Factors That Affect the Onset of PTSD

What one person experiences as traumatic may not necessarily be experienced as traumatic by another person. Two large-scale meta-analyses (Brewin, Andrews, & Valentine, 2000; Ozer, Best, Lipsey, & Weiss, 2003) looking at predictors of post-traumatic stress disorder yielded information on a number of significant demographic and prior history factors, as well as factors directly related to the traumatic event and what followed. In terms of *demographic and prior history factors*, the following variables were found to be significantly and positively correlated to the development of PTSD in adults:

- female gender;
- lower education level;
- lower intelligence;
- a previous psychiatric diagnosis;
- childhood trauma or other prior trauma;
- younger age at trauma;
- minority status; and
- family psychiatric history.

Additional significantly predictive *trauma-related factors* that were identified included:

- severity/intensity of the trauma;
- perceived threat to one's life;
- lack of social support following the trauma;

- greater life stressors subsequent to the trauma;
- intensely negative emotional reactions (during or after the trauma); and
- dissociation (experienced during or after the trauma).

Apparent *mediating factors* regarding traumatic stress include: successful fight or flight response to the trauma; preparation for expected traumatic stressor; one's personal beliefs, developmental history, and internal resources; prior experiencing of similar situations; and perceived social support (Rothschild, 2000).

# 4 Complex Trauma

for every soldier who serves in a war zone abroad, there are ten children who are endangered in their own homes.

(van der Kolk, 2014, p. 20)

For the general population, when PTSD is mentioned, many will immediately think of veterans or first responders. While these are clearly high-risk groups who deserve our support and attention, we need to be mindful that these groups do not comprise the majority of individuals who suffer from PTSD. The oft forgotten and invisible survivors of trauma are those children who grew up in their own familial war zones, where violence, abuse, and/or neglect were constant threats.

The concept of complex trauma is an area of trauma-related knowledge of which we need to be aware prior to entering the valley. This subset of clients who suffer from PTSD appear to have a unique type of presentation with regard to traumatic stress symptoms. They also have a unique set of needs. Given that trauma of this type occurs in a context of interpersonal betrayal, it can take some time and a great deal of sensitivity on the part of the therapist to develop the trust that is central to a strong therapeutic alliance. Education will again be an important tool to help this population to make sense of what they have been through and their reactions.

Herman (1992) proposed the diagnosis of *Disorders of Extreme Stress Not Otherwise Specified* (DESNOS) to capture the symptoms unique to individuals who experienced prolonged, repetitive trauma, i.e., "complex trauma", over a time period of months or years, within a context of living in a state of captivity and under the coercive control of the perpetrator. Within this state of captivity the perpetrator uses threats of serious harm or death of the victim, and/or his or her loved ones, as a means of control. The perpetrator also works to destroy the victim's sense of self and connections with others, in order to foster total dependency on him/her. Examples of the types of living conditions that would fit this description included: prisons; brothels; concentration camps; some religious cults; and some families. While many clinicians were hopeful that DESNOS would be added as a new diagnostic category in the DSM-5, this was not the case. Nevertheless, the proposed concept of complex trauma is clinically useful in understanding the symptomology and challenges of individuals who have survived prolonged traumatic experiences.

## Complex Trauma Symptoms

Several symptoms that extend beyond those that ordinarily define PTSD have been identified as being characteristic of survivors of complex trauma (Courtois, 2004; Ford, Courtois, Steele, van der Hart, & Nijenhuis, 2005; Herman, 1992; van der Kolk, 2002). These include:

- greater vulnerability to repeated harm that is self-inflicted (e.g., self-injury, eating disorders, substance abuse) or at the hands of others;
- altered consciousness via dissociation, suppression of thoughts, depersonalization, denial, and/or amnesia regarding parts or all of the trauma;
- loss of, or injury to, the sense of self—individuals might consequently perceive themselves as less than human, irrevocably damaged, shameful, or evil;
- ongoing somatic symptoms (e.g., gastrointestinal issues; back or pelvic pain; nausea; headaches) with no obvious physiological cause;
- impaired emotional regulation;
- concurrent depression and/or anxiety;
- inability to trust, or feel intimacy with others;
- lack of purpose or meaning in life; and
- development of an internalized bond with the perpetrator.

Such reactions can be means of coping, and for that reason, they deserve our appreciation. The body speaks, or in some cases can appear to *scream*, to request that attention be paid to traumatic stress injuries via these symptoms.

Unfortunately, many survivors of complex trauma come through these experiences with an unquestioning and deeply held belief that they deserved, and continue to deserve, abuse. Consequently, our clients may continue to allow others in their lives to treat them in abusive ways, even when they are no longer living in an environment of captivity, and it would appear from the outside that they have the power to make different choices. Alternatively, some will have come to believe that pain and betrayal are inherent in all relationships, and eschew any close relationships in their lives. Some of my clients who have chosen to close themselves off to relationships (outside of the therapeutic relationship) have explained that this is a well-thought out decision for them, and that the pain of being alone and apart from others is more acceptable to them then the pain of potential betrayal. Both of the aforementioned extreme types of responses to the experience of complex trauma speak to the insidious ways in which trauma and its underlying messages and cognitive templates can become internalized and lead to a chronic reenactment of roles and the entrenchment of survival strategies—even when these strategies are no longer required by the external environment in which a person currently lives.

We will also often witness strong bonds between trauma survivors and the perpetrators of abuse in their lives. The most common situations will be those in which adult children still wish to be in close relationship with an actively abusive parent, or an abused spouse returns to the abusive partner. This can be challenging to untangle since love, fear, violation, and neglect of survivors' needs have become tightly intertwined as one and the same, in their schema for relationships or family. (We will talk about how to approach these complex relationship issues in Chapter 10).

And finally, we need to be aware that the culmination of all of our clients' traumatic experiences can lead to despair. It can be very hard for survivors of complex trauma to find hope and meaning, even in life after the trauma, likely because they continue to relive it on a daily basis within their bodies and minds.

These are some of the unique challenges of working with survivors of complex trauma. At the same time, what sustains us as trauma therapists is the fact that these survivors are some of the most incredibly strong, resilient, awe-inspiring individuals that we will ever meet. Part of our work involves continuously holding up this mirror—reflecting these truths of who our clients are—so that they will start to see and acknowledge their own War-rior Spirit within.

## Understanding the Context of Chronic Childhood Abuse/Neglect

Let us go back to the experience of soldiers in a war zone. The WWII study by Swank and Marchand (1946) indicated that after a period of up to 50 days of ongoing combat, 98% of soldiers experienced some type of psychiatric stress reaction. Let's think about how this translates for children who spend years in their own familial war zone, where violence, abuse and/or neglect are a constant threat. Within this environment of what I call "*familial ter-rorism*", a child must remain constantly hypervigilant in order to maximize chances for survival.

Definitions of terrorism speak to the use of violence and threats of violence to coerce or intimidate people into submission. This is an apt description of what happens within family systems where children are abused and/or wit-ness abuse. In an environment of familial terrorism, the threat of violence is used to silence, control, and ensure compliance. Children and abused partners live in these environments with no sense of safety or stability. They learn to develop and use their senses to try to predict and avoid violence. They listen for the sound of footsteps to hear who is coming and to provide a warning of the perpetrator's mood and state of mind, and to watch the body language and facial expressions of the abuser. They listen for tone of voice, loudness, slurring (to let them know if the perpetrator is intoxicated), and threats. They start to recognize "triggers" that set the perpetrator off. They learn to be hyper-attuned to any indicators which might foretell episodes of violence or abuse.

In this familial war zone, children learn to deny their instincts, sensations, emotions, and needs. Herman (1997) points out that unlike soldiers who may have had the opportunity to grow and reach developmental milestones in a loving and supportive environment prior to entering a war zone, children who grow up within the war zones of their own homes are at a disadvantage. Their emotional, physiological, and cognitive development suffers. Additionally, unlike soldiers who are aware and have been prepared to go to war with an identified enemy (with whom they don't typically have a personal relationship), children are unprepared, untrained, and even unaware that they are in hostile territory. For many children, who don't know differently, they come to perceive their familial war zone as "normal".

It needs to be noted, before we go any further on this issue, that research has indicated that a disproportionately high number of soldiers were also abused as children. A recent study involving military personnel demonstrated the disturbing reality that almost half of soldiers had experienced childhood abuse (Afifi, Taillieu, Zamorski, Turner, Cheung, & Sareen, 2016). Unfortunately for these individuals, combat-related trauma can add an additional layer onto the complex trauma they have already experienced as children.

Max,[1] a client who suffered extensive physical and emotional abuse and neglect as a child, became very skilled at physical and emotional dissociation. (At one point as a young adult he walked on a broken leg for a week because he didn't feel the pain). His ability to totally disconnect from physical and emotional pain served him well in his duties as a military sniper. During one of our sessions, Max shared that he thought it was interesting that one of his senior officers once commented that he didn't know what had happened to Max as a child, but whatever it was, it made him an excellent soldier. This speaks to how the survival skills that children learn within familial war zones can transfer well into war zones in the larger world. Nevertheless, living this way takes a tremendous toll on the individual. When I started working with Max, his ability to dissociate protected him from the pain of negative emotions and physical sensations, but this also meant he didn't have access to any positive emotions or sensations either. Nor did he have access to needed warnings from his body when he was physically injured or ill, which at times placed him in life-threatening situations.

## Unspoken Family Rules

In the early 1980s a number of books and studies emerged that focused on the experiences and psychosocial challenges of Adult Children of Alcoholics (ACOAs). In her book, *It Will Never Happen to* Me, Black (1982) wrote about the often unspoken rules that children of alcoholics learn to live by within their families. These were identified as: *"Don't talk"; "Don't Trust";*

*and "Don't Feel".* Black observed that it was common for ACOAs to have learned not to talk about the "real issues" that were occurring within their childhood home. To do so as children would have upset the system of denial that members of the family had so painstakingly created, and could lead to severe physical and/emotional backlash toward the child. Among ACOAs, it was also common to observe a lack of trust in others, and especially with respect to other adults. They learned, within the context of their families, not to trust that anyone, including the adults upon whom they were dependent, would be there for them emotionally or physically. As a consequence of the previous two rules, Black observed that ACOAs learned it wasn't safe to discuss their feelings. As children, in order to survive, they would have learned "how to discount and repress feelings and some learn simply not to feel" (p. 46). My clinical experience has led me to believe that these rules are more generalizable than initially proposed. My observation has been that these rules are not limited to families in which parental alcohol abuse is an issue, but rather are applicable to most children who grow up within a context of complex trauma.

### *"Don't Talk"*

I've heard from hundreds of adult clients over the years, who have said, that despite the extent of the atrocities that occurred in their childhood homes, they were warned either explicitly or implicitly not to speak about what happened—to anyone. Threats of violence or death against themselves, other family members, or family pets, were often used to ensure silence. Some were explicitly warned that talking about things that happened in their family would be viewed as an unforgiveable betrayal. Others were kept quiet with the threat that if they said anything, they and their siblings would be placed in foster care—and it would be their fault. In some cases, the perpetrator's threats of death made while clients were children have become so terrifying and ingrained, that even as adults who are no longer dependent on these abusive caregivers or may no longer have contact with them, these clients continue to experience shame regarding betraying their family and/or fear of possible reprisal, as a result of speaking about their experiences in therapy— *even though they know our discussions are confidential.*

Children who are abused learn that their family not only demands silence about their abuse and neglect in the outside world, but also within the family itself. A parent, who is angry that the children are making noise upstairs, grabs a gun and shoots through the ceiling while yelling at the children to "Shut up!" The children, who fortunately are not physically injured, become silent. Eyes downcast, they do not look at each other. Nor do they discuss what has happened, either within or outside of the family. Each person is isolated within his or her own terror, physiological reactions, and thoughts. Everyone acts like it didn't happen. A caregiver beats a child for forgetting to put their dishes in the sink. The other children leave the room. One might take care of the beaten child afterwards, but the event is likely never spoken of again. Children see their father punch and kick their mother. When the father leaves, the children take care of her and put her to bed, telling her it will be okay. The next day despite the bruises and mom's two black eyes, everyone pretends things are normal. No one speaks of what happened. To speak about the violence risks further violence.

What do children learn from these experiences? Children invariably learn to compartmentalize in order to survive. They learn that some things are unspeakable and that to speak the truth is dangerous.

### *"Don't Feel"*

Likewise, in order to cope with the pain of chronic and unrelenting familial terrorism and abuse, children have to find ways to shut down their emotions and sometimes even the physical sensations in their bodies.

In these environments, children will often be shamed or threatened if they express sadness or fear, with caregiver comments such as, "Big boys/girls don't cry," or "Stop crying or I'll give you something to cry about." Within these home environments emotions are minimized, belittled, and ignored. They become a potential source of humiliation. Children who are terrified are told they have nothing of which to be afraid. Those who are crying are told they have nothing to cry about. They might be told they are loved, and yet their experience of "love" has been so enmeshed with fear, humiliation, and pain that the concept being loved becomes absolutely terrifying. How confusing all of this can be for a child!

One of the things I have noticed is that when adults who were traumatized as children do cry, they will often express shame and attach apologies to this natural expression of emotion. They will say that they don't like to cry in front of anyone. I have also noticed that this population of clients cries silently, which isn't surprising since as children they would have learned that crying had to be done in secret so as to avoid negative attention and punishment. They learned not to expect that they would be comforted, and thus it became a matter of self-preservation to go off by themselves to release their sadness. For most, this was done in bed at night, alone and in the dark, where no one would see or hear them.

The "Don't feel" rule often extends to physical needs as well. Children in abusive homes are sometimes made to feel that their physical needs are a nuisance and something of which to be ashamed. Control, restriction, neglect, and punishment surrounding physical needs can convey messages of worthlessness and shame to the child. These needs can become another vulnerability that can be exploited by abusive caregivers to inflict pain. I have worked with adults, who as children, grew up in middle-class and wealthy families in which they were denied food. They went to school without lunches because there was no food in their home, nor were they given money to buy food. Food for breakfast and supper was also scarce. Lack of safe and comforting human touch can be another source of trauma. Infants and children require safe and comforting touch for healthy brain development—including the capacity for emotional regulation (Schore, 2016). In some cases, not only is there an absence of this kind of touch, but it is instead replaced by hurtful touch, which adds another layer of trauma. Abuse can also take the form of restriction or deprivation with respect to bodily functions. Within some families, children are made to wait hours to have access to a bathroom to relieve themselves. Sleep deprivation and interruption is also a common consequence of nighttime violence, abuse, arguing, and/or an ongoing fear of the inherent vulnerability of sleeping. I have heard of some sexual abuse survivors who as children learned to sleep with their eyes open and continue to do so in adulthood. Sleep disturbances that result from ongoing hypervigilance in response to very real danger in childhood will often persist into adulthood.

Many children in these situations owe their survival to their ability to dissociate emotionally and, in some cases, physically from their own bodies. This allows them to wall off parts of their pain and provides some relief from unrelenting feelings of powerlessness, terror, and despair. Those who are unable to shut off their emotions will often try to find other ways to deal with their pain. Some turn to drugs or alcohol. Some use self-injury behaviors. Some will also engage in high-risk behaviors or what is often termed "acting out". Suicide might also become a possibility for those who despair that the pain will ever end.

### *"Don't Trust"*

In abusive environments, where children's perceptions and emotions are ignored, dismissed, or invalidated, it is unsafe for children to trust and acknowledge their own feelings and cognitions (Goldsmith et al., 2004; Linehan, 1993). Their instincts also become suspect.

Traumatized children often question if there is something really wrong with them when everyone else is in the family is acting like abuse and violence either didn't happen or isn't upsetting. This can be crazy-making for children in this situation. They might start to mistrust their own perceptions and reactions. Did what they see and hear really happen? Why is everyone acting like nothing happened? Are they the only one who realizes it isn't right? Are they the only one who is afraid and hurting about this? Within such a context, listening to their feelings, bodies, and perceptions would place them in a perilous position within the family. Furthermore, owning these parts of themselves involves owning the unbearable pain and ongoing terror that goes with their reality. To do so would compromise their ability to survive. Thus, this can lead to a fundamental disconnection within themselves as a key survival mechanism.

Children in these environments also learn not to trust others because the most important adults in their lives are either unwilling or incapable of providing them with safety. Their primary caregivers, who are supposed to love and protect them, are instead sources of fear and danger. My clients have often voiced the childhood belief that if they couldn't trust their caregivers who "loved" them, and treated them this way, then how could they trust anyone else? Traumatized children learn that they are alone in their pain and that there are no adults whom they can count on to comfort them and keep them safe. They are on their own with trying to regulate their own overwhelming and intolerable physical and emotional reactions.

## The Abuse Dichotomy

Briere (1992) describes the "abuse dichotomy" as a series of progressive conclusions that abused children reach in order to understand why they are being abused. He suggests that is starts out with a child coming to the realization that he/she is being abused by a trusted caregiver. The child then concludes that the abuse is a result either of the child being a bad person, or the caregiver being a bad person. Since, however, the child has been taught that adults are always right and are supposed to punish bad behavior for the child's own good, it must be the child who deserves the punishment—which means the child is a bad person.

Furthermore, it has been suggested that children will tend to internalize the "badness" because it provides them with a sense of hope and control. If the child believes that they have done something to deserve the abuse, then they can hold onto the hope that if they change, the abuse will stop (Herman, 1997). Some children are directly blamed by a caretaker, and told that they deserve the abuse, which underscores the child's perception that it is their fault. I will often hear my adult clients speak about their abuse as children, saying things like, "I thought if I did better in school", "If I had been prettier", "If I had done a better job cleaning the house." Or they were directly told they deserved or "asked for" the abuse they received. Often still among adult clients, the core or gut level belief is that somehow the abuse was their fault.

It can be helpful to identify and address these unspoken rules and concepts during therapy. This can assist clients to better understand their childhood family environment, as well as their reactions and behaviors within a context of survival. It can also help them to find the words to describe what were once unspeakable experiences.

One of the continuous messages I give my clients who have survived childhood trauma, is that they—like every other child—deserved to be loved, respected, cherished, and protected—no matter what. I think it matters that they are told this, and reassured that there is nothing they could have done to deserve abuse or neglect. One of the other things I will often do is apologize to my clients for what they have been through. Even though I am not responsible for their trauma and I didn't contribute to it in any way, I believe in the power of apology. Several years ago, in 2008, I observed the televised reaction of Canada's First Nations people when the Prime Minister of Canada apologized for the abuses they endured, when decades ago First Nations children were forcefully removed from their homes and sent to residential schools. Families were torn apart as these children were deprived of their native cultures and languages. In these institutions, many of these children suffered through emotional, physical, and sexual abuse. Some didn't survive. The consequences of these traumas have been devastating to generations of First Nations families and communities ever since. What left its mark on me was seeing the tears among the First Nations survivors in the audience as the Prime Minister made an apology on behalf of the country. Some survivors spoke of waiting such a long time for this apology, and how although it didn't erase what had happened, the acknowledgement of what they went through was needed. The Prime Minister did not have any personal responsibility for the abuses experienced by residential school survivors, but he spoke on behalf of the government and Canadian people—and at some level that mattered. As a result of this, I will often tell survivors of childhood trauma that I am sorry that they had the experiences they did, and that they deserved so much better. I tell them that I recognize they are unlikely to hear an apology from those who hurt them, but they deserve one, so I would like to offer one. When I offer this apology, though it doesn't erase anything that happened to them, I see from their expressions, and oftentimes their tears, that it matters.

## Long-Term Impacts of Childhood Exposure to Trauma

Exposure to complex trauma in childhood has been linked to a higher rate of lifetime physiological and psychological vulnerabilities. Comprehensive reviews of the research on the relationship of neurobiology and childhood trauma have highlighted the correlation between childhood exposure to trauma and a profound and lasting impact on brain development and functioning (De Bellis, 2010; Teicher et al., 2010). Moreover, a review of clinical literature on the topic of traumatic childhood victimization suggests that survivors of early life trauma are not only at risk for developing PTSD during adolescence and adulthood, but are also at higher risk for other psychiatric, psychosocial, and medical dysfunctions or impairments (Ford, 2010). Significant increases in specific health issues have been identified:

> We found a strong dose response between the breadth of exposure to abuse or household dysfunction in childhood and multiple risk factors for several leading causes of death in adults. Disease conditions including ischemic heart disease, cancer, chronic lung disease, skeletal fractures, and liver disease, as well as poor self-related health also showed a graded relationship to the breadth of childhood exposures. The findings suggest that the impact of these adverse childhood experiences on adult health status is strong and cumulative.
>
> (Felitti et al., 1998, p. 251)

Hence, childhood trauma exposure can have lasting and life-altering effects in all areas of survivors' lives, which makes it all the more important that these individuals receive appropriate, effective trauma-informed medical and psychological supports and interventions. It also underscores the need for adequately funded early intervention programs for families in crisis.

## Note

1 This client's name has been changed. He provided informed consent to allow me to share parts of his story.

# 5 Recommended Evidence-Based Approaches for Treating PTSD

> You need a guide who is not afraid of your terror and who can contain your darkest rage, someone who can safeguard the wholeness of you while you explore the fragmented experiences that you had to keep secret from yourself for so long.
>
> (van der Kolk, 2014, p. 213)

This passage speaks to our core tasks as therapists. When our clients gather the courage to share their sacred stories with us, we must be equipped with the knowledge and skills that will allow us to accompany them on their journey while effectively keeping them safe and supporting them as they identify, process, and reclaim the abandoned or fragmented parts of the self.

Some of our clients will decide that their goals are stabilization and containment. Once that is achieved, they will be satisfied. Others will want to move beyond symptom management into trauma processing. To do this more intensive work, we will need to have developed the specific knowledge and skills necessary to facilitate evidence-based trauma-processing interventions, which will assist our clients in getting through the individualized pathways that will lead them out of the valley. We will be better equipped to serve our clients if we are effective in two or more of these approaches, since not every approach will be a fit for every client. We will also need to be willing to be flexible in these approaches, and sometimes even creative, in order to adapt them to be culturally appropriate. Fortunately, there are a number of recommended approaches from which therapists may choose.

## Evidence-Based Trauma Processing Approaches

The APA (2017) published *Clinical Guidelines for the Treatment of Post-traumatic Stress Disorder (PTSD) in Adults.* Following a systematic review of the literature in this area, the following clinical approaches were ***strongly recommended:***

- Cognitive Behavioral Therapy (CBT);
- Cognitive Processing Therapy (CPT);

- Cognitive Therapy (CT); and
- Prolonged Exposure Therapy (PE).

Additionally, the following clinical approaches received *conditional recommendation*:

- Brief Eclectic Psychotherapy (BEP);
- Eye Movement Desensitization and Reprocessing (EMDR); and
- Narrative Exposure Therapy (NET).

Furthermore, a large-scale systemic review of therapies for chronic PTSD completed as a project of the Cochrane Collaboration (Bisson, Roberts, Andrew, Cooper, & Lewis, 2013) found evidence to support the efficacy of: individual Trauma-Focused Cognitive Behavioral Therapy (TFCBT); EMDR; individual non-TFCBT; and group TFCBT.

It is of note that all of the recommended therapies have at least some basis in CBT, and some involve imagined exposure to triggering stimuli.

### Cognitive Behavioral Therapies

Developed by Aaron Beck in the early 1960s, and originally called "Cognitive Therapy", this present-oriented, structured, time-limited approach to psychotherapy has taken on many different forms since its inception (e.g., Cognitive Processing Therapy (CPT), Rational Emotive Therapy (RET), Dialectical Behavior Therapy). Beck (1976) explains the role of maladaptive thinking in causing client distress:

> emotional reactions, motivations and overt behavior are guided by thinking. A person may not be fully aware of the automatic thoughts that influence to a large extent how he acts, what he feels and how much he enjoys his experiences. . . . The term "maladaptive thoughts" is applied to ideation that interferes with the ability to cope with life experiences, unnecessarily disrupts internal harmony, and produces inappropriate or excessive emotional reactions that are painful.
>
> (p. 235)

Beck focused on cognitive schemas and automatic thoughts, and how if these were faulty or flawed, they could lead to cognitive distortions and maladaptive thinking.

The primary goal of CBT or CT is to bring these distorted or maladaptive thoughts and schemas into awareness, evaluate the accuracy of these beliefs by testing them against reality, and revise these self-statements and schemas to more accurately reflect reality.

According to Judith Beck (2011):

> the *cognitive model* proposes that dysfunctional thinking (which influences the patient's mood and behavior) is common to all psychological

disturbances. When people learn to evaluate their thinking in a more realistic and adaptive way, they experience improvement in their emotional state and behavior.

(p. 3)

This therapeutic approach recognizes the impact that thoughts have on emotions, physiology, and behavior. Hence, CBT and CT utilize a variety of strategies (e.g., worksheets, mindfulness, imagery, homework, problem-solving training, etc.) to assist clients in identifying maladaptive core beliefs about the self, other people, and the world—and to work to modify these to be more adaptive. When this approach is successful, clients will feel better emotionally and physically, and behave in ways that are more functional and adaptive.

CPT is somewhat unique among the recommended cognitive approaches in that it was designed specifically for the treatment of PTSD. It is structured as a 12-week intervention for individual and/or group administration. It is comprised of five phases of treatment that focus on: 1) assessment of PTSD and other comorbid conditions; 2) education on PTSD and cognitive theory; 3) processing of the traumatic event with special attention to "stuck points" which are impeding client recovery; 4) use of Socratic questioning and worksheets to help clients to get through stuck points; and 5) more directed focus on stuck points and transition to focus on relapse prevention and themes of safety, power and control, self-esteem, intimacy, and trust (Galovski, Wachen, Chard, Monson, & Resick, 2015).

### Exposure Therapies

Prolonged Exposure Therapy (PE) (Foa & Rothbaum, 1998) is a cognitive-behavioral therapy that utilizes repeated imaginal exposure of the trauma, with the goal of habituation of the emotional reaction to these memories. Psycho-education and building of the therapeutic alliance are important components of this treatment. The therapist works with the client to create a hierarchy of trauma-related situations, from those that elicit the least amount of fear, to those that elicit the most. Starting with the safest of these memories, the client describes the trauma-related situation in great deal, to the point that he/she is emotionally engaged. It is within the context of being emotionally engaged in the memory—with the knowledge that he/she is safe in the present moment and although feeling distressed, cannot be hurt further by the trauma—that the traumatic memory is processed and integrated. The client is provided with audiotapes of the session, and listens to them for homework, to assist further processing and identify any areas that might require more attention.

Brief Eclectic Psychotherapy (BEP) for clients suffering from PTSD (Gersons & Schnyder, 2013), begins with a psychoeducational component and then imaginal re-experiencing of the trauma. Trauma-related mementos are used as tools to assist the client in connecting with strong emotions that may have been suppressed. Letter writing is also a tool used in this approach, to assist clients with expressing difficult emotions. One of the final phases of treatment involves helping client to acknowledge that their life has changed following the trauma, and assisting them to integrate the trauma into their "domain of meaning". The final phase of treatment involves creating a farewell ritual to help the client to let go of the traumatic event and move forward with their lives.

Eye Movement Desensitization and Reprocessing (EMDR) (Shapiro, 2001) involves the cognitive restructuring of negative beliefs about the self that were derived as a result of trauma. This approach involves exposure, in that it identifies and works with a targeted trauma memory that is linked to the negative cognition about the self. The client recalls this memory, while the therapist activates bilateral stimulation (e.g., visually through the client's eyes following a light bar or therapist fingers moving from side to side at eye level; therapist alternatively tapping the client's right and left hands; using a recording delivering bilateral tones through headphones). The therapist then supports the client through the processing of thoughts that arise. Shapiro (2001) indicates that the goals of EMDR include: assisting the client to learn from their trauma experiences, desensitizing trauma triggers, and devising plans for dealing with future challenges that might arise.

Narrative Exposure Therapy (NET), is a short-term therapy developed specifically for use with individuals who have experienced multiple traumas, as a result of organized violence (e.g., war, torture, terrorism, etc.) over a prolonged period of time (Schauer, Neuner, & Elbert, 2005). This approach starts with psychoeducation and then next, the client constructs a chronological lifeline in which happy and frightening/sad events are indicated. During the next series of sessions, the client provides a chronological narrative of the events on their lifeline. Particular attention is given to traumatic events, with emphasis on the client's physical, emotional, and cognitive reactions both at the time of the trauma, and at the present time as they tell their story. After the session, the therapist writes up the client's narrative, and reads it at the start of the next session to review it with the client and check for accuracy in their reporting. This process continues until all the traumatic events have been narrated and documented, and the client's emotional responses to these events have been reduced. The client's hopes and plans for the future are discussed. The therapist then provides the client with the written narratives, which end up being a documentation of their life story.

## Pharmacological Interventions

The *APA Clinical Practice Guideline for the treatment of PTSD* (2017) has recommended the use of SSRIs (i.e., fluoxetine, sertraline, and paroxetine) as well as the SNRI, venlafaxine, for their demonstrated efficacy in treating PTSD symptoms. It has been suggested that there is a definite role for SSRIs as an effective front-line intervention to provide PTSD symptom relief (van der Kolk et al., 2007; Stein, Ipser, Seedat, Sager, & Amos, 2006). Furthermore, following a review of all randomized control trials assessing the efficacy of pharmacological interventions for PTSD, researchers concluded that SSRIs have demonstrated effectiveness in significantly reducing the symptom severity of PTSD, as well as related depression and disability, with efficacy over the long term (Stein et al., 2006).

While it might not be within our professional purview to prescribe medications for our clients, we need to be aware that this is an evidence-based support that might be beneficial to our clients, and we need to communicate this to them so that they can discuss it with the appropriate medical practitioners.

## Phase Approach to Therapy

When treating complex trauma, it is recommended that therapy be done in three phases (Courtois, 2004; Ford et al., 2005). These authors recommend that the first phase of therapy focus on: safety and stabilization; building the therapeutic alliance; skill development; and education. The second phase should center on: emotional-regulation strategies to manage distress while clients consciously and voluntary engage in trauma processing; mourning; symptom resolution; and integrating the trauma into one's personal narrative. The final phase should focus on client personal and relationship development with the goal of enhancing the client's daily life.

The aforementioned sequential therapy approach also works, and should be followed, for clients who are dealing with single-event traumatic experiences. All of the phases are important, and none should be skipped. With single-incident trauma, however, it is likely that the phases can be safely transitioned through more quickly than would be the case for complex trauma.

## When Not to Pursue Trauma Processing

Trauma work can be life threatening for some clients due to the level of distress it can elicit. Suicidal impulses are a very real danger if our clients do not have the supports, resources, and tools to effectively manage their distress.

> It may be for some clients that no amount of work to maintain and strengthen self-regulatory capacities is sufficient to prepare them for Phase 2 interventions. The psychic and somatic integrity of the person should never be compromised by attempts at the mastery of traumatic memories.
>
> (Ford et al., 2005, p. 445)

Clients who have not been able to effectively manage distress and/or are at risk for suicide are not candidates for trauma processing. Only if and when distress can be managed without risk of serious injury to a client, should we proceed with this potentially highly distressing therapeutic work.

Some clients will come to counseling because they want to manage distress and wish to do this without going in-depth into the trauma experience. If this is the case, our focus needs to be on stabilization, containment, and resource building. Though we might truly believe that if these clients went through with trauma processing, they would experience much greater benefits, it is not our decision to make, and in extreme cases, could prove fatal to our clients.

Another situation in which it would be unwise to pursue trauma processing is when the client is still living in an abusive or otherwise unsafe environment. Doing trauma processing requires clients to let their defenses down. This is neither safe nor advisable when a client is living in a situation in which those defenses are still required (Rothschild, 2000).

# 6 Clinical Foundations for Working With Clients Suffering From PTSD

Nothing is so strong as gentleness. Nothing is so gentle as real strength.
—Frances de Sales (1567–1622)

The pain caused by trauma and resultant PTSD symptoms, tends to fortify already strong defenses within the individual. These defenses are meant to protect and maximize chances of survival in the face of serious threat. If we approach the trauma survivor in such a way that we are perceived to threaten those defenses, the individual will respond accordingly. Thus, our approach needs to be genuinely non-threatening and transparent. It needs to be based in gentleness, compassion, and respect, while at the same time conveying the message that we are willing and strong enough to hear the truth of the atrocities and resultant pain that our clients have endured.

What kind of foundational tools will we need to bring with us into the valley? Knowledge about trauma is an important tool, but will not be sufficient for the journey ahead. We need to pack a lens that will allow us to see truth through the distortions caused by the darkness and confusion that swirl in the valley. This lens is called compassion. We will also need to invest ourselves in client-centered values—values that form the foundation for the development of a strong therapeutic alliance, which will offer safety and containment for our clients.

## A Compassion-Focused CBT Approach

After witnessing both the immediate and long-term positive impact of assisting clients to shift maladaptive expectations, schemas, and core beliefs, in more adaptive and supportive directions, I found myself embracing the basic components of CBT in my work with trauma clients. Simultaneously, I also found the strength and healing power of compassion—my own and my client's—as a catalyst to healing.

The basis of CBT lies in the premise that maladaptive beliefs negatively impact emotions, physical sensations, and behaviors—and that shifting these beliefs in a more adaptive direction will have a direct impact on the individual at the emotional, physical, and behavioral levels (Beck, 1976). Generally speaking, there are three different types of CBT approaches: 1) coping skills therapies; 2) problem-solving therapies; and 3) cognitive restructuring therapies (Dobson & Dozois, 2010). In the course of this book, the focus will be on coping skills development and cognitive restructuring.

Retraining the mind and body to shift—from a sense of powerlessness in the face of trauma and consequent PTSD symptoms—to identifying and utilizing coping strategies to manage and reduce distress, is not only vital to assist clients in understanding that they have some control over distress in their daily lives, but it is also essential within the context of therapy in order to establish safety prior to progressing to trauma processing.

Cognitive restructuring or reframing, through a lens of compassion, is a dominant theme in my approach to working with clients suffering from PTSD. Genuine compassion is the balm to shame, which is a toxic component of PTSD. Shame can cause our clients to hide the most vulnerable and injured parts of themselves, not only from others, but often from themselves as well. Shame is a roadblock to understanding and embracing all the parts of the self into wholeness once again. Cognitive restructuring allows us to address the most insidious part of the traumatic experience, i.e., the undermining of the sense of self, and one's inherent value as a human being. In the process of cognitive restructuring, we must first help clients to identify these shame-laden beliefs, recognizing that "most central or core beliefs are enduring understandings so fundamental and deep that they often do not articulate them, even to themselves" (Beck, 2011. p. 32). The cognitions or core beliefs that form (often unconsciously) during the worst parts of the trauma experience, or very soon after, are a source of ongoing emotional, physical, spiritual, and/or cognitive distress for trauma survivors. The reason that these cognitions are so negative can be understood by considering the context in which they are formed. During trauma, as discussed previously, the mind is not functioning rationally, but rather is in survival mode. The lens through which the traumatic experience is viewed, is one of unbearable fear, horror, pain, and/or powerlessness. What kind of self-concepts will be ingrained during such moments? The most common ones I've heard have involved variations of the following: "I am permanently damaged", "I am worthless", "I am unlovable", "I am shameful". These beliefs have been maintained, often over many years, via the unconscious tendency to selectively attend to data that supports them while ignoring or minimizing data that is contrary (Goldsmith et al., 2004). In cognitive restructuring, our first task is often to bring unconscious core beliefs into consciousness. Until they have been identified, we can't start to assess their level of adaptiveness and accuracy, and or work to change them if needed.

Education, metaphors, and reframing are tools that can be used for the purposes of cognitive restructuring. Providing accurate information on trauma, such as how it can affect the mind and body, including typical reactions and symptoms can, for example, shift clients' beliefs that there is something weak or shameful about their responses to trauma. They learn instead that their responses fall within the normal range of what is expected, given what they have been through. This is a very important initial shift that can begin to reduce distress. The use of metaphors, such as that of the Warrior Spirit and the valley of the shadow of death can also help clients to reframe how they see themselves, to feel hope instead of hopelessness, and to begin to glimpse their own strength and resiliency and how this will serve them on the journey that lies ahead of them.

One of the interesting things about cognitive restructuring is that you can often visually witness the transitional moment when a new cognition starts to take root. This is a significant transformational moment in the therapeutic process. It doesn't mean our job is done, but rather lets us know that something important is starting to happen in the brain. It is the "ah-ha" moment for the client, where you as the therapist might notice a change in the client's facial expression that denotes some relief and/or a reduction in distress. Sometimes it begins with a look of skepticism or surprise, followed by one of consideration and then understanding. You can often see these thoughts play out in the clients' non-verbal reactions as they work through a new concept in their mind that they realize fits for them in a positive way and helps to make sense of that which has been troubling them. You may actually observe the physical release of tension in their body. In these moments it is essential to process all of this—any changes in thoughts, physical sensations, and emotions that occur. I've observed that noticing these changes and bringing them into the conscious awareness of clients seems to help to strengthen the cognitive restructuring that is occurring.

## Underlying Values of This Approach

### *Client-Centeredness*

I let my clients know that because trauma is about loss of control, fear, unbearable pain, and/or a sense of powerlessness—*healing cannot be*. In trauma therapy, clients must have control over determining what their goals are and how they would like to proceed. At the start of counseling with trauma clients I let them know that they will be in control of setting counseling goals, what topics we will discuss, and to what depths. It is my responsibility to offer a safe and supportive environment and therapeutic relationship in which to do this work. My role is to be up-to-date on perspectives, theories, and interventions that might be helpful to my clients and to offer these for their consideration. My role is that of a guide, but clients choose the paths we will take. They are the experts on themselves. They will judge what fits or doesn't fit for them in terms of the strategies and interventions I offer for their consideration. Some clients will want assistance with stabilization and managing their distress only. Others will want to go all the way through to processing parts of the trauma. It is imperative that we hear their goals and be respectful of them, even if we believe they might truly benefit from trauma processing.

Doing trauma counseling requires humility. We are not above our clients. We do not walk ahead of them on this journey. Nor are we shouting commands from the sidelines. Instead we walk beside them. We are professional guides and therapeutic facilitators of healing. We have an idea as to what to expect and what provisions are needed in advance. We help to prepare our clients, to ensure they have the internal and external resources that will be needed to address challenges along the way. We call upon our skills to help to facilitate the healing process on this journey. Throughout, we need to keep in mind the honor that has been bestowed upon us, as our clients allow us to accompany them.

## Transparency

Transparency flows out of the intention to be client-centered. We must provide information in a manner that clients can understand, so that they can make informed choices about how we will proceed. This might mean offering information in several different formats such as verbal, written, experiential, etc. This also means avoiding professional jargon and acronyms, so that we speak to our clients in everyday language that does not require them to have a background in psychology or social work to understand what we are saying.

Psychoeducation needs to be a large part of the counseling process for clients who are dealing with trauma. Education and knowledge about trauma, typical reactions during and following traumatic experiences, and the stages of the healing journey, can provide clients with the words and language to describe what might have previously been elusive and/or unspeakable for them. It can help to normalize their experiences and in doing so, can relieve the added distress that often comes with mistaken perceptions that their bodies and minds are reacting in ways that are abnormal following the trauma. Psychoeducation also needs to include information on the types of trauma-processing interventions that are being offered (including risks and benefits), to allow clients to make informed choices about the therapeutic process and what pathways they would like us to travel with them.

Likewise, transparency applies to the therapeutic relationship. Interpersonal trauma inherently involves personal boundary violations. For those who have survived long-term traumatic relationships, boundary violations might be the norm in their significant relationships. It is imperative that we clarify roles of the therapeutic relationship at the outset. This helps clients to know what to expect and can provide them with some relief. In addition to the usual administrative information (e.g., length of appointments, cancellation policies, roles, etc.), I make sure I tell my clients that I will not touch them even when they are very upset. I explain that I'm aware that touch has been used to hurt many of my clients in the past, and that it can also trigger flashbacks. Instead I will offer my caring, undivided attention and either respectful silence or words depending on what I believe will be most helpful to them in the moment.

## Reverence

An individual's trauma story is sacred. By "sacred" I am referring to the Merriam-Webster dictionary definition, "entitled to reverence and respect". At the core of any trauma story is human vulnerability. These stories expose injuries for which the pain can still be overwhelming. As we know now, there are physiological reasons that finding words to tell their story can be difficult, and at times impossible, for the trauma survivor. It takes tremendous courage, on the part of our clients, to face these memories, which may result in reliving rather than simply recalling.

When a person chooses to reveal their trauma story to us, they are bestowing an honor. Our clients need to be reassured that it is healthy for them to discriminate regarding with whom they share their story. The truth of the matter is, there are some people who will not respond with the respect and compassion that is deserved. Thus, I remind my clients that their story is sacred, and it is their right to decide with whom they will share it. I remind them that this applies within our relationship as well. I will not press for details of their story because to do so could be perceived as a boundary violation, and might be retraumatizing. I might ask some questions to try to understand their story better, but I am clear that it is important to their healing that they not provide these details if it makes them uncomfortable. It takes tremendous trust to share a trauma story. As therapists, our actions and words need to reassure our clients that we will treat them and their story with reverence and respect.

## Compassion

Compassion combined with safety, knowledge, and professional skill is the cornerstone of our work. The levels of pain, vulnerability, and often shame, to which we will bear witness, require tremendous trust on the part of our clients. Compassion is about connecting with our clients on a level playing field. It involves genuine, non-judgmental caring. Compassion can be conveyed in our open and leaning forward posture. It can be conveyed in our eyes, tone of voice, and words. It can be conveyed in the way we interact and collaborate with our clients as equals on their healing journey.

I truly believe that compassion is the antidote to shame and where healing starts to happen. When our clients trust us enough to share that one thing they've never told anyone before . . . or that one thing they've tried so hard to forget; when our clients trust us enough with these things and we respond, often to their surprise, with compassion rather than disgust or derision—healing starts to happen. This can lead to a shift in the schema within their minds that led them to believe that they are inherently bad or evil—that if anyone found out what happened they would be abandoned. When this compassionate acceptance of our client happens consistently over time within the therapeutic alliance, the client's perception of self starts to soften. I have witnessed those same clients who hated and despised parts of themselves, move into a place of self-compassion. I have heard them internalize my words of compassion, in relation to themselves, and speak them out loud. This is not only a moving experience, but is also evidence of the client's successful cognitive restructuring.

### Belief in Clients' Strength and Resiliency

At the core of this work lies our belief in our clients' inherent strength and resiliency. Traumatic stress symptoms and coping strategies that no longer serve a helpful purpose might be hiding these truths from our clients. As therapists, however, we must train ourselves to see through this. Our clients are with us now because of their strength and resiliency. We work with them to unmask it so that they will be able to recognize it within themselves. It is through harnessing their internal strength, their Warrior Spirit, that they will find the direction and stamina needed to travel their individual healing pathways.

Our role, as therapists, even when our clients are seemingly drowning in the darkness, despair, and pain of PTSD, is to keep our eyes on the light. It is an ongoing balancing and timing task for us. While acknowledging our clients' distress and validating their perceptions and responses to the atrocities they have experienced, we must also gently challenge them with reframes of their strength, courage, and perseverance in the face of these atrocities. In PTSD, a tremendous source of pain comes from negative beliefs of the self that often unconsciously become anchored in the mind and body during and following trauma. It is part of our work to help our clients to identify and address these, in order to reduce distress.

### Recognizing Client Self-Determination

> By offering trauma victims choice, control, empathy, and respect, the therapist's behavior contradicts aspects of the traumatic experiences and facilitates healing, awareness and empowerment.
>
> (Goldsmith et al., 2004, p. 458)

There have been times in my work with clients, where part of me is convinced that if only my client would (fill in the blank), they would be much better off. While I've developed a pretty good set of prediction skills, based on what I have learned in life regarding cause and effect, the bottom line is that I am not aware of all of the internal and external factors with which my clients are dealing. Nor can I truly know all of what they experience from within their own bodies and minds. As adults, our clients have the right to make their own decisions without the influence of our personal biases. Being professionals who strive to be both culturally sensitive and trauma-sensitive in our work, means that we must make a conscious effort not to impose our own values, choices, or cultural lenses on individuals who have already suffered the boundary violations that are part of the trauma experience. This means not trying to pressure clients to adhere to our values, suggestions or "advice" on how they should live their lives, even though we might believe we have their best interests at heart. We can express genuine concern if our clients are placing themselves in dangerous situations, and we can talk with them about ways they might consider to improve their safety, but it isn't our place to tell them what to do. To do so would place us in a parental role, thereby communicating that we perceive that we are deserving of more power in the therapeutic relationship than the client, thus setting up a breach in the foundation of the alliance.

It is not always easy to bear witness to clients who engage in ongoing high-risk behaviors and/or relationships, without wanting to firmly warn them that this needs to change for their own well-being. This is a very delicate place in our work, and requires a great deal of gentleness and respect on our part. Our clients have likely heard from their loved ones how they need to stop doing (fill in the blank), or to end an abusive relationship, and yet that hasn't resulted in the suggested changes. If we take a similar stance, our clients will likely go on the defensive. They will see us as part of the group of "others" in their lives who don't understand. I visualize this as my clients standing facing me with their backs to whatever high-risk behavior or relationship they are defending. Their arms are spread out to the sides as they face me and protect what is behind them. In this posture they can't see what is behind them. They are too busy digging in their heels to protect against a possible attack on something that is important to them.

Our role is to provide a safe space in which clients can take down their defenses and turn around to look behind them, without fear of attack. This is necessary if we are to work together to assess how their current behaviors and relationships are affecting them, and give them the opportunity to decide if they wish for things to be different. If so, we can then work with them to figure out how to work toward desired changes.

If I am working with a client who has been traumatized and has been told by loved ones to talk to me about a behavior or relationship that they are engaged in that others want them to stop, I will ask why they think their loved ones are concerned. I will then explain that it isn't my place to judge them or try to make them change, but rather to provide a place where they feel safe enough to take down their defenses without fear of attack, to look at what they have been protecting, and to make their own decisions. It is my job to try to understand the situation from their perspective, to provide information that might help them to make sense of what is going on, and to assist them in identifying what they want for themselves. To do any more or any less would be unprofessional and disrespectful.

### Inclusivity—*Not* Us *vs.* Them

As a college counselor, a few years ago I was invited to a meeting of community clinical placement supervisors for one of our health science programs. In this meeting, supervisors were expressing their concerns about the stress that some of their placement students appeared to be under, and how this was affecting their performance. I shared information on available counseling services and offered to do a workshop for these students on stress management. A few supervisors expressed concern about students who were suffering from depression or anxiety and asked about how we could better support these students. I provided information on the types of supports we offer and provided my contact information that they could share with students about whom they were concerned. It was then that a faculty member suggested that perhaps, students who were suffering from depression, anxiety, etc., shouldn't be in the program. He suggested that *they* might not be a good fit for this program and might be a danger to the patients with whom they worked. (I had to take a deep breath as I swallowed my anger, and checked myself to ensure I would respond as a professional). I then proceeded to cite my previous research (Porter, 2011), which indicated that students who sought counseling had a higher retention rate than their peers who had not utilized our services. I pointed out that among students who used our counseling services, the most prevalent presenting concern was in fact anxiety-related symptoms. I further shared that even our most at-risk students, (i.e., those who expressed suicidal ideation), did very well academically once they received the appropriate supports (Porter, 2010). I also reassured faculty and clinical supervisors that if we, as counselors, believed a student was at imminent risk of seriously harming themselves or others, we would take appropriate actions. I reminded the group that students in their clinical program were a reflection of our society as a whole. *They* are *us*—and there are many successful medical professionals currently in the field who are also dealing with depression, anxiety, PTSD, etc. After this meeting, a few of the clinical supervisors came up and thanked me for speaking at this meeting and for the perspective I provided. As therapists, we will have many opportunities to educate others and confront the stigma that unfortunately continues to be associated with many of these illnesses.

Not only in the community, but also within our workplaces and offices, an "us" vs. "them" mindset can seriously undermine the effectiveness and integrity of the therapeutic relationship. It can set up power differentials, which place our clients in a lower power position that can be reminiscent of interpersonal trauma experiences. Those who have never experienced PTSD can choose to live in the privileged illusion of believing that they are somehow above this—that it could never happen to them. As therapists, we might need to check any such privileged beliefs and set ourselves straight about them. If we truly accept that individuals who suffer from PTSD are not deficient in any way as human beings, that it is not a matter of character flaw or weakness, then we need to also face the reality that this can happen to *any of us*. Being a therapist does not make us exempt any more than a cardiologist is exempt from the possibility of having a heart attack. It's not about *us* and *them*, it is about *us* as human beings, period. When we accept this reality, we can then begin to approach our clients as equals in the therapeutic relationship. While we have different roles that are both vital in this relationship, the core of the work is about creating an alliance to achieve the goals of the client.

It can be powerfully connecting when we speak to our clients in a manner that acknowledges that we, too, are vulnerable. When I say this I am not talking about getting into extensive disclosures about our own struggles, but rather, choosing our words to reflect this reality. This is why when I explain how PTSD can affect the mind and body, I'm using language such as, "When we experience a situation in which our own or another person's lives are threatened". The "we" acknowledges that it could happen to me, too. This is also why when I explain concepts (e.g., window of tolerance, the difference between a traumatic and non-traumatic memory, etc.), I use myself as the subject. I want to reassure my clients that this applies not just to them, but to all of us generally as part of the human condition. I can tell you that when I speak this way, I invariably notice a shift in clients' non-verbal communication. Their attention becomes sharper. Usually they will lift their eyes to meet my own. It is almost as though they are surprised, and then a bit more relaxed. I imagine that this is because, at first, they look at me and think that I have it together, and am somehow immune to the struggles they have. I want them to know that this is an illusion and contributes to a sense of isolation. How many times do our clients come in and tell us that "everyone else" seems to be doing better than they are? My usual response is, "It's interesting to me that so many of the clients I meet with, think the same thing. If you think about it, do all of your acquaintances, friends, and family members know what you are going through?" (In most cases, they don't). "Like you, some of them will be dealing with their own challenges that you don't know about, and they might be thinking that you are one of those people who have it all together, too. What I have learned from doing this work over many years and through my own personal experience, is that we all have our challenges in lives. *You are not alone.*"

It is not important for my clients to know whether I have dealt with PTSD personally. What is most important is that they know that I honestly don't see myself as above them or stronger than them, and that I am genuinely there with them in the moment, willing to accompany, support, and guide them—as an ally—during their journey through the valley.

## *Accessible Language*

As therapists, we have become immersed in the language of our profession, which is to be expected. We talk about depression, anxiety, PTSD, and use terms such as EMDR, CBT, and DBT. We discuss different forms of dysfunction, emotional regulation, attachment, and resiliency. Every profession has its own second language. However, it is incumbent upon us to make sure that when we are communicating with our clients we do not expect them to have the vocabulary and understanding that we have worked on over years of study and immersion within this profession. If we fail to make information accessible to our clients in ways that are meaningful to them, then we fail in an important part of our work.

About 15 years ago, my father began his battle with cancer. It started with bladder cancer. Seven years later he was diagnosed with skin cancer. A few years after that we learned that the skin cancer had spread into his brain. (He has been fortunate beyond belief, however, in that although we were told to expect that he would die within a year due to the cancer in his brain, it is now more than four years later and he recently learned to parasail, went on a vacation to Ireland, and continues to live a very active and busy life). I still remember how, at the beginning of this journey, I was reading all kinds of medical websites and journals trying to understand what was going on and what to expect. I recall that it felt like I was struggling with a new language. My sisters and I often had to look up terminology because we didn't understand what his doctors were saying. I still remember how, after the surgery to remove my father's bladder, the physician came out of the operating room and told us that my dad had one of the most aggressive cancers he had ever seen. He warned us that our dad would need very aggressive chemotherapy that would require him to be hospitalized during treatment. We asked the doctor when he was going to tell our dad this and were told that after the biopsies came back, his office would call my dad to come in for an appointment where they would discuss how to proceed. Given my dad was still in denial that he had cancer at all, none of us had the heart—or courage—to tell him it had spread. We thought he would be more likely to accept it from his doctor. We waited for the doctor's office to call my dad with the appointment date, with the intention of going with him when he received this news. For the next few weeks my sisters and I tensely waited for news of this appointment. We kept checking with my dad to find out if he had heard from his doctor's office. He finally said he received a call and had an appointment scheduled in a few months. We didn't understand why the appointment was so delayed when it was so serious. One of my sisters called the doctor's office. A nurse spoke to my sister and said she had told my dad when she called to schedule the follow up appointment that "the margins were clear." My sister asked what this meant and was advised it meant that the cancer had not spread as thought. It turned out my dad didn't know what the nurse was talking about and was too embarrassed to ask. For me, this experience felt like a wake-up call. It made me think about how I communicate with my clients. Did I sometimes convey important information in language that my clients didn't understand but were too embarrassed to ask about? I probably had, because it wasn't something I had, up to that point, made a conscious effort of which to be mindful. This experience also fueled my commitment to try to find ways to use metaphors, everyday language, and practical examples to help my clients to better understand trauma. It is also the reason I wrote my first book on trauma, to make the concepts that surround trauma and healing from trauma accessible, through simple language and meaningful metaphors. I've come to realize that I have an obligation to communicate to my clients in ways that are understandable *within their context* first and foremost—rather than my own.

## The Therapeutic Alliance

A strong therapeutic alliance is the foundation for trauma counseling. A meta-analysis of research studies on this topic has confirmed, "the strength of the alliance is predictive of outcome" (Martin, Garske, & Davis, 2000, p. 446). In this study, an "alliance" was broadly defined as the affective and collaborative bond between therapist and client. The therapeutic alliance is a unique type of relationship. The therapist sets the tone via unconditional positive regard, empathy, and congruence (i.e., genuineness, openness, and honesty), as well as ensuring confidentiality and appropriate boundaries:

> let myself express positive attitudes toward this other person—attitudes of warmth, caring, liking, interest, respect.
>
> (Rogers, 1961, p. 52)

The focus within the therapeutic relationship is on the client and achieving client goals, though the relationship between the therapist and client can be part of the means of achieving those goals. For it is through this relationship, and the reframing, strengths mirroring, support and interventions provided by the therapist, that schemas about the clients' views of the self and world will often begin to shift.

### *Therapist as the Holder of Hope*

Another of the key roles of therapists in this work is to be the holder of hope. With all that they are dealing with, most clients will have times when they are overwhelmed by the darkness of their physical, emotional, cognitive, and/or spiritual PTSD symptoms. In those moments, hope might be beyond their grasp. It is at those times that I will often say to my clients something along the lines of:

> *"I can see that right now it's hard for you to imagine that things will get better. That's not uncommon in moments when we are feeling exhausted and overwhelmed. It can be hard to find hope and hold onto it. I want you to know that I truly believe that you can and will get through this. Until you can believe it too, I will hold onto the hope for you".*

This can take a burden off clients' shoulders and allow them to hear our belief and confidence that they will get through the worst parts. They need to hear this and know that we will hold fast to the hope when they cannot.

## Culture and Context

In all counseling work, but especially in trauma work, cultural sensitivity is a must. To clarify, I am referring to culture in the broadest sense: country of origin, race, socio-economic status, education level, religious affiliation, gender identity, ability/disability, age, sexuality, language, etc. While it is likely impossible to be knowledgeable about every culture, it is our obligation to continuously work at educating ourselves about different cultures and particularly those of the clients we serve, and to do so with humility and curiosity. Sue and Sue (2016) describe the characteristics of "culturally competent helping professionals" as ones who:

> are actively in the process of becoming aware of their own values, biases, assumptions about human behavior, preconceived notions, personal limitations . . . actively attempt to understand the *worldview* of their culturally diverse clients . . . are in the process of actively developing and practicing appropriate, relevant, and sensitive intervention strategies and *skills* in working with their culturally diverse clients.
>
> (p. 56)

Of note in these competencies is the emphasis on the fact that this is an *active* and *ongoing* process of self-awareness, knowledge acquisition, and skill development. Developing cultural competency in our work begins with self-awareness and reflection regarding how our own cultures influence our attitudes, beliefs, motivations, behaviors, and cultural projections (Leach, Aten, Boyer, Strain, & Bradshaw, 2010). This is where we begin, but it is not sufficient.

Self-awareness can be the most personally and professionally difficult part of being culturally aware. As Sue (2001) adeptly points out, as therapists we like to think of ourselves as moral, respectful, and decent people. Thus, increasing our self-awareness in such a way as to identify and confront our own privilege, biases, and experiences of discrimination can be quite painful. I think of privilege as referring to unearned advantages that we receive for being part of a particular group, in comparison to others who are not part of our "group" and cannot take for granted that they too will have access to these advantages. Our privilege and biases are often hidden from ourselves, until we search them out. What does it mean to be White, Black, Asian, Middle Eastern in our culture? Christian, Atheist, Jewish, Muslim? Rich, poor, middle-class? Have a visible or invisible disability? What is it like to have an English, French, Spanish, East Indian, . . . accent? What does it mean to be identified as a woman, a man, or a child in our cultural contexts? What is the experience of LGBT members in our community?

I teach a graduate level Cross-Cultural Counseling course at Western University. At the outset I warn my students that this course can be very difficult on a personal and emotional level—for all of us. I make a commitment to them, that I too will be examining my own biases and privilege as we work through this topic. I believe that as a professor I have to model the openness and non-defensive self-awareness that I am asking of my students. I share with them some of my own experiences. One of the examples I share with them is that a couple of days after the terrorist attack in Paris, which I heard about through continuous news reports on the television and on news websites, I was walking my dog. As we were walking, a group of teenage boys was walking toward us. I could see them talking among themselves. They were not behaving in any way that was threatening. Yet, I noticed a physiological fear reaction happening in my body. My stomach knotted. My muscles tensed. And I felt fear through my chest. I didn't understand why I was reacting this way. As they passed by us, I noticed they appeared to be Middle Eastern. I continued to try to understand my reaction and realized that it was connected to the coverage I had seen on the terrorist attack. Horrified by my reaction, I realized that I had to work on freeing myself from the newly internalized belief that these young men were inherently dangerous, because I was not willing to accept it into my belief system. This story was, and is, embarrassing to share. I know better than this, and yet somehow, fear of a cultural group crept in without my awareness and permission. If I had ignored it, denied it, or rationalized it, I would not have dealt with it and it would have stayed. It would have come out in unconscious ways.

Developing self-awareness and knowledge is a difficult process. Occasionally, there are times in my cross-cultural counseling class when students shed tears as they become aware of their areas of privilege and realize how others in their lives may have been denied the same privileges. They reflect back on things they have done or not done, things they have said or not said, and they see these instances from a different perspective. At times, those who have experienced marginalization and discrimination have also shed tears. Based on what I have heard from individuals in such situations, I imagine that the reasons for tears can be complex: relief that their peers are finally starting to "get it"; relief that for once they don't have to be the one educating others; remembrance of the layers of pain associated with past experiences; possible traumatic flashbacks; maybe some hope mixed with frustration, and anger with hurt. Even in a safe environment, it can be a painful process for all of us, but it is a necessary part of our development.

As therapists, we are obliged to be generally knowledgeable and informed about the cultural groups with which we work. We also need to be aware of the types of challenges these groups might face within our communities. Similar to ourselves, our clients will live within a variety of cultural contexts or communities (e.g., work environment, family, religious institution, broader society). Within these contexts, each person will have his/her own individual roles and experiences. While we should not assume that diverse clients are coming in to counseling to discuss experiences of discrimination or marginalization, it is important that we are aware that this could be a possibility and be open to hearing these narratives if they arise. If these types of narratives do become a focal point in the therapeutic process, we might need to be mindful of our own defenses. The vicarious pain of hearing about experiences of oppression, abuse, and discrimination might trigger our own defenses of minimization, denial, or rationalization. Horrified by how a client has been treated, we might impulsively want to offer alternative explanations for the offenders' behaviors, or try to play down the intent. The purpose of these defenses is likely to try to lessen our clients' pain, and possibly to protect our own belief that we've progressed so much as a society that these things don't happen anymore. To respond in these ways, however, is naïve and unsupportive. It conveys the message that we are assuming we know better about our clients' experiences than our clients, that we are doubting their perceptions, we "don't get it", and ultimately that we can't be trusted to hear their stories. Such therapist responses risk shutting down and retraumatizing our clients.

Another part of the knowledge piece of being trauma-informed and culturally sensitive in our work is to be aware that the experience of chronic marginalization or oppression by individuals, groups, and systems can be traumatic in and of itself. Ongoing threats of violence, overt and subtle discrimination, and isolation can result in the need for constant hypervigilance. This experience can be akin to living in a war zone, in which one's survival depends on the ability to identify and respond to potential threats. (For some of our clients it won't have been "akin" to living in a war zone, it will have been their reality if they have lived in war zones or countries where particular cultural groups were targeted). We witness the realities of life and death struggles of specific minority and/or oppressed populations in our society, and the world in general, in the news on a daily basis. Depending on whether individuals in these groups belong to communities of safe refuge, they might never be able to take their guard down. Hence, we need to be mindful that racism, sexism, and other forms of discrimination can be a valid source of PTSD among our clients.

Skill development in terms of meeting the needs of culturally diverse groups is likewise a very deliberate and active process. It involves being aware of our clients' individual cultural contexts, and adapting our approach, strategies, and interventions to fit those needs and contexts. This might involve a more directive approach, involvement of family members, use of story-telling, adapting our verbal and non-verbal communications, seeking consultation with traditional healers or spiritual leaders, etc. (Sue & Sue, 1999). It might also involve focusing on advocating for our clients and focusing on systemic change, rather than on changing our clients (Sue & Sue, 2016).

## The North American and White-Middle Class "Bubbles"

In my experience of working with clients who have emigrated from countries outside of the U.S. and Canada, I have become aware of a concept that I will refer to as the "North American bubble", though my clients have used a few different terms to describe it. After we have developed trust within the therapeutic relationship, several of my clients who have come from some of the most dangerous Middle Eastern, South American, and African countries have shared stories of mind-boggling human atrocities (i.e., systemic rape, "disappearances", kidnappings, torture, and murder). Most have told me that I am the first person in this country with whom they have shared their story. They have gone on to explain their observation, that we, who are privileged to have grown up as part of the middle class in North America, live in a "bubble" such that we take for granted that people everywhere live in society where justice prevails and safety is the norm. This perceived, and likely true, naiveté within North American culture in general, is what stops them from telling their stories. They expect not to be believed or heard. These clients have taught me that we need to be continually mindful of the socio-political realities that exist throughout our world, and be ready and open to hearing the individual consequences of these realities.

Likewise, among individuals who have lived all their lives in North America, and have grown up within marginalized groups, there appears to be a perception of a "White bubble", whereby those of us from a White, European-descent middle-class background, are living in an alternate reality, and have no idea what society is like for those outside this bubble. Again, I believe the perception is, unfortunately, accurate. By staying within the safety of this bubble, those of us who reside there do not have to face: the painful realities of our fellow human beings who are subjected to discrimination and oppression on a daily basis; the collapse of any delusions we hold that life is fair and justice prevails; any threat to our own privilege if systemic discrimination were eliminated; and/or overwhelming frustration regarding how difficult it can be to facilitate societal change to end discrimination and oppression. However, the fact of the matter is that doing this work involves gathering the courage to choose to live outside the bubble.

As a Caucasian woman, who works in an educational system, when my biracial child experienced racism at school at the hands of an older child, I was furious and demanded action—which I received. I didn't expect anything less and would have gone right up the supervisory levels within the school board—and outside—if I hadn't received a prompt and appropriate response. When the incident occurred, however, my husband, who is a Black man who experienced unchecked racism throughout elementary school, had no confidence that the school would deal with it. He was surprised when they responded so quickly and effectively to my complaint. This situation reminded me of the reality of my White privilege. Having never personally experienced racism prior to my marriage, I had taken for granted that it was wrong and would be seen that way by others who were in positions of power and could address it. My husband, on the other hand, because of his experiences, had no such faith that people in positions of power would do the right thing. This, as one of many experiences in our life together, makes me painfully aware of the privilege of the White person bubble I have been living in and can still access. It also makes me aware of the obligation I have to try to not only level the playing field for members of diverse groups by advocating for systemic change, but also to use any privilege I have to advocate fiercely for my clients from diverse cultures to ensure their rights are being respected and they are receiving access to the resources and supports they need.

As mentioned previously, self-awareness, knowledge, and skill development related to cultural diversity and cultural competencies in counseling should not be limited to our time as students, but rather needs be a continuous process throughout our careers. We know that our attitudes directly impact our behaviors in ways of which we might not consciously be aware. Thus, as therapists we need to be vigilant about biases that might take root in us, and "uproot" them as needed.

## Systemic Change and Advocacy

Sometimes in doing our work we will hear stories of how individuals are being traumatized by discriminatory systems or practices within our community. Advocacy is part of our role. We might be presented with opportunities to do this at the community level as part of a larger organizational response, or on an individual level. This is a pathway that our clients might not feel strong enough to travel, or one that remains too treacherous for them. We might have to go down this avenue on their behalf.

The first example that comes to mind, of working at the systemic level, is when the state of Tennessee passed Senate Bill 1556 in 2016 which allows therapists to turn away lesbian, gay, transgender, and other clients based on "sincerely held beliefs". The American Counseling Association, which planned to hold its annual conference in that state, moved its conference to another state in a show of protest toward the discriminatory and unethical nature of this bill. I understand that the ACA has continued with advocacy efforts on this front. This action speaks to our responsibility as therapists to speak out and advocate for marginalized communities who are facing systemic discrimination.

Advocacy might also be required at an individual level. Our clients might need us to step up and advocate on their behalf with their physician, their workplace, their professors (if they are students), funders, etc. As professionals, we possess a level of credibility and expertise which can provide much needed information and support to others, from whom our clients need some flexibility. For example, if I am working with a client who was sexually assaulted on the weekend, I will offer to contact their professors (with client's written and informed consent) to say that I can confirm the client is currently dealing with significant personal/health issues, and request extensions on assignments or rewrites of tests scheduled for that week. There are often things we can do in a practical sense to support our clients by advocating for different types of accommodations in school or the workplace, without disclosing the confidential nature of their struggles.

Advocacy sometimes has a research component. Research is important because it allows us to demonstrate more objective evidence, of what we already "know" is true as a result of doing this work, in ways that can be more difficult for others to dispute or dismiss. Research might not be a favorite pastime of front-line therapists, but I encourage you, if there are opportunities, to take advantage of them. In the counseling department where I work, positions have been saved from cuts, and even added, as a result of research that provided senior administration with a more accurate understanding of the nature of our work and the positive student outcomes associated with accessing counseling. Our own inner knowing that we are making a difference with marginalized populations, and belief that others will also value this, is no longer enough in many settings which are being threatened by cutbacks and downsizing. Counseling does make a difference. We know this from our daily experiences with clients, but the confidentiality of our work can often make it difficult to communicate our experiences in meaningful ways to those who don't do the work. We need to find ways to convey this important message to our funders and senior administrators, in quantitative and qualitative ways.

## Examples of Typical Client Presentations[1]

### *Keisha (29-Year-Old Female)*

Keisha is a full-time accountant who enjoys her work. She lives with a room-mate whom she describes as very supportive. She comes from a very loving family who lives nearby. Keisha's presenting reason for coming to therapy is that she has been feeling "really stressed out" recently. She said she has been irritable, reacting to small things, with anger that is way out of proportion. She used to be very social, spending evenings out with friends (e.g., din-ner, movies, theater, sports events), but has become very withdrawn. When friends ask her to go out, she said she makes up excuses. She just wants to sleep. She said that sometimes on the weekends she doesn't get out of bed. When asked to what she attributes her stress, she said she is in tax season and there are a lot of demands on her at work. When asked if this is her first tax season, she said it is her fourth. She admitted she didn't feel like this during the last three. When asked when her symptoms began, Keisha was quiet and thoughtful. She said she noticed that she first started making excuses to avoid going out with friends in November. When asked what was going on at that time in her life, she said that things were normal at work. She was busy but happy. She was enjoying time with her friends. She paused. She added, "Oh yeah, that's around the time my cousin, Maya, died. It was a suicide". She explained that Maya had been suffering from depression. Keisha had been trying to be supportive, and had been encouraging Maya to get out with friends rather than spending so much time alone. The night Maya died, they were supposed to go out to dinner with friends. Maya canceled at the last minute. She said she didn't feel up to it. After dinner, Keisha decided to stop by to check on her. Maya didn't answer the door. Keisha tried texting and calling her. There was no answer. Keisha had a key for emergencies and let herself in. She found Maya in her bed. There were empty pill bottles on the nightstand. Keisha called paramedics but it was too late.

### Stephen (42-Year-Old Male)

Stephen is a veteran from the war in Iraq. During his last tour of duty, he lost four of his closest friends when an IED exploded under their jeep. He was in a vehicle following behind. He said he has felt dead inside since that moment. The only emotions he can temporarily experience are rage and deep sadness. He said when he looks at his wife and children, he knows he should feel love, but inside he feels nothing but a coldness and distance. He said he has been consuming a lot of alcohol recently to try to forget, but doesn't like the person he is when he is drinking. He has been considering suicide.

### Simon (36-Year-Old Male)

Simon is married and recently became a father. He said it was the happiest moment of his life, when his wife gave birth to a baby boy. When they brought the baby home, however, he found that when the baby would cry, he started to remember how often he cried in his own childhood. Simon's parents had been very physically abusive toward Simon and his younger sister. They were physically beaten and verbally berated for even small mistakes. He recalled a time when he came home from kindergarten and proudly showed his parents that he had printed his name for the first time. They used a belt on his hand because his "S" was backwards. They told him that this punishment would help him to remember how to do it correctly. Simon also recounted instances of being taken to hospital for broken bones after beatings, which his parents told hospital staff was due to his clumsiness. Simon has been having nightmares about the abuse. He said he has been bombarded with memories of the abuse that he hadn't thought about for years. He has also been avoiding being alone with his son and admitted he is terrified that he might become like his parents.

### M. J. (20- Year-Old Female)

M. J. came into the office in obvious distress. A female friend accompanied her to the appointment. M. J. immediately began to cry. Her eyes were downcast and she appeared physically agitated. She explained that she had gone to a birthday party at a friend's home on the weekend. She remembers having a drink and then doesn't remember anything until she woke up around 4:00 a.m. in the bed of a guy that she doesn't know. She said she was disoriented and felt nauseous. She gathered her things and called a cab to go home. For the remainder of the day she was vomiting and had a headache. She said she hasn't been able to stop crying.

### Reflection Questions

*   *What are your initial thoughts regarding these cases? Did you make any cultural assumptions?*
*   *How might your case conceptualization be affected if these clients were members of the following cultures: Caucasian? Asian? Black? Native American Indian? Transgendered? Christian? Muslim? Physically disabled?*

## Note

1   The examples presented are not actual individual cases but rather are representative of the types of client presentations one might experience in this work.

# 7   Therapist Self-Care

> If I can form a helping relationship to myself—if I can be sensitively aware of and acceptant toward my own feelings—then the likelihood is great that I can form a helping relationship to another.
>
> —Carl Rogers (1961, p. 51)

If we cannot accept ourselves, shadow and light, how will we be able to truly accept all parts of our clients? This is one of the ongoing challenges for us as therapists as we look in the mirror. This work is difficult and makes demands on us at a very personal level. Self-acceptance first requires self-awareness—to be aware of and respectful toward our own emotional, physical, cognitive, and spiritual needs. Self-care efforts, which serve to protect and support us in this work, can then follow. We will need to move beyond developing the knowledge, skills, and abilities specific to trauma counseling/processing, into developing these areas in relation to our own individual challenges, needs, and related self-care. Failure to do so can result in us also becoming injured and lost in the valley.

I must confess that originally this was planned to be the last chapter of the book. Furthermore, my intention was to present you with a multitude of evidence-based strategies to help protect you from the effects of compassion fatigue and vicarious trauma. However, two things happened to change my plans. The first was that, when I conducted a literature review to find evidence-based strategies to counter the effects of compassion fatigue and vicarious trauma for clinicians who engage in trauma counseling, I was taken aback by the paucity of studies in this area. Second, when I spoke to a colleague about this, she wisely pointed out that this fits with the fact that we, as therapists, tend to relegate our own well-being to the bottom of the priority list. We talked about how this important topic was never discussed in detail in our graduate-level counseling courses—other than references being made to the importance of "self-care". She commented that it seems like for many of us, learning how to protect ourselves as we do this work is often an "afterthought"—something to which we don't necessarily give a lot of thought—until we find that we have been injured by the work. I had to agree. It was then that it dawned on me that placing this chapter at the end of the book was mirroring that pattern. So I decided to move it closer to the front, to emphasize the important fact that we need to develop the knowledge, skills, and abilities to support our own well-being *prior* to entering the valley. Our own self-care is vital if we are to do this work safely.

## The Distinctive Risks of Trauma Counseling: Compassion Fatigue and Vicarious Trauma

While burnout is a hazard for all therapists, therapists who do trauma work are exposed to additional risks:

> the potential effects of working with trauma survivors are distinct from those of working with other difficult populations because the therapist is exposed to the emotionally shocking images of horror and suffering that are characteristic of serious traumas.
>
> (McCann & Pearlman, 1990, p. 134)

As a result of bearing witness to the painful details of the traumas of our clients, we are at risk for experiencing compassion fatigue/secondary traumatic stress, and vicarious trauma. Studies have found that 5–29% of therapists experience symptoms in the "high" or clinically significant range (Bride, 2007; Choi, 2011; Kadambi & Truscott, 2004; Salloum, Kondrat, Johnco, & Olson, 2015). While the terms compassion fatigue and vicarious trauma are often used interchangeably, we will use the following definitions for the purposes of our discussion.

Compassion fatigue (CF) has been described as:

> The natural behaviors and emotions that arise from knowing about a traumatizing event experienced by a significant other—the stress resulting from helping or wanting to help a traumatized person. . . . Compassion fatigue is identical to secondary traumatic stress disorder (STSD) and is the equivalent of PTSD.
>
> (Figley, 1995, p. xv)

Consequently, therapists might experience PTSD symptoms including painful affect, as well as intrusive and disruptive trauma imagery related to their clients' trauma narratives, in the form of flashbacks, intrusive thoughts, or nightmares (McCann & Pearlman, 1990).

Alternatively, vicarious trauma (VT) refers to changes in therapists' core beliefs regarding self, others, and the world, as a result of the cumulative effects of empathizing with clients and being exposed to their traumatic narratives (Pearlman & Mac Ian, 1995). Examples of the types of shifts in cognitive schemas that might occur along dimensions of trust, safety, power, and independence include: heightened suspicion of others; increased sense of vulnerability;

helplessness; and restriction of one's sense of personal control and freedom (Collins & Long, 2003). These changes in the way the therapist perceives the self, others, and the world can have a devastating impact on the therapist, both personally and professionally (Trippany, Kress, & Wilcoxon, 2004).

For some of us, the costs of doing this work can indeed be very high, which is why the lack of research into this area is disappointing and problematic, to say the least.

### The Research (or Lack Thereof) for Prevention and Treatment of CF and VT

In a large-scale systematic review that focused on identifying effective interventions to address the effects of secondary traumatic stress among mental health workers, over 4100 citations were reviewed, and *not one* met the inclusion criteria (Bercier & Maynard, 2015). As a result of this "empty review", these researchers concluded:

> Although there has been a priority on developing and rigorously assessing trauma interventions for those who directly experience various types of trauma, it appears that little effort is being made to rigorously test interventions to help the helpers. While there may be some aspects of techniques or primary trauma treatment that can inform and be adapted to treat CF, STS, and VT, we should be careful to not assume that trauma interventions intended to treat primary trauma will be effective in treating CF, STS, and VT.
>
> (p. 87)

Consequently, there are very few studies available to provide us with evidence-based protective and intervention strategies to address the risk of CF, STS, and VT among trauma therapists. Among the few additional studies that looked into evidence-based protections for therapists who work with trauma survivors, there was consensus regarding caseload, but differing opinions regarding the role of counselor coping strategies.

There is evidence that therapists who work with a higher percentage of trauma survivors experience more PTSD and VT symptoms than those who see fewer survivors (Brady, Guy, Poelstra, & Brokaw, 1999; Schauben & Frazier, 1995). Moreover, in assessing the effectiveness of a range of commonly recommended strategies to reduce VT, Bober and Regehr (2006) found that "time spent with counseling trauma victims was the best predictor of trauma scores" (p. 1). Thus, reducing our caseload in terms of the number of survivors to whom we provide trauma counseling in a given week, and/or advocating for the organizations we work for to do this, appears to be a practical health and safety issue that can be effectively addressed in the workplace. It is unclear, however, what the maximum caseload would be. As a starting point we might nevertheless want to take into account that

Trippany, Wilcoxon, and Satcher (2003) found that counselors who provided trauma counseling to an average of 14 clients per week did not experience statistically significant levels of VT.

In terms of coping strategies, Schauben and Frazier (1995) found that among their sample of counselors, the five most frequently reported self-care activities—i.e., addressing the problem directly; seeking emotional support; seeking direction; planning; and using humor—were significantly associated with lower PTSD, burnout, negative affect, and VT symptoms. Seemingly conversely, a study by Bober and Regehr (2006) found no association between the time therapists allotted for specific categories of coping strategies (i.e., self-care, leisure, supervision, and research and development) and their trauma scores. However, the difference in these results might be due to the way coping strategies were measured. The former study used a frequency measure (i.e., a 1 to 5 scale with 1 = never and 5 = very often) of therapist use of particular types of coping strategies, while the latter study measured how much time trauma counselors devoted or allotted to these types of activities. Thus, these studies are measuring two very different things. Not all of the coping strategies we engage in take hours of our time. Often the most effective self-care activities that I and my colleagues frequently use, within and outside of session, only take minutes rather than hours of our time, and yet if you asked us, we would say that these are the factors that both protect us, and help to heal us when we are injured by the work.

## Strategies for Therapist Well-Being

While we await identification of conclusive evidence-based means to protect us from CF and VT injuries, there are some evidence-based strategies that we can use to support our general well-being as we work in the area of trauma. Mindfulness, self-care/personal coping activities, peer supervision, education and training, and spirituality have been identified as such means.

Mindfulness-based stress reduction training has been found to be related to significant reductions in anxiety, perceived stress, negative affect, as well as increases in self-compassion and positive affect, when comparing treatment and control groups (Shapiro, Brown, & Biegel, 2007). In a review of the literature regarding the benefits of mindfulness-based interventions for therapists, Davis and Hayes (2011) highlighted the following findings: increased empathy and compassion for self and others; positive effects on counseling skills; significantly increased self-awareness; reduced stress and negative affect; as well as reduced anxiety, depressive, and PTSD symptoms.

Similarly, a significant correlation has been identified between the frequency of self-care activities and well-being (Richards, Campenni, & Muse-Burke, 2010). In this study, self-care was defined as "any activity that one does to feel good about oneself. It can be categorized into four groups which include: physical, psychological, spiritual, and support" (pp. 252–253). In a qualitative study by Killian (2008), clinicians who worked with trauma survivors indicated that quality time with friends and family, and exercise, were strategies that played a significant role in their self-care. Pearlman and Saakvitne (1995), suggest that VT symptoms can be decreased through physical activity, creative activities, and socializing with loved ones.

The potential benefits of peer supervision for trauma therapists are many. Peer supervision can: provide social support and decrease a sense of isolation; set norms; challenge cognitive distortions; provide opportunities for reframing; and increase objectivity (Catherall, 1995; Killian, 2008; Trippany et al., 2004). It can also be very helpful as a forum in which knowledge regarding particular clinical issues, interventions, and resources are shared. Pearlman and Saakvitne (1995) suggest that it is imperative to receive clinical supervision when doing trauma work, in order to enhance clinical skills.

As discussed previously, prior to doing trauma therapy, we require training to help us to develop competencies in terms of the knowledge and skills that are essential to providing this service in a professional, ethical, and safe manner. Participating in professional development can help to broaden our own resources as clinicians and reduce a sense of isolation (Brady et al., 1999).

Work environment is also an important factor. Having one's own workspace, having a say in one's work, and having control over how many hours one works in a day are factors that can positively contribute to therapist well-being (Killian, 2008).

Clinicians who work with trauma clients have also identified spirituality as a significant factor in their self-care (Killian, 2008; Pearlman & Mac Ian, 1993). VT can disrupt a therapist's schema for meaning and sense of connection. Conversely, spirituality tends to provide a sense of meaning and connection within a person's life, which might explain why it is viewed as an important component of self-care among some therapists.

## Some Reflections on Personal Distress Management Strategies

> There are things we can do to help our colleagues. . . . The first is to speak openly about our own struggles with compassion stress and compassion fatigue. The conspiracy of silence among the profession about this compassion fatigue is no different than the silence about family violence, racism, and sexual harassment in the past.
>
> (Figley, 2002, p. 1440)

A few months back I presented at a conference in San Francisco. After my presentation, there were two young women waiting to talk to me. They were newly graduated therapists who had been working with trauma clients for less than a year and were feeling discouraged that they were already feeling overwhelmed by the work and were questioning if it was something they would be able to manage. We talked for quite some time. They asked me how I had coped with doing trauma work during the course of my career.

I shared some of my personal strategies with them, and as I did so, found that I felt a bit uncomfortable in doing so. I reflected on this later to try to understand my discomfort and realized that it is because these strategies aren't ones that I can necessarily present in an objective way as being evidence-based, but rather are ones that I learned on my own and through colleagues, and in many ways they are deeply personal. At the same time, I realized that if we are to work together to figure out what helps to reduce and manage our distress in doing trauma work, the first step is often to begin with sharing our subjective experiences regarding what has worked for us, so that others might possibly benefit from this knowledge. Thus, I would like to share my observations and experiences as to what has been helpful to me and some of my colleagues in managing and reducing our distress as we do this work, in hopes that these ideas might be helpful to others, too. You will likely notice that spirituality plays an important role in some of my coping strategies. I recognize that this isn't a fit for everyone. My hope is that you will take what fits for you and leave the rest. If nothing fits, maybe this section will spur you to reflect on what works for you.

### Use of a "Filter" or "Shield"

Something that caused me a tremendous amount of pain during the first two decades of my career was an overdeveloped sense of empathy. I could not only feel what my clients felt emotionally, but I could also feel their physical pain in my body. I was able to reflect back to my clients where the pain was, exactly in their bodies, and what it felt like. While it might have been a strong way to connect with my clients, it was causing me a great deal of pain and emotional exhaustion, and eventually was starting to make me physically ill. After a particularly difficult few months, through prayer and meditation, it came to me that it wasn't necessary or even healthy for me to connect with my clients at this level in order to be helpful to them, and that I needed to do something to protect myself from taking on my clients' physical and emotional pain. What I began to do at the start of my day was to ask the Divine to stand between my clients and me in session to filter out toxic emotions and material so they would become neutralized and could no longer harm my clients or me. My experience upon utilizing this strategy was an immediate shift in how trauma narratives affect me. I no longer feel my clients' physical pain, and while I can still read their emotions accurately, I no longer feel them to the degree that hurts me. Other therapists I know use the imagery of light or a personalized shield to protect themselves in a similar way when they do trauma counseling. We each need to find what works for us.

### Breathing

Similar to our clients, we too might hold our breath or no longer take deep, full breaths when we are listening to trauma narratives that are frightening or particularly painful. When this happens, our bodies go into a kind of panic as they begin to operate without sufficient oxygen. Thus, for me, being mindful of my own breathing both during and following difficult sessions can help me to become aware of my own reactions, and allows me to take steps to reset my breathing when needed to help me to get re-centered.

## *Dual Awareness—Stepping Into Our Warrior Spirit*

As therapists, we are the holders of hope and compassionate anchors for our clients who find themselves in the valley. I've found that in order to maintain my ability to be a steadfast anchor in the therapeutic alliance, I have to make a conscious decision to "step into" my Warrior Spirit prior to beginning these trauma therapy sessions. Approaching therapy from my Warrior Spirit allows me to be genuine, to lean into my own strength, and to view my client from a lens of compassion—while protecting the integrity of my own body and mind.

Dual awareness is what allows us to do this work safely and effectively. For not only do we need to be in our bodies to monitor our own physical and emotional reactions to the trauma stories to which we are bearing witness, but we also need to keep our lens of compassion focused on the resiliency of the client. If we instead start connecting with the client's despair and fear, our lens can become clouded, and we too might get lost in the valley.

## *Scheduling*

In addition to managing the number of clients I see for trauma counseling in my caseload per week, I also try to manage how I schedule them in a day. While I've found that five clients per day is my maximum, I've learned that all five of these sessions cannot be trauma-related sessions. For me, seeing five clients in a day who are dealing with trauma-related issues is more than I can handle physically, emotionally, and cognitively. On days where I have made a scheduling error and have had to do this, I find that after work I am exhausted on every level. We each need to assess and respect our own maximums with this work.

In terms of scheduling, I have further learned that it important for my well-being to take time for a lunch break, to go for a walk mid-afternoon with one or more of my colleagues to the cafeteria to pick up hot tea, and to leave on time at the end of most days. At lunch, I go to the gym for 30 minutes, or for a walk, or spend time in the lunchroom with my colleagues chatting about anything other than work. Our midafternoon walk to the cafeteria to pick up coffee or tea gives us the chance to check-in with each other. This is a time to which we all look forward. Getting out of our office for a few minutes provides us with an emotional and cognitive break from the work. Likewise, leaving work on time most days is important to me, because it represents respect for the other important people in my life, and my commitment to them and myself. I need a break from the valley if I am going to be strong enough to go back in day after day.

When my clinical interns begin their placement, I have always made a point of telling them that during their time with us, they are not to do work on their lunch breaks. I explain that it is not a healthy habit to get into and suggest that they read, socialize, go for a walk, exercise, or do anything else they would like—not related to work, in order to give themselves a mental break. I also advise them that they are to schedule sufficient time for client notes during their workday so that they are not staying late every night. While there are days when circumstances are such that we must complete our notes prior to leaving, staying late is to be the exception, not the rule. To emphasize these points, I let them know that part of their clinical evaluation will focus on self-care. I want to help them to be mindful of their personal-professional boundaries, and make a commitment to self-care a priority right from the start of their career.

### Writing Clinical Notes

I've observed that I find writing clinical notes, related to my trauma counseling sessions, to be distressing. I believe that this is due to the fact that in order to write these notes I must relive parts of the session. Reviewing the painful material that is often part of trauma counseling can be difficult, especially when we are tired at the end of the workday. Given that I know that this part of my daily work causes me distress, I make a conscious effort to increase my distress tolerance during writing by routinely doing two things that work for me: turning on spa music, and getting a cup of hot tea. I'd suggest that if there are particular parts of the day that you too find distressing, it might be helpful to integrate some of your own distress tolerance strategies into your routine.

### Vicarious Flashbacks

Frequently, after hearing vivid descriptions of client trauma, I have experienced visual flashbacks of their traumas. It is a disturbing experience that can last over long periods of time if not addressed. What I've found most effective has been to imagine that I am seeing the image through the lens of the camera, and then to close the lens to shut out the image. I do this as many times as necessary until the image is completely gone. This has been very effective for me.

### Informal Peer Supervision

While the counseling team of which I am part has scheduled formal bi-weekly group supervision for which I am very grateful, one if the invaluable aspects of my work environment has been the opportunity for informal peer supervision "as needed". In our office it is accepted practice that we consult with our colleagues, as needed, when we are dealing with difficult cases.

This has been especially useful when it comes to complex cases, brainstorming potential resources and supports for our high-risk clients, or to review suicide risk assessments. I tell my counseling interns that there is no shame in asking for a consult. It is something all the counselors in our office do, regardless of years of experience. This is what makes us stronger as a team, and allows us to provide excellent service to our clients.

Informal peer supervision can also be helpful when dealing with intense countertransference reactions to a client and/or their narratives. It can provide a safe, supportive, confidential consult which can allow us the chance to debrief and sort ourselves out so that we are able to go into our next counseling session or task. This is an important piece of developing the necessary self-awareness, in relation to others, which is part of the basis for safe and effective therapeutic work.

## Use of Ritual

It was during a 13-week group I facilitated with paramedic students, as part of a study looking at how to increase resiliency, where I first noticed the difference in students' demeanor between when they were wearing their uniforms to group, versus when they came dressed in casual clothes. On days they wore their uniforms I noticed they seemed more emotionally reserved. They weren't cold, but it seemed like they were more "professional" and protected somehow. I connected this with my observation that the police officers I knew personally, who I had seen both off-duty and then at other times in uniform, presented similarly. As a result of these observations, I've come to believe that there is something in the physical act of wearing a uniform that provides a type of protective mental shield to these professionals, and I've wondered how we could similarly protect ourselves as counselors. For some, the use of a simple ritual of some sort appears to meet this need.

One of my colleagues, who I first met when I was his clinical internship supervisor, began each workday when he arrived at the office by changing from his casual watch to his work watch. He said he did this as a way of preparing himself mentally for the work he was doing. He would then change watches again when he left at the end of the day, to signal to himself that he was leaving his work at the office. Another colleague who worked in a hospital setting would use the lanyard that held her hospital ID in the same way. I have been doing the same for several years with my college ID card which I put on when I get to work, and take off when I leave—as an acknowledgement of consciously preparing myself for the work as my day starts, and consciously letting it go when my workday ends.

## Addressing Personal Challenges

For each of us there will be times when we are struggling with personal challenges. Sometimes we can effectively manage these challenges on our own, and other times we will require help—just like every other human being on this planet. In this profession we know the signs that indicate when a person needs to seek help; however, we might have some difficulty in recognizing these signs when we look in the mirror.

We care deeply and we try to help other people. It's what we do professionally, and quite likely in our personal lives, too. We are busy people. We are trying to make a difference. In doing this work, there are some important questions that we need to continue to ask ourselves: Do we make time to take care of ourselves physically, psychologically, medically, and spiritually? Or do we put our needs at the end of a long "to do" list so that we never quite get to the end? Are we mindful of the pain we carry physically, emotionally, spiritually, and in relationships, and are we taking the time to address it? Are we also mindful of when our pain starts to impede us in our professional obligations? We have a responsibility to our clients, and to ourselves, to recognize when personal issues are interfering with our abilities to act according to our profession's professional practice and ethics standards, and to actively take steps to address these issues.

This is my third attempt at writing a personal example on this topic. The first two attempts included other, less vulnerable examples, than the one I am going to share with you. I know that part of me is avoiding sharing this example. And yet, I expect that it will be the best example that I can give of what I am talking about. It was about 20 years into my career. At this point, I had already worked with hundreds of suicidal clients; however, none of them had completed the act. It was the week after my dad was diagnosed with inoperable brain cancer, that a high-risk client with whom I had been working closely, died by suicide. At our last meeting she had verbally committed to attending our next session and promised not to take her own life in the interim. I became very worried when she didn't show for our appointment. When I heard of her suicide I was devastated. In retrospect, I believe that prior to this event I was already experiencing some symptoms of CF and VT; however, in the months that followed this suicide I developed severe PTSD symptoms. At one point, two of my colleagues who are also good friends of mine, pulled me aside and told me they were worried about me, and encouraged me to take steps to get the supports I needed. For me, it was the concern of my colleagues, combined with the moment when I realized that I no longer had it in me to hold onto the hope for my clients and had lost confidence that I could help them find their way out of the valley, that I realized that I needed to take a leave from my work to focus on healing from my injuries. With the help of a good trauma therapist and knowledgeable medical professionals, I was once again able to find my footing and to regain confidence in my ability to hold the hope and to help my clients once again.

I share this very personal example because I want you to know that if you get injured in this work, there is hope. The shame does not belong to me and it does not belong to you. Sometimes injuries just happen. It is a hazard of the work. The thing is, it's how we treat ourselves and what we do about it that matters. In such moments, we deserve the same level of compassion, support, and respect from ourselves that we give to our clients. We also deserve the benefits of external professional supports.

Before we move on from this important aspect of self-care, I want to point out that at times we might need to help each other to recognize when we are in need of external help. When we recognize the signs that a colleague is struggling to cope in some way, it is incumbent upon us to gently and respectfully communicate our observations, express our concern, and encourage our colleague to get the support they need. I know this wasn't an easy thing for my friends to do, but they did it because they cared. I am grateful. Our colleagues will likely be some of the first people in our lives to pick up on it if we are suffering. After all, many of us spend more waking hours in the company of our coworkers than in the company of some of our family members. If a colleague approaches us with concerns of this type, we need to take them seriously, do an inventory of ourselves in terms of where the sources of distress are in our lives and how we are managing them, and take steps to obtain any needed medical, psychological, and/or other supports. This is about living in congruence with the messages of self-care and compassion that we promote among our clients.

## Use of Prayer

A number of counselors have privately shared with me that they pray for their clients—asking God to bless them and help them. These same counselors also ask God to grant them wisdom and guide their work with their clients. I share their use of prayer as a personal strategy to deal with the demands of this work. I can attest that inviting the Divine in on my work provides me with some reassurance that it isn't "all on me". Aside from having peers to support me through my fears around the safety of high-risk clients, I also feel that I have a powerful ally on this journey. There are times when I'm fearful for the ongoing safety of my clients, but in many of these situations, my hands are tied. In these moments I go before God in my heart, asking for my client's protection, for guidance in my work with them, for the activation of other supports in their lives, and for quite simply whatever it is that my client needs most at the moment. Since I believe that prayer is an effective response to fear of the unknown, it has been a valuable, calming resource for me.

## Identifying and Staying Connected to Your "Tribe"

The work we do is tough. Only people who have done it will understand how physically, emotionally, cognitively, and spiritually draining that trauma counseling can be. Thus, it has been important to me to be connected to people who work in similar fields and/or share similar values and outlooks on life—so that I don't have to educate, defend, and explain why I am passionate about this work. Sometimes it is wonderful to "just be" with people who "get" who I am and what I am about. This is why I think it is important for each of us to find our people, our "tribe", so that we can spend time together, support each other, laugh, and share the journey of life in a meaningful, respectful, and fun way together.

About a year ago I started a Bookless Book Club. I noticed that many of my friends were very busy with their own medical challenges, as well as dealing with the demands of raising children and/or taking care of ill parents. I knew that if we formed a Book Club that required them to read a book a month, many would not be able to attend since they honestly don't have the time to read for leisure. Thus, I suggested we have a Bookless Book Club that includes all the best part of traditional Book Clubs (i.e., food, wine, laughter, and friends) without the reading. Hence, our "Bookless" Book Club has been a success. More importantly, these women are my tribe. They are a source of strength, humor, and inspiration in my life. I think that in this work, we owe it to ourselves to find and connect with our tribe in whatever way makes sense for us.

# Part II

# Engaging in Trauma Therapy

# 8  First Things First

> The challenge—not so much to accept the terrible things that happened but learning how to gain mastery over one's internal sensations and emotions. . . . Sensing, naming and identifying what is going on inside is the first step to recovery.
>
> (van der Kolk, 2014, p. 68)

As stated, one of the challenges that we need to assist our clients with is to understand, observe, and name what is going on within themselves; helping them to find the words and concepts to explain that which at times can seem beyond words and comprehension.

Hence, one of our first tasks upon entering the valley is to assist our clients in getting their bearings by identifying and assessing their injuries, providing information on trauma, and normalizing their reactions. This will typically involve an assessment of the injuries they have sustained, in terms of how current PTSD symptomology is impacting different areas of functioning in their lives. We will then begin to work with clients to identify and mobilize supports and resources. At this point, and throughout trauma counseling, client crises will take precedence over trauma processing. In dealing with crises, we need to be prepared, as needed, to assess for suicide risk, create safety plans, advocate on behalf of clients, and/or mobilize additional supports and resources as appropriate.

## Identifying, Assessing, and Addressing Injuries

I will usually start with new clients by asking how I might be of help to them. Some have a ready answer to this question, while others will tell me they don't know where to begin. In the latter case, I will suggest it might be easier for them to start with what happened to bring them to the point of one day waking up and deciding they were going make a counseling appointment. The response to this question can be quite helpful. In many cases, our clients will have come to counseling at the urging of loved ones who were very concerned about them. Their loved ones might even have accompanied them to their first appointment, or be waiting for them in the waiting room. For some, there may have been a particular incident that was a catalyst, or perhaps they came to a realization that despite their best efforts, they weren't able to handle their distress alone anymore. Whatever the response to this question, it will provide us with key information about what our clients' value and are motivated by.

In the first session, if the client is reporting distressing symptoms, I will inquire as to how long these symptoms have been occurring and what was going on in their lives around the time they began. Oftentimes when we are talking about what turns out to be PTSD, I find that clients (and sometimes their physicians) have not yet made the connection between their symptoms and a traumatic experience or the experience of complex trauma. If in my initial assessment of symptoms, it seems that traumatic stress might be involved, it is at this point that I ask clients if they would be willing to fill out a Traumatic Stress Symptom Screening Checklist—TSSSC (Appendix 1).

In creating the TSSSC, I divided symptoms into sections based on diagnostic criteria from the DSM-5, and have included a section related to symptoms commonly associated with complex trauma. It is not intended to be a diagnostic measure (thus, there is no scoring key), but rather is intended to provide a base-line understanding of the specific trauma-related symptoms and associated levels of distress that our clients are experiencing. This information can then be used to assist us in developing treatment plans and prioritizing interventions.

When asking clients to complete the TSSSC, I explain that completing this checklist will give us a better idea as to what symptoms they are dealing with, so that we will know how to proceed. I further explain that this checklist will be helpful at a later date, for comparison purposes, to allow us to measure improvements in their symptoms. When offering this checklist, I ask clients if they would prefer to read and complete it on their own or if they would like me to read it out loud and have us fill it out together. (This is an important accessibility piece given that some clients might have undisclosed learning disabilities or be struggling with English as a second language, and we don't want our clients to feel alienated at the outset by our lack of sensitivity). I also encourage clients to ask for clarification if they are unsure what some of the symptom descriptions mean.

Starting with identifying, assessing, and addressing injuries that have resulted from traumatic experience(s) provides a non-threatening and validating place to begin with new clients. This exercise can also serve to challenge the tendency among some of our clients to deny and minimize their pain. I find it especially helpful with clients who might be reticent to be in counseling in the first place. Talking about symptoms can feel less vulnerable and likely be less triggering than discussing the trauma itself. Some might not have realized that injuries aren't always physical. Completing the checklist can be illuminating for our clients, in that it can provide them with visual confirmation of the scope of their injuries and disruption in their lives. This can provide a sense of validation and normalization of their PTSD symptoms and the level of distress they experience on a daily basis. It can also help them to begin to realize that PTSD symptoms are wide-reaching and can affect all aspects of their functioning—physical, emotional, cognitive, social, behavioral, and possibly spiritual—and that this too is normal given what they have been through. This realization is a first step in helping our clients to get their bearings and start to make sense of what has happened to them. Although I am unable, as a psychotherapist and social worker, to diagnose PTSD, I can use the responses on this screening checklist to inform my case conceptualization and treatment plan.

If, from the results of the TSSSC, I believe that clients are suffering from PTSD, I will share with them that it looks like we are dealing with a traumatic stress reaction. I explain that I am unable to provide a diagnosis, but that I don't require one in order for us to work together. (If clients want a diagnosis and/or medical treatment is required, I will offer to include the screening checklist in a referral to the appropriate health professional). I will then ask if they have ever experienced trauma, either as a single incident such as an accident, a witnessed death, sexual assault, etc., or a number of traumas over a longer period of time. While most clients are aware that childhood, physical, sexual, and/or emotional abuse can be traumatic, some might not have considered that neglect, bullying, harassment, racism, sexism, and poverty—for example—can also be traumatic. Thus, I explain that when I am asking about traumas, I am including all these of types of potentially traumatic experiences, and that getting a sense of whether it was one traumatic event or multiple/long term traumas, will help me to better understand with what we are dealing and to come up with a plan as to how we might proceed.

Unless clients start to talk about their traumatic experience spontaneously, that is not where I will typically start. Talking about the trauma for individuals with PTSD can activate painful traumatic stress reactions. Before we get into details of the traumatic experience(s), clients need to be equipped with the tools to handle the distress that will invariably come with these discussions. If, however, clients need to start by talking about it, I will listen to them, without probing further, and will offer support and validation. If it appears that clients are reaching a level of distress that is activating their survival responses (e.g., flashbacks, dissociation), I will ask if we can stop and focus on getting them grounded again. I explain why:

> *I'm going to ask if we can take a step back from getting into the details of your trauma experience, because I can see that it is causing you a great deal of distress. I want to make sure that before we get into any in-depth discussions about your trauma experience(s), we have equipped you with the tools you will need to be able to reduce any distress that might be triggered*

by us talking about what you've gone through. So would it be okay for us to focus on getting you grounded first? Then we can talk for a bit about how the trauma has affected you so we can get an idea of where we need to start to focus our efforts to reduce your distress. (At this point we might do some breathing exercises, get them focused on what they can see and hear in the office, and/or I might get them a glass of cold water or hot tea, etc.).

## Identifying and Mobilizing Client Supports and Resources

Within the confusion and despair that often accompanies PTSD, clients might initially perceive that they have no supports or resources. This is simply not true. The most powerful resources they have lie within them, but they often can't see through the darkness to realize this. Our task in this beginning stage is to help them to begin to identify their inherent resiliency, as well as the people in their lives who are supportive. We might also need to provide them with information on external resources in their communities.

### The Self

We need to begin in the very first session, not only to validate the distress that PTSD symptoms have caused in the lives of our clients, but also to hold up a mirror to our clients' strength in surviving the atrocity/atrocities that they have faced. Viewing themselves through the lens of PTSD can make people forget who they are as persons. It can undermine their sense of self, their worth, their sense of competency, safety, and strength. One of our tasks is to help them to see through a different lens—one of compassion and wisdom—into the truth of their strength, courage, perseverance, and resiliency.

There are four common misperceptions about the self that we may need to address with clients in the initial sessions.

### 1) I'm Losing My Mind

One of the first reassurances we might need to provide our clients is that although it might feel like it, PTSD symptoms are not a sign that they are losing their minds. Rather, these are symptoms that indicate that a significant injury has occurred which requires attention. The Traumatic Stress Symptom Screening Checklist (TSSSC) (found in Appendix 1) can be used to help to reassure our clients that their symptoms are within the normal range. The psychoeducation on trauma that you provide can also help clients to make sense of their reactions and symptoms, so that added fear caused by the existence of these symptoms can be put to rest.

## 2)　*PTSD Is a Sign of Weakness or Character Flaw*

Unfortunately, this piece of misinformation is still prevalent in some parts of society, and in particular pockets of the military and emergency responder services. The stigma caused by this fallacy results in a great deal of unnecessary suffering and lives lost. It adds a burden of shame onto those who are already suffering tremendously, and can prevent them from seeking the help they so desperately need, which we know sometimes results in suicide.

It can be incredibly reassuring for our clients to know there exists evidence from MRI studies of the brain that PTSD is related to changes in the way the brain functions. (See Chapter 2—Overview of the Neurobiology of Trauma). They need to know that there is scientific evidence that PTSD is a very real, physiological condition that affects the functioning of the mind and body. It is not a matter of weakness or character flaw, any more than a broken leg is. It is an injury that deserves to be attended to like any other injury.

## 3)　*I Should Be Able to Handle This by Myself*

Clients, particularly those that consider themselves to be the ones whom others go to for help, can have difficulty admitting they need help. PTSD can challenge one's sense of autonomy. Oftentimes, clients will not come to us until their backs are against the wall, in that they have tried everything they can think of, to no avail. One of the ways to reframe this is to share the following multiple-choice question:

> *In the course of going about your day, you trip and break your foot. You notice that the pain is excruciating and your foot cannot bear weight. You (circle one):*
>
> a)　*refuse to seek professional/medical treatment because you believe you should be able to deal with the injury yourself*
> b)　*become angry when anyone notices that you are hopping/limping and suggests you get professional care for your injury*
> c)　*try to ignore and deny the pain while hopping/limping through your life*
> d)　*obtain appropriate professional/medical assessment and treatment services to treat your injury in order to reduce your pain and help you move toward recovery*
> e)　*a, b, and c*
>
> *Then, I pose the following question: What if the injury was different. . . . What if you experienced post-traumatic stress disorder instead? Would your answer change? If so,* **why***?*

## 4)　*If I Were Strong, I Wouldn't Be So Exhausted*

It is not uncommon for our clients to misconstrue the fact that they are exhausted as a result of dealing with PTSD symptoms, as proof that they are not strong. We need to remind them that in fact they are exhausted because they have had to be *so very strong* in order to cope with their symptoms. Traumatic stress symptoms take a tremendous toll on the mind and body. This again can help to reframe self-perception in a more accurate and helpful manner.

### Connecting With Others

It is not uncommon that we will be the first person that clients confide in regarding their traumatic experience(s) and resultant PTSD symptoms. We are often the beginning of the resource network that they will need to support them on their journey. Trauma work is most successful when our clients have a team of professional and non-professional supports. Helping our clients to identify and connect with safe and trustworthy others will likely be part of our work together.

Our clients might require additional professional supports. If they are experiencing ongoing psychiatric symptomology that is significantly disrupting areas of their lives, they might require the support of a psychiatrist and/or a physician who can monitor their symptoms and perhaps prescribe and manage medication. If our clients have experienced physical injury or disability as a result of trauma, or ongoing pain as a result of somatic symptomology, they might require other medical supports (e.g., specialists, physiotherapists, occupational therapists, massage therapists). Also, psychoeducational groups facilitated by psychologists, counselors, social workers, or other mental health professionals may be helpful.

In terms of non-professional supports, trying to identify just one friend or family member, whom they have learned they can trust over time, can be a good place to start. We need to be mindful there are many possible reasons why family members might not be the people to which our clients will be comfortable talking. The cultural and individual contexts of our clients are especially important in these discussions. Some clients might be more comfortable connecting with others who have experienced similar types of trauma in a confidential peer support group setting. With those who have experienced complex trauma, in which interpersonal betrayal and violation was the norm, they may want us to work with them on how to develop new relationships with healthy boundaries, and to guide them in how to cultivate friendships where trust and respect are the basis.

Ultimately, as clients learn that they can trust at least one person (e.g., their therapist), who will hear their truth without judgment and will respond with respect and support, they are more likely to consider the possibility that there might be others who can do the same. I believe that the reason the therapeutic alliance can be such an effective predictor of outcome is because it has the potential to totally upend the client's schema for relationships, particularly in cases where trauma is rooted in relationship betrayal. Only through learning to trust again, and allowing themselves to believe in the possibility that there are still others in the world who can be trusted, will our clients be able to fully reclaim their lives.

## Crises Take Precedence

When dealing with clients suffering from PTSD symptoms, there will be times when the focus on historical trauma needs to wait such as when clients are dealing with an immediate crisis. If a client is suicidal, if they are currently in a domestic violence situation, if they have no place to live or lack money for food, if they are experiencing significant medical issues, etc.—these situations will take precedence over trauma counseling per se. Stabilization is one of the primary goals in our work and, therefore, dealing with threats to safety and other immediate crises will be required prior to getting into trauma specific material that could further destabilize clients. Therefore, there may be times, at any point in the counseling process, when we need to put the brakes on with respect to dealing with trauma material in order to assess risk, advocate, make referrals, and/or provide crisis intervention to our clients.

### Suicide Risk Assessment

Sometimes clients are very straightforward about suicidal ideation and impulse, "*I've been thinking a lot about suicide lately.*" Other times they might be more vague, "*I just want this to end. Sometimes I want to go to sleep and not wake up again.*" If we have any inkling that our clients are considering suicide, we need to probe and be very direct, i.e., "*Have you been having thoughts of suicide? How intense do those thoughts get? Have you ever attempted to end your life before?*" It is a topic about which new counselors often, understandably, feel squeamish. I've found, however, that clients appreciate the direct approach, respond to it, and often express relief that someone finally knows the truth of what they are going through. By asking direct questions, we are letting clients know that we are willing to hear the answers. It gives them permission to speak about that which might have been unspeakable, up to that point in their lives. Due to the fact that physical, cognitive, and emotional pain can be very severe with PTSD, and that despair is often part of it, suicidal thoughts/attempts are not uncommon among this population of clients. In fact, the majority of my clients who have suffered from PTSD related to complex trauma report chronic suicidal ideation as one of their symptoms.

Therapists need to be prepared to conduct suicide risk assessments as needed with trauma clients. In Appendix 2 you will find a copy of a Suicide Risk Assessment Form, and in Appendix 3 a Safety Plan template. I have adapted these forms specifically for use with trauma clients, from ones we developed for use with clients in our Counseling Department at Fanshawe College. The Suicide Risk Assessment form is to be used in discussion with clients who express suicidal thoughts. It is not to be handed to clients to fill it out on their own, but rather is to be used to direct the conversation between the therapist and client. It is the information on this form, in conjunction with the clinical interview, which assists us in assessing both immediate and future risk, and mobilizing resources as appropriate.

This is how I introduce the Risk Assessment protocol to my clients:

> *"Whenever any of my clients mention that they are having suicidal thoughts, I use a risk assessment form to help us to better understand what you are going through right now so that we can put the appropriate supports in place to help you through this. I find this form helpful so that I don't miss anything."*

In the included Suicide Risk Assessment we are asking for the current address and phone number for the client at the time of the risk assessment, since it might be in flux and/or have changed since the last time we obtained this information. If we ever require emergency services to check on the welfare of the client, or to respond to an emergency at the client's home, this will provide us with the necessary up-to-date information. We also ask for a personal emergency contact, a physician contact, and information on current diagnoses and medications.

The priorities for a risk assessment are to assess current imminent risk, as well as ongoing risk. Imminent risk obviously involves an immediate crisis response. Crisis response options will vary depending on the resources available within your community. Some of our clients will be suicidal over a long period of time. When this is the case we might need to do brief check-ins, as needed, over time to monitor risk. Thus, resources and supports that are needed might change over time.

A past suicide attempt tells us that an individual has crossed this line in the past and might be more likely to do so again. It is also very concerning if a person has a well-thought-out plan and the means to put that plan into action with little effort. For example, a person whose plan is to overdose can usually quite easily obtain medication at their local pharmacy to carry out their plan. Likewise, a person who plans to jump and lives on the 10th floor of a high rise also has very easy access to put their plan into action. We need to ask directly to obtain specific information about suicide plans (if clients have thought this far ahead) and how accessible the means are to enact their plans. Do our clients have access to weapons? How many, what type, and where they are located can be vital information to inform our clinical assessment of risk. We also need to consider high-risk behaviors such as active alcohol and/or drug abuse since these can alter rational thought and might increase suicide risk. Knowing how frequently clients are using alcohol and/or drugs, and how much they are using, can help in assessing risk. Self-harming behaviors may or may not contribute to the risk of suicide depending on the details. Having the aforementioned information can help us to focus our safety plan (e.g., talking with a client to ask if during high-risk times, they would allow a family member or friend to remove alcohol, medication, razors, knives, other weapons, etc., from their home in order to reduce risk).

Furthermore, given that these clients are suffering from PTSD, we need to assess what is happening with their symptoms. Are there certain symptoms that are causing unbearable distress that have led to thoughts of suicide? If so, these symptoms will require immediate attention. Also we need to find out if there was a recent triggering event or new trauma that has exacerbated their symptoms. If we have time, we might want to complete an updated *Traumatic Stress Symptom Screening Checklist* (Appendix 1) with our client.

The Risk Assessment also involves our asking about deterrents. Knowing what has stopped our clients from acting on suicidal thoughts and intentions in the past can not only help us to assess risk, but also give us some direction as to how we might work with them to build up their deterrents. It is concerning and an important source of information if clients cannot identify any deterrents whatsoever.

The emergency and supportive resources that are listed as options for mobilization on the Suicide Risk Assessment form are not exhaustive. It might be helpful for each community to prefill their own resources and contact information so it is readily available to therapists conducting risk assessments.

One of the most important parts of this Suicide Risk Assessment is the Counselor Assessment of Risk. This is the clinical judgment of the counselor derived from all of the available information. Sometimes the counselor will need to consult with a peer or supervisor to come to this determination. The truth is that there are times, even after more than two decades, where I will consult with a one of my colleagues to help me to process the information I have heard to make sure I haven't missed anything in my assessment. In situations where I am on the fence about whether to send a client directly to hospital, I will try to consult with a colleague immediately. On these occasions I will tell the client that I want to take a moment to consult with one of my colleagues about their case because it is very important to me that I haven't missed anything and want to provide them with the best care possible. I have never had a client object or leave my office because of this. My impression has been that they are surprised and/or relieved that I am taking their distress so seriously and am willing to consult to ensure I am doing the best I can for them.

### Non-Suicidal Self-Injury

There is an important distinction to be made between suicidal behaviors and non-suicidal self-injury or self-harm behaviors. Suicidal behavior has the intent of ending one's life while self-injury behavior is intended to change an emotional state. (See Window of Tolerance in Chapter 9). Sometimes our clients will use self-injury as a means to feel something when they are experiencing unbearable numbness or disconnection from themselves and the world. Or conversely they might use self-injury as a means to shift themselves from a state of being emotionally overwhelmed, to experiencing a release of those intense emotions. For some individuals, self-injury behavior allows them to localize their pain in a specific area of the body and to feel a sense of control over it. Unlike the pain caused by PTSD, self-injury provides some of our client with a sense of control over when pain begins and ends, as well as where it is located.

With clients who engage in self-injury, we need to find out the form(s) of self-injury that they use and, if the risk of accidental suicide is present, to work with them to find ways to reduce this risk. Some clients might be willing to try holding ice in their hands or snapping an elastic band on their wrist instead of cutting or burning themselves. Another common strategy is to ask clients who self-injure if they would be willing to move the site of injury from a higher risk place on the body such as the wrist, to a lower risk site, such as the outer thigh. In cases where the risk of accidental suicide is high and imminent, immediate crisis response intervention will be required.

### Suicide Risk Safety Planning

Safety planning is an integral part of the Suicide Risk Assessment protocol and comes into play after any imminent risk has been dealt with first. Creating a safety plan is a collaborative task with our clients. Together with them we write out a plan that they can put into action whenever they are feeling suicidal. This provides them with a concrete plan—identifying actions they can take to distract and soothe themselves, connect them with resources and supports, and remind them of their motivation and deterrents not to act—that they can take with them and refer to whenever needed. A template can be found in Appendix 3.

### Current Abusive Relationships

Some of our clients will still be involved in abusive relationships when they come to us for counseling. The perpetrator might be a partner, parent, or a family member. The perpetrator might live with the client, or if not, might still be in contact with them. These are usually complex situations that require a lot of understanding on our part, as well as some restraint if we are feeling compelled to pressure our client to change the dynamics of the relationship when they are neither interested, nor willing, to do so.

The first thing we need to do is assess risk, and develop safety plans where appropriate. If our client is living in an abusive or violent home, this is a crisis situation that will definitely require safety planning. If the client is not living with the perpetrator, but is still in contact with him or her, information about the nature and frequency of contact will help us to assess whether this is a crisis situation and whether a safety plan is needed. In these situations, if clients are open to it, we can discuss ways that they might safely begin to limit contact with the unsafe person. Even if we are dealing with a crisis situation, however, it doesn't mean that we can take over. (The exception would be if children were involved, in which case we would obviously have to notify the appropriate child protection agencies). If we are afraid for the safety of the client, it is okay to express this. It is genuine caring. It is also important at the same time to remain mindful that as adults, our clients have the right to make their own decisions. In these situations we can provide education on trauma, the power and control dynamics of abusive relationships, and support. We can offer information on community supports (such as police, medical services, shelters, etc.), and offer to contact them with our clients and/or advocate on their behalf, if they would like us to do so.

### Safety Planning—Abusive Relationships

Developing safety plans with clients who are being subjected to abuse and/or violence requires attention to detail, and often the mobilization of community supports. We need to talk to our clients about any patterns they might have observed that indicate to them that the probability of abuse or violence is high or impending. Are there specific days of the week or times of day? Are there non-verbal or verbal cues from the perpetrator? Are there rooms or places where our client feels more vulnerable? Are there places (e.g., library, shopping mall, a friend's) where they could go during higher risk times? In some cases it might help to draw a diagram of their home and plan escape routes. We might want to suggest that our clients keep money on hand and a phone number to call for a ride to get away if needed. Providing information on shelters and abuse hotlines might also be helpful.

Safety planning has to be tailored to the individual situation of the client. In my community, there are community agencies that have expertise in this area and offer legal, financial, counseling, and other services to individuals who are in abusive relationships. It is important, given the prevalence of domestic abuse in our society, that we are aware of local services and ready to advocate for our clients if needed.

## Explaining PTSD to Our Clients

I try to explain PTSD to clients in a few ways. I tend to use information handouts and concrete examples to make the information easy to understand. I've found that my clients respond very positively to the example below.

> *I've found that providing an example of the difference between a trauma memory and a non-trauma memory can be really helpful in explaining how trauma affects the mind and body. Is it okay if I share this with you?*
>
> *First I'll start with the non-trauma memory. Let's imagine that I am driving to work in my car one morning. I'm listening to the radio. Feeling relaxed. Thinking about what I have to do at work that day. I notice the*

*cars around me. I notice the people walking on the sidewalk . . . the kids with backpacks on the way to school . . . the woman walking her dog. Then all of a sudden my eyes catch a glimpse in my rear-view mirror of a car driving erratically behind me. The survival part of my brain sounds the alarm to alert me to the presence of a potential threat. Stress hormones flood through my body. My muscles tense up. My breathing becomes shallow and rapid. My heart rate increases. My attention narrows so that I am focused on this car behind me. I shut off the radio to reduce distractions. I notice the car is weaving in and out of traffic at a high rate of speed and is all over the road. I look ahead. I see the woman and her dog approaching the crosswalk. She is not looking down the street and has not noticed this car. She steps out onto the crosswalk as this speeding car comes up behind me. I am afraid for her safety. I am afraid for my own safety.*

*Now the stress hormones in my body are taking over and I am no longer thinking rationally. What happens next is determined in an instant by the survival center of my brain. My brain has a few options. Based on the information it has, it might decide it is best for me to try to escape—and if so, my actions will be directed toward trying to flee or driving away from the danger. Or, the survival part of my brain may decide I have a better chance if I fight somehow and will cause me to take actions to engage with the threat—maybe by trying to force this other car off the road—or I might sound my horn to try to alert the woman at the crosswalk to the danger. If I were a soldier or police officer, and had been trained to deal with this type of threat, my training would kick in, and I would do what I had been trained to do. Or, my brain might decide that fight and flight aren't options, and that my only option is to freeze, watching in horror, unable to act, as the situation unfolds.*

*Let's imagine I freeze. Then the speeding car somehow goes out of control and winds up stopped on the curb. No one is hurt. Police are called. When they arrive and I leave the scene, I will likely let out a sigh of relief. That breath is a very important moment in all of this. That breath or sigh of relief signals to the brain that this event, not only had a beginning and a middle—but it also has an end. This is important. This tells the brain that the threat is finished and the body can relax. My body and mind will "reset". My breathing and heart rate will return to normal. My muscles will relax and my attention will widen again to take in all that is happening around me. If, later in the day I were to tell you about my day, I might feel some emotions about what happened but they will not be as intense as they were when the incident occurred. Also, I won't relive the same muscle tension, shallow breathing, and increased heart rate that I felt at the time of the incident. This is a non-trauma memory.*

*Now let's go back to the story and change the ending. So, let's imagine I freeze when I see this speeding car behind me. I watch in horror and feel powerless, as the car plows through the crosswalk and runs over the woman and her dog. The car keeps going for a while then stops down the road.*

*Police and ambulance are called. The woman and her dog have been seriously injured. We are unsure if they will make it.*

*Let's imagine that this is a traumatic event for me. So when I drive away, I do not breathe a sigh of relief. My body continues to release stress hormones. My brain is so overwhelmed by the stress hormones in my body that it does not receive the message that this event, which in reality had a beginning, middle, and a horrible end, is now over and the threat has passed. The stress hormones might be so elevated in my body that my mind is unable to record my conscious memories of all or part of what happened. I am overwhelmed physically and emotionally as I continue to feel the horror and powerlessness of the event. My muscles stay tense. My heart continues to race and my breathing is still fast and shallow. If I were to see you later in the day and talk to you about what happened, there is a good chance that I might have difficulty describing to you what happened, but would feel the same intensity of emotions and physical sensations that I felt during the initial incident. Also, if I wasn't thinking about the traumatic event but then a sound, smell, sight, physical sensation, or emotional reaction reminded me of the event, I might go back to the event in my mind and relive fragments of what my body and mind experienced, as though the accident were happening in the present moment. This is a traumatic memory. The mind and body have not registered that the trauma has ended, and continue to relive it over and over again.*

When I explain it like this to my clients, I invariably witness a non-verbal shift in them as they begin to understand. The light goes on. They begin to make sense of their experience. I can feel some of their shame dissipating regarding how they responded to their own trauma, and how their minds and bodies have responded since.

Knowledge itself is an important coping tool. It helps our clients to regain their balance and to approach their trauma experience and reactions to it with understanding and curiosity, rather than shame, denial, and avoidance. It is up to us to present the information in ways that are accessible to our clients.

## Introducing the Valley of the Shadow of Death—as a Metaphor for PTSD and Healing

What follows is an example of how I explain this metaphor to my clients:

*When we experience PTSD, it is like finding ourselves in the valley of the shadow of death. I like the image of the valley of the shadow of death, because it seems to fit with PTSD really well. The valley is a dark and desolate place that exists in the shadow of some kind of significant ending—a real or symbolic death. It is in this place we are apt to feel a profound sense of loneliness, fear, and hopelessness. We might struggle to think clearly. Old coping strategies don't work as effectively here. We are likely exhausted and are starting to despair that we will ever find a way out. The terrain looks treacherous and foreboding. Here the days are dark and the nights are starless. There are no obvious pathways out. It can be difficult for us to know where to begin.*

*I have studied the valley and my role is much like that of a guide. My job is to know what to expect and to help you to prepare for it. No two people follow the exact same pathways out of this valley. The paths you take will be unique to you and it will be our job to figure out what they are. You will make the decisions on what pathways we go down and how fast and deep we proceed. If you ever want to rest or change course, you have the right to make that decision.*

*Our first task is to help you to get your bearings. That is what we were doing when we talked about how trauma can affect the mind and body. It is important that you know that what you are going through is normal, given what you have experienced. It is also important that we acknowledge that you have been injured, and start to gather supportive people and resources to help address those injuries.*

*Our second task is to work on ensuring you have access to the tools you will need. It can be a steep climb so naturally you will need some tools, strategies, and supports to get through the more difficult parts. For some people, once they gather tools that help them to manage their distress effectively, that will be enough for them. They are able to block out the trauma and are comfortable to leave it alone. That is as far as they wish to go on this journey. That is definitely an option and one you can decide to take at any time.*

*If you choose to continue and undertake the journey out of the valley, we will talk about the options available to you for working through your trauma. The trauma-processing pathways are the most difficult part of the climb, but we will make sure you are comfortable with using the coping tools and supports available to you to effectively manage any distress that arises. Also, you will continue to be in charge of the pace and can take breaks as needed. There might be a number of pathways we will need to go down during this part. Some of the common ones involve dealing with anger, grief, guilt, fear, and relationships. Whatever pathways you go down will be unique to you and what you need for healing.*

*After we have helped you to get through your climb, we move into the next phase, which is preparing you to live with the scars and reclaim your life. This is the more fun, celebratory, and creative part that involves relocating the trauma into your history, so it's no longer the first thing you think about in the morning, and demanding your time and attention throughout your days and nights. Then we can focus on how you would like to move forward and reclaim your life when you are no longer living in the valley.*

I've found that using this metaphor to explain the trauma experience and the phases of the healing journey has been very effective with my clients, regardless of their cultural and religious backgrounds. It has invariably been one of those deep connection moments that happen in therapy, where something clicks for the clients so that they can understand it in a new way. A few have even responded to this metaphor with tears in their eyes, explaining that it resonates very deeply with the truth of their experience.

## When to Make Medical Referrals

The question of when to make medical referrals is one with which therapists often grapple. If a client is struggling with high intensity suicidal ideation and impulses, or if they are struggling to function in areas of their lives due to PTSD symptoms, I do, with their permission, make a referral to their family doctor or a hospital emergency room (if they are imminently suicidal).

For clients who are finding it difficult to get out of bed in the morning because they are overwhelmed by their symptoms, sometimes medication is necessary to help them to find their footing so that they have the strength to begin to implement coping strategies. Given the fact that PTSD can cause life-threatening symptomology in the form of despair, hopelessness, and/or severe pain symptoms that might lead to suicidal thoughts, our clients have a right to information about medication that might decrease this risk. (See the section on Pharmacological Interventions in Chapter 9).

# 9 Gathering Tools for the Journey

The recovery process includes exploration of and reconnection with the neglected realms of the self, as it becomes safe to do so.

(Bruner & Woll, 2011, p. 27)

Safety is paramount in trauma work. We cannot begin working with clients to reconnect with the traumatized, neglected, and abandoned parts of self, unless and until they have the capacity to manage moments of intense physiological and emotional distress that are likely to arise. Once clients have an understanding of PTSD, the valley, and what to expect, our task is then to help them to gather tools for the journey ahead. Even if our clients have decided that they do not wish to pursue trauma processing, but rather want to focus only on stabilization and distress tolerance, these tools will serve them as well. This part is about continuing to tend to injuries. It is about safety, sometimes it involves rest, and it always involves assisting clients in identifying and becoming proficient with the tools they will need to help them to get through the rough patches. The tools that will be provided in this section can help our clients to learn not only how to better manage and reduce their distress levels, but also to increase their tolerance for distress when it arises.

## The Window of Tolerance

The "window of tolerance" is a wonderfully helpful concept that was first introduced by Daniel J. Siegel in 1999, and was later adapted to understanding traumatic stress reactions by Ogden, Minton, and Pain (2006). I've adapted this concept in a way that allows me to provide clients with a simplified visual depiction to explain how we can experience distress and the need for coping tools. You will find a handout for use with clients, in Appendix 4 (called Understanding Your Window of Tolerance).

I explain it to my clients like this:

*In Figure 9.1, the vertical axis denotes the intensity of emotions experienced. The horizontal axis refers to time. Depending on the person, the time frame might be hours, days, weeks, etc. The shaded area between the lines is the*

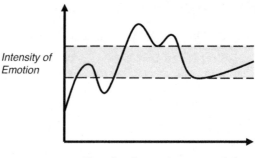

Time (i.e., hours, days, or weeks)

*Figure 9.1* Window of Tolerance

*window of tolerance for that person and shows the intensity of distress that they can handle at a given point in time. The intensity of emotions that we experience within this window might not necessarily be comfortable, but these emotions can be managed in such a way that we can still think, problem-solve, and cope. This window will widen or narrow depending on our circumstances. If we are dealing with major stressors such as physical pain, illness, financial or relationship issues, PTSD, depression, anxiety, etc. our window will likely narrow.* (This concept extends beyond trauma and can be used to explain how we handle emotional distress generally). *If we find ourselves outside our window, either above it or below it, we experience that as overwhelmingly painful. Above the window the pain is connected to intense emotions. Despair, sadness, anger, shame, fear, guilt, etc., become unbearable. Likewise, if our emotional intensity falls below the window, the pain is also unbearable, but in this case is caused by emotional experiences of numbness, disconnection, or "feeling nothing at all". When outside the window, either above or below it, we struggle to think clearly and rationally. Problem solving and coping become an issue. Consciously or subconsciously, the mind and body will desperately seek out ways to reduce the pain and return to inside the window. There are many ways this can be done.*

*Let's imagine that this is my window of tolerance for a given day. I've been working for weeks on a project and have just finished it. The deadline for me to hand it in is in a couple of hours. I've just saved it on my hard drive and was going to print it, when I received an e-mail from my manager with a subject line that reads "Urgent". I open the e-mail. Strange text appears across my screen and then the screen goes dark. The e-mail I opened contained a virus and everything on my hard drive has been erased. Notice the* **X** *on this figure (Figure 9.2). This is where this event ranks for me. It's just outside of my window of tolerance. I feel intense panic and frustration and because I'm outside and above my window, I cannot*

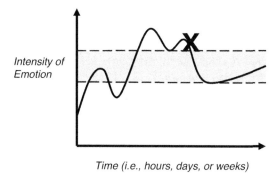

*Figure 9.2* Example of Distressing Event That is Outside of Window

think rationally or problem solve. I decide I need to walk away from my computer for a few minutes to clear my head and calm down. I get a glass of water and decide to talk to one of my coworkers. My colleague listens and suggests I talk to my boss and explain what happened. She reminds me that I still have all the information that I used for the report, and the words came from my mind and are still there. By walking away, getting a drink of water, and talking to a supportive colleague, I am able to get back into my window of tolerance. I'm still upset but I can think and act in a rational way once again.

Now let's imagine that the exact same scenario happens on a different day when my window of tolerance is much narrower. Maybe I have not slept well the night before. Maybe I am dealing with symptoms related to PTSD, depression, anxiety, or chronic pain. Whatever the reason, when my hard drive is erased, I find myself quite far above my window of tolerance (*Figure 9.3*).

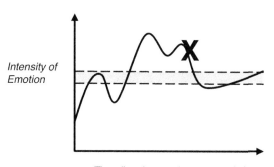

*Figure 9.3* Window Narrow with Distress

*The despair, frustration and sense of helplessness are overwhelming and unbearable. How might I handle it? . . . I might cry. I might slam my hand down on the desk. If my reaction instead was below my window of tolerance I might totally shut down. Regardless of how I act outwardly, on the inside I will struggle to think clearly. My ability to think and problem-solve in a logical way is significantly impaired. Human beings are incredibly driven to survive, however, and I will turn to whatever ways have become habitual for me, to try to get back into my window of tolerance.*

*What is fascinating about us as human beings is that we are naturally drawn to find ways to get ourselves back into our window of tolerance, often without consciously thinking about it. We tend to use distress reduction strategies that are readily available and/or familiar to us. Some will turn to exercise, meditation, talking to a friend, or journaling. Others will turn to alcohol, substance use, self-injury such as cutting, or high-risk behaviors like unprotected sex, or gambling. What we need to be clear about is that all of these behaviors contain underlying good intentions, i.e., to get back within our window of tolerance and/or to make it wider. I've observed that when people turn to the higher risk coping strategies, it's typically because either they feel unbearable nothingness or numbness and want to feel something, or alternatively, they are experiencing emotions that are so intense and unbearable that they need to get to a place where they feel less. The intention is good and in fact these coping strategies do provide short-term relief; however, there are often long-term negative consequences—like shame, physical effects, legal problems, or relationship issues—that can add to distress.*

I find that understanding this can help clients to *let go of the shame* they might have about some of the coping strategies they have been using. (I've actually witnessed a sigh of relief at times when clients who have been using substances or self-injuring to manage their distress, finally make sense of *why* they have been doing this).

I then refer to Figure 9.4 and explain that in counseling, when it comes to the window of tolerance, we have two main goals:

*Our first goal is to work together to add to your distress management toolkit by identifying healthy and effective strategies that fit for you, which you can then use to move back into your window of tolerance when you find yourself outside of it. Our second goal is to work together to find ways to increase the width of that window so that your tolerance for distress is greater overall.*

Clients understand this concept. It makes sense to them. It's practical and meaningful in terms of their own experiences. It's a concrete representation of what we are aiming for. It can also be instrumental in commencing cognitive restructuring. What has been overwhelming, confusing, and unbearable, has been made understandable and hopeful. Clients are introduced to

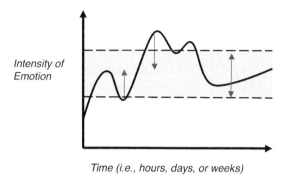

*Figure 9.4* Goals of Counseling

the hope that there are tools that will allow them to effectively manage their distress. They learn they have some control, and that they are no longer powerless.

For those with addiction issues, we can add the support of a counselor who specializes in addictions (if that isn't us) and medical support. We let them know that as they try out new distress management strategies and evaluate their effectiveness, we will eventually figure out which strategies and combination of strategies will work for them. Over time, when they are ready, and with appropriate supports, they can begin to replace their substance and/or alcohol use coping strategies with healthier, more adaptive ones—likewise with self-injury or other higher risk-coping mechanisms. This stated expectation provides our clients with much needed, realistic hope.

## Explaining Distress Tolerance Strategies

I share with clients my observation that there are seven categories of tools that appear to be effective for people who are dealing with PTSD, in managing distress and increasing their window of tolerance. (See accompanying handout in Appendix 5: Individual Distress Tolerance and Management Plan).

### *Counseling and Medical Support*

Two of these categories involve working directly with professionals. One of these is working with a counselor, which our clients are already doing, to help with resetting how the brain works following trauma. The other involves clients working with their physician to assess whether any of the physical distress they are experiencing needs to be treated in a medical way. For individuals who are unable to cope with the functions of daily living as a result of PTSD symptoms, I do recommend a medical consultation and am happy to send a referral to their doctor to outline their concerns—because sometimes clients aren't sure what to say or how to say it.

## Distraction

PTSD symptoms will often include spiraling thoughts that focus on reliving aspects of the trauma (i.e., flashbacks) as well as fear-based spiraling thought patterns that are focused on the future. Both cause considerable distress and can increase distress the longer one stays within these spirals. For some, distraction will be an effective tool to break these patterns in the mind and body. To use distraction tools, there needs to be a degree of dual awareness so that clients are able to recognize when they are in these spirals of thought, and have the capacity to try to disrupt these neural patterns by doing something outside of the pattern. Thus, if a person is lying in bed and experiencing a fear-based thought spiral in which they are imagining all the terrible things that might happen in their future, if they have the capacity of dual awareness and are able to disrupt this pattern, for example, by getting out of bed and making a hot drink or watching a funny video, or reading a supportive letter from a friend, then they can start to take control of reducing their distress. Likewise, if they are at work or school and start to experience flashbacks or fear-based thought spirals, if they can disrupt this neural pattern by texting a friend, or by looking at a picture of their loved ones or a favorite vacation spot, then this might allow them to escape the distressing thought pattern. These are the kinds of tools we want to help clients to identify for themselves, so that they come to realize that they have some power to manage their distress.

## Mindfulness

Some clients will find that mindfulness is a helpful addition to their toolkit. I suggest to them that there are three different mindfulness strategies that they may wish to try. One is specific mindfulness about what is happening internally within the body—with non-judgmental observation of physical sensations and emotions—experienced in the moment. The second is observation and attention to one's external surroundings. These are sensory observations that can bring one's attention back to the present through observation of what one can see, hear, touch, smell, and/or taste. The third type of mindfulness involves noticing what is being asked of them at the present moment.

I use the following examples to explain this concept:

> *If you and I are sitting in my office where it is safe and non-threatening but one of us is reliving the pain of the past or are worried about imagined horrible things happening in the future, then our body and mind will experience pain and distress—despite the fact that we are safe and unthreatened in the present moment. There are three mindfulness tools that we can use, however, to bring us back to this moment. One is just to notice what is going on inside our bodies—noticing what is happening physically in our bodies and our emotions. Sometimes observing these things without judgment can*

have a calming effect. Another mindfulness tool for getting ourselves back to the present moment involves shifting our attention to what we can observe outside of us, through our senses—things that we can see, hear, smell, touch, and/or taste. For example, if I look around the office to find my favorite color, or pick up this rock and notice its texture, weight, and temperature—I can only do this if I am in the present moment. I can't be in the past or the future. The last mindfulness tool is one that I like to use when I am trying to go to sleep but find that my mind won't cooperate and instead is focused on worries or fears for the future. In those moments I find it helpful to ask myself, "What is being asked of me at this moment?" It is then that I come to the realization that all I am being asked to do at the moment is to relax and go to sleep. Nothing more. There is something calming in that. Sometimes we need to remind ourselves what the demands on us really are, at a given moment in time, in order to let go of imagined ones.

## Self-Soothing

A third type of distress tolerance tool that many of my clients have found helpful is self-soothing. This involves consciously choosing to surround oneself with healthy and calming comforts—especially at times, or in situations, when PTSD is likely to be activated. The focus here is on one's senses and identifying what sounds, textures, sights, smells, and tastes will contribute to a sense of calm and safety in that moment. For some, it might be comforting to wear a favorite sweater or other type of clothing. For others a scented hand lotion, or scented candle might help. Music, hot drinks, or a hot shower or bath are common self-soothing strategies among my clients.

## Accepting Support From Others

Accepting support from others, for some unknown reason, seems to be quite a challenge for many of my clients. What is interesting is that so many of them are helpers in their careers, i.e., first responders, health care workers, or in some type of human services field. Alternatively, many are unofficial helpers, i.e., the individuals who others in their social circles come to for help and support in their lives. I've learned that it can be useful, with these individuals, to continue to remind them that in life, the reality is that at points in time we will be the helper, and at other points in time we will be the ones who need help. Sometimes we will be in both roles in the same day. This is how life works. There is no shame in it. It isn't about weakness as a person. To make this point, I will often ask my clients how they feel about the loved ones they support when their loved ones are dealing with challenges. I ask my clients if they think less of their loved ones. Do they think of them as being weak for accepting help? Most clients are appalled by this suggestion, and only take a moment to realize that they are using a double standard. I will then challenge them to afford themselves the same levels of compassion, understanding, and respect that they give their loved ones. I remind them that accepting help from loved ones, local organizations that can provide support, and/or peer support groups can make a significant impact in terms of reducing the distress caused by isolation, loneliness, or the stresses of daily living which might be more than one can handle when PTSD symptoms are at their worst.

### Education

Another important tool to reduce and manage distress is education and knowledge. When clients better understand trauma, how it can affect their minds and bodies, and what they can do to support their own well-being and healing, they become empowered. Knowledge is a light in the darkness. It provides clarity in confusion and hope in the face of despair. Therapists have an important role to play in the education of their clients, but clients can also learn about trauma and healing through other credible means. Providing interested clients with reading lists, including workbooks focused on stabilization and/or healing, can be helpful. There are also a number of websites that clients might find useful.

## Creating an Individualized Distress Management Toolkit

After explaining each of the seven categories of tools available to support them in managing distress, I ask my clients if they would be willing to work with me to create their own *Individual Distress Tolerance and Management Plan* (worksheet can be found in Appendix 5). If so, we start with two copies of this worksheet—one for the client and one for me. Also, we each have a highlighting pen. I ask clients if they would like to read through it on their own or if they would prefer to have me to read it out loud as we work through it. (I do this because I am aware that some clients might have difficulty with reading, due to any number of challenges and I do not want to put them in an uncomfortable position.) I suggest to the client, that as we go through the list of possible strategies, they highlight any that have worked for them in the past, they are currently using, or they are willing to try. If they are reading through the handout on their own, I ask them to let me know what items they are highlighting, so I can do the same on the handout I have—which I will keep for my records.

At the end of this process, I point out the strategies that the client has highlighted which will take the least amount of energy and time. I suggest that when they are starting to feel overwhelmed, these might be best as their "go to" strategies. When our clients are already feeling overwhelmed and having difficulty with daily functioning, we need to be sensitive to this. The goal is to help our clients to learn how to move back into their window when they are feeling overwhelmed. While some might have the time, energy, and inclination to engage in the more demanding strategies, it is best if they make this decision on their own. We don't want to add to their burden, by setting up expectations about what they "should" be doing, when in some cases, these suggestions might not be within the realm of possibility for our clients at that point in their journey. I've found that it makes more sense to suggest that they use the easier strategies, like texting a friend, spending a few minutes in nature, changing into comfortable clothes, or getting a hot drink. This takes the pressure off and provides hope that they can succeed, since these tools are more accessible when they are struggling.

I challenge my clients, suggesting that on days when they are feeling up to it, to do the more time- and energy-consuming strategies as a way to widen their window of tolerance. Building one or two of these more intensive strategies into their daily or weekly routine, when it becomes possible for them, can be an ongoing way of supporting a wider distress tolerance window.

We also take time to focus on those strategies that might be portable, with a little prep. So if chewing gum helps them to be mindful, then they can pack some with them for when they go to school or work. If scented lotion or a picture of loved ones helps, these are things they can easily carry with them in a backpack or bag throughout their day. Or if music helps, they can ensure that what they need is available to them on their phone.

Another suggestion I make is that they prepare an individualized toolkit. A shoebox or other small box works well. They can decorate it if they like. In it they might pack things such as art supplies, a scented candle, a book they want to read, a picture of loved ones, a shell or rock from a favorite place, bubble bath, etc.—anything that might help them to employ their distress reduction strategies when they are having a hard time. Having them all in one place that is easily accessible can make it more likely they will use them.

I use Figure 9.5 as I explain to my clients, that in all likelihood, using one of the tools they have identified isn't going to make things entirely better when they find themselves outside their window. However, if a hot drink reduces their distress by 5%, and going for a short walk outdoors by

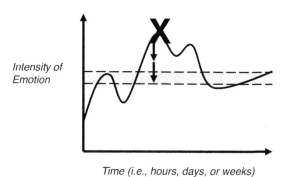

Time (i.e., hours, days, or weeks)

*Figure 9.5* Cumulative Efforts to Get Back into Window of Tolerance

10%, and listening to favorite music by another 5%, then that overall 20% reduction in distress might be enough to get them back into their window and make their experience bearable.

Our clients need to become effective at using these strategies not only in their daily lives but also in therapy, because these strategies are also key to our doing safe and effective therapeutic work with them.

## Teaching Our Clients How to "Apply the Brakes"

Babette Rothschild (2011) came up with the brilliant metaphor of teaching a person to drive a car to explain how we need to approach trauma therapy. She pointed out that in learning to drive, we don't first teach a person to accelerate, but rather how to apply the brakes:

> Just like driving a car, safe trauma therapy requires knowing how to stop before speeding ahead. It is unwise to set a volatile process in motion—regardless of the method applied—before clients know how to regulate affect and control flashbacks. They will be safest when they are readily able to calm themselves down even when strongly provoked by their trauma memories.
>
> (p. 14)

When I first read these words, a light went on for me, and I changed the way I approached trauma therapy. As a result, not only did my clients fare much better, but they also developed confidence in their ability to manage their emotional distress and flashbacks in session, which then transferred into their daily lives. Practically speaking, this is about making a decision not to start trauma-processing interventions with our clients, without first ensuring they have the tools and supports to handle potential distressing reactions that may arise, both within and outside of session. Thus, explaining the metaphor of applying the brakes can help clients understand why we will progress slowly, and give them confidence in our commitment to ensuring their safety throughout this process.

Therapists can assist clients to learn how to apply the brakes by working with them to consciously monitor their distress level during session. Identifying physical and emotional symptoms that typically precede flashbacks or dissociation can be helpful in identifying when to apply the brakes. Since we know that when clients dissociate or go into flashbacks they are no longer processing the trauma, it is in the clients' best interest that we do our best to ensure that we operate within their window of tolerance.

Working with clients to develop agreed-upon strategies as to how they will apply the brakes in session is a good plan prior to beginning to discuss the trauma experience(s), since for some, this will be triggering. Some examples of options I provide, for when either the client or myself notices that the client is moving toward dissociation or flashbacks, include: having the client take a drink of cool water or hot tea and focus on taste; doing a breathing exercise; asking the client to look around the office and point out their favorite color; changing the subject to something less threatening for a few minutes.

I was working with Ella[1] on managing frequent flashbacks by focusing on distress management tools. We hadn't begun trauma processing yet. Ella came into session, very distressed. Her eyes were large and her breathing was shallow and rapid. I asked what was happening. She said she heard some people talking at lunch and they were saying how most times women make up rape accusations because they regret their decision of having sex with someone. She said the comments being made about women were terrible. Having recently survived a violent rape, Ella was experiencing flashbacks. I asked if I could get her a glass of water or tea. She chose the latter. Upon giving it to her I asked her to smell it and notice the scent. I asked her to feel the warmth of the cup in her hands. I then asked her to look around the room and see the details of where she was—to recognize that she was safe and that it was just the two of us in the room. In doing this, Ella was able to stabilize her emotions. I empathized with her about what she heard, and agreed it was a horrible experience. I reminded her that she has the power, which she used, to leave situations like the one she left, if she is feeling threatened or triggered. We also talked about how she could use the strategies we used in session, in her life to help to regulate her distress when she is triggered.

## Body Awareness

Helping our clients develop body awareness is important to their healing, since so much of trauma memory is often sensory (Rothschild, 2000). When I notice clients becoming physically tensed up, I ask them to do a body scan from head to toe, to notice the physical and emotional sensations they are experiencing. Once they become aware of physical tension in their body, they can do gentle, slow movements to release the tension. Alternatively, changing the position of parts of the body can sometimes relieve distress. This is another way of teaching our clients how to apply the brakes and reduce distress.

Matt[2] was talking about a situation in class in which he had been triggered. The discussion was about war and this "young punk who still lived at home with his mommy and daddy", was talking about peace and making disrespectful comments about the military. As a veteran, Matt said he was livid and wanted to go over and "punch the kid in the head". Instead he walked out of class. I congratulated him on his self-control and empathized with how difficult that must have been to hear. While discussing it, I noticed Matt's fists were clenched and his knuckles were white as he clutched the arms of his chair. He was leaning forward and looked like he was ready to pounce. His feet were hooked around the front chair legs. He appeared ready for battle. I shared my observations with him. He expressed his surprise that he hadn't noticed his posture. I asked him to notice how he felt physically and emotionally when in that posture. He responded that he did feel ready to physically fight someone. His chest was tight. His body was super tense. Emotionally, he said he felt cold and angry. We talked about how this experience in class had triggering his PTSD, such that he was reacting as though his survival was at stake. He agreed that this is how it felt, even though objectively he knew it wasn't a life or death situation. We discussed that we needed to find a way to communicate this to his mind and body. I asked if he would be willing to try sitting back in his chair and allowing his feet to sit firmly on the floor, and his hands to relax on his lap. I asked if he would take a deep breath. He did what I asked. After a few seconds, I asked what he noticed. He said that his body felt less tense. His chest wasn't so tight anymore. He felt more relaxed and said he didn't feel like he wanted to punch his classmate anymore. Physically, he said he felt warmer, and emotionally, though still angry, less so. He said he also felt more rational.

Our bodies show incredible wisdom. They remember and recognize trauma reminders, often before we are consciously aware of them. Helping clients to become sensitized to these physical reactions can be useful information in understanding their initial responses to trauma, and helping us to focus efforts to resolve these responses in order to reduce distress. Initially, we teach our clients how to apply the brakes. When they become proficient at this, we can then go back and process the source of the trauma response.

During the past decade, I've worked with an increasing number of young women who have been drugged (against their will and knowledge) and then physically and/or sexually assaulted. Most of these women have not had any conscious memory of the assaults. They recall what happened up to a point in the evening, but then their memory stops, and doesn't resume until sometime the following morning. In these cases, the physical and emotional sensations they experience can often help us to understand something of the missing hours of their memories. However, these bodily and affective memories can be quite overwhelming for them, and they will also need to know how to apply the brakes before we proceed to trauma processing.

## Medical Support and Pharmacological Interventions

I've noticed that oftentimes my clients are reluctant to speak with their physicians about their severe PTSD symptoms. These symptoms tend to be related to insomnia or other sleep disturbances, gastrointestinal complaints, concurrent anxiety/depression, and/or in some cases, chronic suicidal thoughts and impulses. Much of this reluctance is attributed to perceived stigma. My clients express fears that they will not be taken seriously, that they will be considered "crazy", or that they will be hospitalized against their will. I wish I could reassure them that this would never happen, but unfortunately, experience has taught me that I can make no such guarantees.

Whether individuals suffering from PTSD, possibly with concurrent depression and/or anxiety, should be accessing medication to address some of their symptoms has been a complicated issue. My clients differ widely on their stance. Some indicate that they will not consider medication—ever. Some are willing to try anything. Still others are in the difficult spot of wanting to try medication but are fearful of the response of their loved ones who don't "believe in" medication, PTSD, or both. Some have been told outright that if they take medications they will be disowned by their families because it means they are "crazy". Many have said they want to "do this on their own", believing that taking medication means that they are weak. I've spoken to therapists who vary in their opinions as to whether clients should be taking medication as well. The bottom line is that it is the client's decision and they should be provided with what they need to allow them to make an informed decision.

The evidence regarding the use of medication (i.e., SSRIs) in addressing PTSD symptoms indicates that it can be effective in reducing symptom severity and accompanying disability (Stein et al., 2006). Moreover, the use of medication in the treatment of PTSD has been included as a recommendation within the *APA Clinical Practice Guidelines for the Treatment of PTSD* (2017).

I have repeatedly witnessed how the use of medication can reduce physiological and psychological pain for my clients, and allow a person, who was not functioning, to reengage with their lives. Jenna[3] had been chronically suicidal for years as a result of complex trauma symptoms. She had already completed four years of trauma therapy. She had never considered medication, believing she needed to do this on her own. When we met, she informed me that she could no longer live with this unending, unbearable pain. She wasn't willing to do it for much longer and in fact had read up how to effectively end her life by suicide. I asked her if she would be willing to talk to her doctor about the possibility of medication. She decided she had nothing to lose and made an appointment with her doctor who prescribed an anti-depressant. She told me that within 3 weeks of taking the medication she woke up one morning and started to cry. She said her tears were tears of relief, because the intolerable emotional and physical pain that she had experienced her entire life had subsided. She wondered aloud if this is what life felt like for most people. She asked why she had suffered for so long, and why her previous therapists had never mentioned medication as an option. With the reduction in pain and disappearance of suicidal thoughts, she had the strength to engage in EMDR therapy with me, which she found to be very helpful.

Medication can allow a person to find the strength that is needed to do trauma work. For some it is a means to help them to stay within their window of tolerance while developing strategies to effectively manage their distress in healthy ways and/or while doing trauma-processing work. With that said, medication isn't an option for everyone—due to side effects, conflict with values, etc. However, it is an evidence-based option that should be presented so that clients can make an informed decision as to whether this is something they wish to discuss with a physician. The bottom line is that untreated severe PTSD will make it harder for the client to stabilize and to gather the strength for the climb out of the valley. Our clients might require multiple resources in order to embark safely on this journey, and we need to support them in obtaining whatever supports they feel they require.

I've found that when clients decide to discuss the option of medication with their physician, sometimes they feel less nervous about this discussion if I send a letter to their physician prior to their appointment, explaining what I have observed and my concerns. Given that the language of PTSD symptoms is often new to my clients, I can sometimes present the information in a straightforward and comprehensive way to which physicians might be more open. Further, it has been my experience that receiving such a letter from another regulated health professional might make them less willing to discount their patient's concerns. (I'm including a Sample Referral Letter to a Physician in Appendix 6).

## Strategies for the Client Toolkit

### Sleep

Sleep disturbance, in the form of insomnia, nightmares, and night terrors can result in significant sleep deprivation and distress for our clients who are struggling with PTSD. The prevalence rates for nightmares and insomnia among individuals suffering from PTSD have been reported to be as high as 71% and 91%, respectively (Leskin, Woodward, Young, & Sheikh, 2002; Neylan et al., 1998; Ohayon & Shapiro, 2000). These sleep disorders are related to increased agitation, decreased emotional regulation, and poor concentration (Spoormaker & Montgomery, 2008). Furthermore, recurrent nightmares have been linked to increased risk of suicide (Nadorff, Nazem, & Fiske, 2011; Sjostrom, Waern, & Hetta, 2007). Thus, assessing and addressing sleep disturbance will be a priority with this client group.

As noted above, sleep disorders can lead to increased physical, cognitive, and emotional distress for our clients. Nevertheless, it can be difficult for clinicians to tease out which of these symptoms occur as a result PTSD, and which will disappear once adequate sleep is achieved. Treating both the PTSD symptoms and the sleep disorder simultaneously, if possible, is recommended (DiViva & Zayfert, 2010). Recommended therapeutic interventions for dealing with recurrent nightmares and insomnia include CBT and Imagery Rehearsal (IR), as well as consideration of pharmacological treatments (Brownlow, Harb, & Ross, 2015; Spoormaker & Montgomery, 2008). Consequently, we will sometimes need to refer clients to their personal physicians so that they can discuss whether a prescription sleep aid or anti-depressant might be appropriate. I've observed that in many cases of PTSD sleep disturbance, clients will start to self-medicate using street drugs or alcohol. Given the potential long-term negative consequences of this approach, I encourage them to talk with their physician to discuss a non-addictive and controlled treatment plan. Another option is for clients to work with a sleep specialist (usually a psychiatrist) who understands the impact of PTSD on sleep.

## Mindful Breathing

You may have noticed, at times, that when clients talk about their trauma experiences, their breathing becomes shallow, or ceases altogether. In such cases this is a sign that their distress levels are rising and they are reliving parts of their physiological trauma response. If our clients hold their breath when they are speaking about aspects of their trauma experience, it is quite possible that this was their reaction at that point in the actual traumatic experience. It is natural to hold our breath when we are terrified. However, to help the body to understand that the trauma is over, and one is safe, we need to get to the point of breathing through trauma reminders.

Breathing exercises can be very helpful tools for our clients. There are many guided breathing exercises available on-line. A simple one that I like to use with clients (and in my classes), is 60 seconds of mindful breathing. It can be a nice start, or end, to a counseling session or class. To begin I ask clients if they are open to this exercise, and if so, we start by having them close their eyes or finding a place in the room to softly focus their eyes—whatever feels most comfortable for them. I then gently direct them to notice their breathing—to go inside themselves and let the external world fade into the background for just 60 seconds. Sometimes I suggest they focus on noticing the transition point between inhaling and exhaling. Mindful breathing is a great tool for grounding. It seems to have the capacity to reset the body and mind. It is also a tool that is easy to use and portable.

## Routines

Routines in our daily life can provide a sense of stability and safety due to their predictability and consistency. Routines can also help with feeling like we are accomplishing something. In the midst of traumatic stress symptoms, which can be incredibly disruptive and exhausting, it can be difficult to maintain or try to reestablish ordinary routines. Thus, we might want to work with our clients on simplified routines that focus on self-care to reintroduce this type of stability in their lives. Routines can be based on some of the self-care strategies our clients identify when they complete their *Individual Distress Tolerance and Management Plan* (Appendix 5). An example of a simplified bedtime routine for a client might be: a half hour before bed, they begin by washing up, then turn on relaxing music, do a few yoga stretches, and then go to bed. That might be the extent of the routine we are working on to begin with. Our clients will know what they can manage at a given point in time. Encouraging them to start with what they are certain they can manage, will help them to build confidence and see progress in the short term.

### Readjusting Performance Expectations

This is often a big challenge for trauma survivors. For some reason, it is quite common for trauma survivors to believe that despite the fact that they are dealing with acute stress or PTSD symptoms, they should be functioning at peak performance. I hear a lot of self-criticism among my clients when they become frustrated that they don't have the energy to do everything they did before, and/or they aren't doing things to the standard they have come to expect. Some report feeling like a failure. My response in these conversations is to draw a circle. I ask them, out of 100%, how much of their energy is currently being used dealing with the trauma and its impact on their body and mind. I typically get estimates that range from 40% to 80%. I then divide my circle into a pie chart to visually represent the stated estimate of their energy that is being used to cope with trauma. We then acknowledge how much energy is left, which is typically somewhere between 20%–60%. I then point out how much they are still accomplishing given the limited amount of energy currently available to them, and suggest that how they are performing is not disappointing, but to the contrary, is usually in fact *incredible*. I remind them that the amount of energy required to cope with PTSD symptoms can vary over time, but that to be fair to themselves, they need to keep in mind what their current circumstances are.

### Simplifying

If clients are having difficulty with all of the tasks on their plate, we might need to talk with them about trying to reduce commitments where possible and simplifying aspects of their lives. I will usually suggest to clients who are doing this work, that now is not the time to take on additional commitments, and that it's perfectly okay, and healthy for them, when asked to do more than they can handle to say something like, "That doesn't work for me right now." No further explanation is needed, and if pushed for one, to firmly reiterate their statement. Sometimes clients are new to saying "no", and role playing or providing them with ways to say "no" that feel more comfortable to them can be helpful.

Simplifying might also involve identifying areas in their lives where small or big changes can be made to reduce stress and energy expenditure. It might be as simple as clients making a menu for meals, and cooking enough so that they can rely on leftovers every other day. For those who have financial means, it might involve hiring someone to do their house-cleaning. For those who have supportive family or friends who want to help but don't know what to do, it might involve asking for help with such things as transporting children to and from activities, preparing a meal, providing childcare so the client can rest, running interference with difficult others, etc.

### Dealing With Dissociation and Flashbacks

Dissociation and flashbacks are both indications that a client is being trig-gered and/or has exceeded their window of tolerance. When either of these responses occurs in session, it is a signal to us that we need to back off and move more slowly. We might also need to reinforce distress tolerance tools and strategies with our client prior to moving forward. Getting our clients grounded is the priority when this occurs. Thus, we need to commit with our clients to being mindful of this possibility, to notice precursors, and try to keep our work within their window of tolerance—at times possibly right on one of the edges of that window—but always trying to stay within it, in order to keep our clients safe and be effective. By doing this, we teach our clients how to stay within their own window and to recognize when they need to back off because they are getting too close to the edges.

When working with a client who has become dissociated or is dealing with flashbacks in session, it can be helpful to speak slowly and softly. Doing a breathing exercise with them if they are able, can also help them to reconnect to their bodies and the present moment in a non-threatening way. I might ask them to try to feel their feet on the floor and their body in the chair. I might ask them to look around the office and point out their favorite color. If a client is having flashbacks, I will usually remind them that they are safe and the trauma is over. I will ask, if they are able, to step into their Warrior Spirit—that observing part of their awareness that knows they are safe, and can allow them to observe the flashback from that perspective. These strate-gies are meant to help clients to anchor at least part of their awareness to the present moment where they are safe and the trauma is over. The focus for the remainder of the session will, in most cases, be on client self-care.

Asking clients to describe the sensory mode that their flashbacks typically present in can be helpful in identifying strategies that they can use to deal with them. If flashbacks are visual, I will suggest they imagine them on a projection screen whereby they can shut off the images with a remote, or to imagine seeing the flashback through a camera lens, and closing the lens. If it is an auditory flashback, I suggest they imagine hearing it through a headset and changing the channel to the sounds of the present moment. I encourage clients to use their chosen strategy every time a flashback occurs so that the brain will eventually rewire itself. If flashbacks are somatic, I sug-gest clients observe the sensation or pain and ask what message their body wants them to hear, writing it down with their non-dominant hand while not censoring the message. I've found that identifying the message is sometimes sufficient for somatic flashbacks to dissipate. Breathing through the sensations while reminding oneself the trauma is over can also be helpful. All of these strategies require the client to have dual awareness, i.e., of the past trauma that they are reliving, and of the present moment simultaneously, which can help to bridge the survival and rational parts of the brain to integrate the trauma experience.

## The Five Times Critiquing Rule

I came up with this because I was frequently hearing from my clients that they were spending an enormous amount of time going in circles in their minds trying to determine how they might have handled their traumatic experience(s) in ways that might have resulted in more favorable outcomes. While it is normal to review difficult situations we have gone through to try to learn from them, in hopes of avoiding something similar in the future, there is a point at which continuous critiquing becomes maladaptive. I explain to my clients that it is not healthy for them to spend endless amounts of time critiquing what happened. The possibilities imagined can be endless, and this activity might end up taking not only hours, but days, weeks, and months from their lives, when the bottom line is *the event has happened*, and no amount of critiquing is going to change that. I suggest they choose a number, which will be the number of times they allow themselves to critique the trauma either alone or with others outside of therapy. I have chosen "5", but they can choose whatever number they want. (Chances are, in most cases, they will have already surpassed their number.) I then suggest that once they reach their limit, they resist any more critiquing unless we are working through the trauma in therapy. Many of my clients have reported that they have found this suggestion to be helpful.

## Establishing Safety

In addition to working with clients to develop safety plans for those who struggle with suicidal ideation or who live in domestic violence situations, we might need to work with them to identify steps they can take to increase their sense of safety overall.

If clients feel there are specific threats to their physical and/or emotional safety (e.g., particular people in their lives, having to work alone late at night, living in a dangerous neighborhood, etc.), we can brainstorm with them possible steps they might take to increase their safety. As we know, the intense trauma-related fear that can be triggered by such perceived threats can decrease problem-solving and creative thinking abilities. By working together to brainstorm, we might be able to help our clients to move out of a sense of powerlessness and paralysis, into proactive action.

If the threat is not specific, but instead has been internalized as a general fear, there might also be practical things that clients can do to increase feelings of safety. What follows are just a few examples of steps some of my clients have taken to increase their sense of safety. Some have found that installing a deadbolt or alarm on their exterior doors, and/or an individual lock on their bedroom door helps to reduce hypervigilance. Some have found that placing a rod or stick in patio doors and windows to prevent them from being opened can also help them to feel safer and sleep better. Some have found that they feel safer in their apartment or home if they have a roommate.

Others have adopted a pet so they aren't alone. Some choose to sleep with a light or nightlight on. If they are working late, some will talk to a friend on their cellphone until they arrive safely at home. I've worked with some clients to develop detailed strategies regarding how to limit contact and keep themselves safe with people who are potentially volatile. What helps individual clients to feel safe will need to be explored with them.

### Nighttime Strategies

Nighttime is often the hardest time of day for individuals who are suffering with PTSD. In some instances we can link this to the fact that the trauma these clients experienced happened, or happened most frequently (if multiple incidents), at night. Thus, for many, nighttime can be a trigger for PTSD flashbacks.

There are also the real sensory and social changes that come with the night. Our ability to see clearly and to have accurate perspective in the dark is diminished. Hearing seems to become more attuned and we are likely more apt to notice sounds that we wouldn't notice during the day. Due to the fact that most people are sleeping at this time of day, it can also lead one to feel, and in fact be, very isolated and alone. Sleeping itself is inherently vulnerable. It requires that we let our guard drop, physically, cognitively, and emotionally. For some, this is terrifying at every level.

Given all the reasons above, it is easy for flashbacks, nightmares, and night terrors to intrude. Feelings of despair, isolation, hopelessness, and terror can overwhelm. Hence, establishing a safety plan or self-care plan for nighttime will be essential in our work with some clients. In addition to helping clients identify distraction, soothing, and mindfulness strategies they can use from their individual self-care plan when they are having a difficult night, I have suggested that they write themselves a letter. This letter is to be written during the day when they are feeling stronger. The goal is to use this letter to remind themselves of their strength and to provide the hope and reassurance they need during the night.

### Know That Past Traumas Might Be Activated

Past traumas that a person has experienced might be activated by a recent experience of trauma. This is not uncommon, but can be frightening for clients who all of a sudden start having flashbacks to things that sometimes happened several years ago. These clients may be stymied because they never experienced intense traumatic stress reactions to the previous event(s), but all of a sudden are experiencing tremendous distress related to these past events, that might be even more disturbing than distress related to the most recent trauma(s). It can be helpful for clients to be reassured that this is not uncommon, and can be dealt with all at once. This is another instance where knowledge is a distress reduction tool. Highlighting shared themes between the traumas (e.g., interpersonal betrayal and violation, witnessing serious injury or death of another, one's own life being threatened) can help clients to understand and make sense of the connections, particularly in cases where the content isn't obviously related on the surface.

### Recognizing Self-Medicating Activities

Individuals dealing with active, excruciating, and unbearable PTSD symptoms will sometimes turn to drastic means to manage their distress (Herman, 1997). Many of my clients, who are suffering from active PTSD, turn to alcohol or substance abuse, disordered eating behaviors, self-injury, promiscuity, and/or other high-risk behaviors as ways to try to manage their pain. Most of these clients are aware of, and can articulate how these behaviors help them to sleep or feel better, at least for a time. They have also been clear that they would find it difficult, if not impossible, to give these behaviors up unless they had alternative effective means available to them.

A challenge we, as clinicians have, is that the shame that clients attach to self-medicating behaviors can keep them from sharing this information with us. (Explaining the Window of Tolerance can sometimes help with this). Thus, it might be necessary to talk about these types of behaviors when talking about coping strategies and tools. Reassuring clients that the intention behind these activities makes sense, can help to alleviate some of the shame. Acknowledging that these strategies can be effective in the short-term, but can often cause complications in the longer term, is information that clients are usually willing to concede, and can be a door to starting to discuss harm reduction strategies and ways to substitute more adaptive coping behaviors over time. In-patient treatment programs for addictions or eating disorders might be something we need to explore with clients, depending on the severity of these potentially life-threatening illnesses.

### Grounding Objects

One of the insidious things about PTSD is that it can make someone forget who they are as a person, and anything good or hopeful in their lives. The despair that accompanies PTSD is like a dark, narrow pathway through the valley. The moon and stars are absent. It is disorienting and frightening. In the darkness of this place, clients may not be able to remember any of the goodness that has been in their life. They cannot recall the warmth of the love of others, or find light to give them hope that at some point the pain will end and all of this will be behind them. Hence, concrete tools to help our clients to remember their life beyond the darkness of the valley may be required.

Grounding objects are things that can remind a person of who they are, and what their lives and hopes are—beyond the dark pathways they are on. These objects are portable and have personal significance to our clients.

Some examples of common grounding objects my clients have used to this end include things such as: a piece of jewelry or clothing; a picture of loved ones or a favorite place; a shell or stone from a favorite place; an inspirational quote or poem; a letter; or a keychain.

When my clients are going through a particularly dark time, I will some-times offer them a grounding object in the form of a letter. I will write a personal letter to them to remind them of their strength, courage, resilience, and how far they have come. These letters focus on reassurance, hope, and strengths mirroring. Several of my clients have commented that they've found this very helpful to read when they are starting to move into despair. A few have told me that they've carried this letter with them for periods of time so they could reread it whenever and wherever they needed. (A *Sample Therapist Letter to Client* can be found in Appendix 7).

I know of some therapists who keep a collection of polished stones in their office. They allow their clients to choose one to take with them. This provides clients with something concrete they can touch, to notice shape, texture, and temperature as well as color—to anchor them to the present. I expect that the other part of this is that it reminds them of the therapist—someone who believes in them, sees the good in them, and cares about them unconditionally.

### Physical Comforts

Physical comforts have a role to play in reducing the distress associated with PTSD. Their role is two-fold: 1) to provide sensory comfort, and 2) to assist clients in reconnecting with their bodies.

Physical comforts are individual, although there seem to be some com-mon favorites. These comforts provide a sensory feeling of relaxation and support. In terms of tactile senses, some examples of favorites among my clients include: massage therapy (but this is less common for individuals who were sexually or physically abused); a hug from a loved one; soft clothing; a blanket; a stuffed animal; petting an animal; and holding a shell or polished stone. Regarding the olfactory senses some of these are: baking bread or cookies; scented candles; scented hand lotion; fresh air; and flowers. For taste, many of my clients prefer: coffee, tea or hot chocolate; comfort foods; fresh fruit; and chocolate. Comforts regarding sight could include most of the abovementioned ones, but common ones I've heard also include: photos of loved ones or favorite places; candles or low lighting; seeing a loved one or pet in person; looking at nature; or viewing a starlit sky. For sound, favorite comforts among my clients include: relaxing music; sounds of nature; quiet; a waterfall or waves on a lake or ocean; and the voice of a loved one.

Clients who were traumatized as children, or adults who experienced prolonged trauma, may have cut themselves off from physical sensations to defend against overwhelming pain. Unfortunately, this also shuts down the ability to notice and experience comforting physical sensations as well.

Thus, we might need to do some work with our clients as we help them to reconnect with their bodies. Reconnecting with their bodies will mean that they will start to feel the painful sensations too, but this time we will have worked with them to identify effective ways to find comfort. In these cases, we might need to challenge our clients to try a number of different physical comforts to figure out what works for them, because they might not have thought of this or paid attention to it before.

As I've mentioned previously, when I began working with Max, who had a history of complex trauma throughout his life, he was so disconnected with his body that he walked on a broken leg for a week before he realized it was broken. We realized that he began disconnecting from his body as a child when he went through painful and invasive cancer treatments. Disconnecting from his body and emotions also allowed him to survive a subsequent car accident in which he was severely injured and had to be resuscitated. It allowed him to survive years of childhood abuse, and later his working conditions as a military sniper. We spent a lot of time in our sessions on self-care, which was new to him. The first time I gave him "homework", it was to start to notice when he was tired and go to sleep, to start to notice when he was hungry and to eat, and to start to notice when he needed to go to the bathroom and do that. He smiled at this and asked how I knew. He then agreed to try to work on this. During our work together, I often asked him to do body scans to help him to begin to connect with his physical sensations and emotions—both of which were new experiences for him. I still recall the session where he came in and excitedly told me that for the first time in his life he felt a food craving—it was for ice cream. I also recall the many sessions where he told me about different emotional and physical sensations he had started to notice—one of which was chest pains. He said he thought about just going to sleep but could hear me telling him to listen to his body, and he called an ambulance instead. We were both grateful he did, because it turned out he was having a heart attack. What I will also never forget is that near the time we were ending counseling, he told me about how he felt peaceful within himself for the first time he could remember.

### Externalizing the Pain

The pain associated with PTSD can be huge. I recall one client who described her anger as "bigger than this office". Beneath the anger are often sadness, helplessness, despair, and/or hurt. The pain can be all encompassing and immobilizing. It is not healthy and can be toxic to the body and mind. Thus, finding ways to externalize it, or get it out of the body and mind, can transform this energy into something positive, or at least neutral. When it is inside, the bigness of it can be confusing and overwhelming, so that it is difficult to understand and get a handle on. Getting it outside can allow clients the opportunity to see and understand the bigger picture.

How do we externalize this kind of pain? Some of my clients do this by talking it out or writing in a journal. Sometimes I will give my clients a large piece of flip chart paper in session and ask them to write down all of the negative or painful messages about themselves that they are carrying inside them. This can be a powerful exercise, as they come to realize the extent of the burden they have been carrying, and understand why they have been so tired and feeling so badly about themselves. This also gives us a chance to challenge these messages through a lens of compassion and understanding. Some of my clients will externalize their pain in creative ways: painting, sculpting, drawing, or writing a song. I had one client who would come in and ask to sing new songs that she had written related to her trauma. This was a transformative experience for her. There are also clients who don't want to get into the details of their pain but just want it out of them. These clients will often use physical activity to release and transform their pain into strength. It is important that our clients follow their instincts and path on this, not ours. Our role is to provide options, and their role is to choose or decline the options we present.

### Bodywork

From a clinical perspective I've observed that fully healing from PTSD often requires more than mind work. Cognitive restructuring is an important part of the work, but will not necessarily be sufficient. PTSD affects mind and body, and thus, to fully recover, our clients will often also need to engage in bodywork at some point. There are some complementary approaches that have demonstrated effectiveness in decreasing physical symptomology. These include trauma-sensitive yoga (Nolan, 2016), and mindfulness-based therapy (Hofmann, Sawyer, Witt, & Oh, 2010). As well, some of my clients have reported relief from physical pain as a result of using massage therapy, Reiki, or osteopathy. The bottom line is that it is important that we remain open-minded and support our clients as they explore the types of body-focused interventions that will best meet their needs.

### Patience and Recognizing Progress

I can't count the number of times my clients have asked, "When will I be done with this work?" or "Why is this taking so long?" Doing this work requires patience on the part of the client, but especially on the part of the therapist. I let my clients know that there is no defined timeline and "it will take however long it takes". I encourage them to trust their body and mind in this work. I let them know it is okay to take breaks from therapy if they feel they need to do so. At these times we will often review their progress, which sometimes can be difficult for them to recall.

It can be helpful to set short-term goals to help clients to stay focused and notice their progress on a more frequent basis. Initially, encouraging clients to set modest goals regarding self-care actions can be a good place to start. As therapists, part of our work will be to continually point out the small steps our clients have taken and to commend them on these. Unless these successes are made conscious, our clients might dismiss or not even notice them. Noticing that they said "no" to someone for the first time in favor of doing what is best for themselves, or that they took steps to advocate for themselves, or that they experienced a feeling of anger when someone treated them disrespectfully—these are amazing accomplishments for many of our clients—that need to be acknowledged and celebrated.

### Delaying Major Decisions

When clients are in the throes of active PTSD, I don't encourage them to make major decisions. Their abilities to think clearly, see the whole picture, and understand consequences are likely to be impaired. Thus, I will gently encourage them to hold off for a bit on making big life-changing decisions, if possible, such as changing careers, moving to another part of the country, or ending a significant relationship. In doing this, I am clear that I respect their independence and right to make decisions for themselves, but am concerned, given the level of distress they are in, that they might see things differently when the distress subsides. I will then leave it to them and will support them through whatever decisions they make. I will not, however, encourage them to wait to make a decision if they are in an unsafe living situation or in an abusive relationship. Client safety is always paramount, and it is important that we support them in identifying their options and in making the best decisions of which they are capable to ensure their safety.

### Cocooning

Often times we as a society view social withdrawal as a concerning sign. While this is generally true, I have found that in dealing with PTSD, sometimes people, and especially extraverts who are typically very outgoing and busy, might need to take some time to "cocoon". I found the definition of the verb cocoon which resonates the most with me in the Oxford Dictionary: "to envelop in a comforting or protective way". This in some ways describes the therapeutic relationship, and also what clients might need to continue to do for a time outside of therapy to support their own healing.

Due to the fact that PTSD and trauma work can be so exhausting, there can be times when cocooning is vital. In order to support their health and well-being, rest and self-care is essential for our clients as we do this work. Clients might express concerns about changes in their behavior when they find themselves wanting more time alone to rest. They might need to be reassured to trust their body in this, as the work they are doing takes a lot of energy. The cocooning in their personal life will likely be temporary until they are sufficiently rested and then they will be able to resume the busyness of their life. (If the withdrawal, however, also includes difficulties with daily functioning and other depressive-like symptoms, then a consult with their physician may be warranted).

### Identifying Motivation

As indicated many times already, trauma work can be very difficult. Despite our efforts to strengthen and equip our clients for the climb, at times they will find the work to be extremely taxing and frustrating. Hence, helping clients to identify and connect with their motivation as early as possible can provide them with the impetus to continue during the darkest moment.

We need to ask our clients to think about what they will hold onto and what will give them the strength to keep going when they feel frustrated or exhausted. For some, connecting with their inner strength and wisdom, their Warrior Spirit will be enough. For others, their motivation will be their children or families. For still others, it might be determination not to allow the trauma, or its perpetrators, to take anything more from them. Faith, or determination to help others, may be the motivator. Whatever makes sense to the individual, that which gives them strength, courage, and provides an anchor when the road becomes treacherous, is what we need to identify. This will be something that as clinicians we need to make note of so that we can remind our clients to hold onto this when the road gets rough.

### Scheduled Grieving/Worrying

Oftentimes, one of the trauma-related challenges that my clients find most debilitating in terms of trying to function at work or school is grief or worry that ambushes them at different points during their day. We've found, however, that if they schedule time to grieve or worry (e.g., 20–30 minutes per day, at the same time each day), and they honor that commitment, then they are more successful at containing it during their day. In doing this I suggest that clients set an alarm at the beginning of their scheduled time to let them know when it is finished. During the allotted time they can worry, grieve, cry, etc., but when the alarm goes off they are to stop, wash their face, and move on to some other activity. If the grief or worry pokes itself into their day outside the scheduled time, they are to firmly tell it that it's not time yet, and not engage with it. Many of my clients have been surprised by how well this works.

### Laughter, Joy, and Celebration

My colleague and friend, who works in the office next to mine, has occasionally commented on the laughter coming from my office. It's true. Sometimes my clients and I laugh a lot in session, which might be surprising to people when they think of trauma counseling. However, laughter and a sense of humor can be a tremendously powerful tool in the valley.

What is there to laugh at when we are doing trauma work? There are so many things in life that are funny, joyful, and worth celebrating. It is truly a blessing and a sign of progress and health when clients can connect to this despite the challenges of walking through the valley. Sometimes I laugh at myself, and my clients join in. Sometimes my clients laugh at themselves, and I laugh with them. Laughter can be healing as we come to gently accept our flaws, weaknesses, and the things we've done that surprise even ourselves.

With one client, I recall that we laughed with joy about the fact that he was finally able to sit in the waiting room in a chair without his back against the wall. He had struggled a very long time to try to let go of his military training, which required constant surveillance of his surroundings. When I saw him sitting in a chair without his back against the wall—we both smiled and later laughed about it in my office. What a wonderful success that was for him! With another client, an international student from a country where war had broken out during his studies, I recall I had many sleepless nights as we awaited the results of his refugee hearing. He had been through so much trauma already. When he came into my office that day to share the results of his refugee application, I was trying hard not to show my fear and worry. When he told me he received refugee status and wouldn't be sent back to a country where he had no home to return to, I know I shouted, "Yes!" and had to wipe away a few tears. We laughed and celebrated. With another client, we laughed when she spoke of finally standing up to someone who had been bullying her—and both she and the bully were surprised. What wonderful success! Even in the midst of the climb there are plateaus. Places where we can rest and see the stars in the sky. Places of joy. These moments sustain us—clients and therapists alike.

## Notes

1 This is a variation of a scenario I have heard several times in working with clients who have been sexually assaulted. The name is fictional.
2 This is not the client's real name. He has provided informed consent to allow me to share parts of his story.
3 This is not the client's real name. She has provided informed consent to share parts of her story.

# 10 Beginning the Climb— Trauma Processing

Shadow work is the path of the heart warrior.

—Carl Jung

To confront a person with his own shadow is to show him his own light.

—Carl Jung

As mentioned previously, trauma work is atrocity work. It involves working with the shadow parts of the self that have been seriously injured as a result of trauma, and consequently have been hidden, abandoned, or neglected to protect the rest of the self from unbearable pain. Trauma processing involves working with clients as they consciously seek out these shadow, injured parts of the self in order to understand, and eventually accept them. We assist with these latter two tasks by continuing to reflect back clients' strengths, resiliency, and adaptability via a lens of compassion. This is how we try to assist clients to see the light within the shadow parts of themselves.

## How to Know It's Safe to Begin the Climb

Knowing when and when not to proceed with trauma processing is important. While each situation is individual, I have come up with the following general guidelines.

It may be time to consider trauma processing if the client:

- wants to proceed with it;
- is not in crisis, suicidal, or living in an unsafe situation;
- has learned to effectively utilize coping strategies/tools/resources to manage distress;
- is able to make an informed decision about treatment (i.e., after being made aware of how the intervention works, possible benefits and risks, etc.); and
- has developed a safe and trusting relationship with the therapist.

# Potential Pathways Through the Valley

Pathways in the valley are not marked. Individuals have to create their own. While there are some common types of pathways that people travel through in the valley, their length, the specific issues dealt with along the way, and the order in which they are taken is individualized. As therapists, we have some idea as to what is possible. Our role is that of guide and companion as we help our clients to determine which routes they need to take and to facilitate trauma processing. The following sections focus on potential pathways that our clients might need to travel in their journey out of the valley. Additionally, in this chapter, we will focus on two new specific compassion-focused CBT interventions that can be used for trauma processing. Both of these interventions harness the power of dual awareness. One utilizes the clients' Warrior Spirit to process and reframe traumatic experiences. The second uses the lens of compassion to help clients to view themselves in a more accepting, positive, and accurate light.

### *Addressing Ongoing Depression and Anxiety*

We know that the co-occurrence of PTSD with Major Depressive Disorder (MDD) and Anxiety Disorders can be quite high. A national survey of more than 34,000 civilian respondents in the United States found that the rate of concurrent PTSD and Major Depressive Disorder (MDD) diagnoses was 35.2%, and the rate of concurrent PTSD with any Anxiety Disorder diagnosis, was 59% (Pietrzak et al., 2011). A meta-analysis involving 57 studies looking at concurrent PTSD and MDD found an even higher rate of 52% (Rytwinski, Scur, Feeny, & Youngstrom, 2013).

The Beck Anxiety Inventory (BAI) (Beck & Steer, 1993) and Beck Depression Inventory—Second Edition (BDI-II) (Beck, Steer, & Brown, 1996) can be helpful for assessing clients' anxiety and depressive symptoms over time. These are not diagnostic tools, but rather are brief screening instruments, which can allow us, along with our clients, to get a clearer picture of how their distress is presenting. These measures only take minutes for clients to complete and can provide invaluable information to assist with client case conceptualization and treatment planning. Whenever clients rate in the severe range on the BAI and/or BDI-II, I suggest they share the screening with their physician to keep him/her in the loop and provide a basis for discussion of potential medical supports.

The BDI-II contains an item that asks clients about suicidal ideation and their intention to act on these thoughts, which can also be a very helpful starting point for discussion. Many times I have gone from scoring the BDI-II, into conducting a Suicide Risk Assessment and developing a Safety Plan with the client. Clients, who are initially hesitant to mention suicidal ideation out loud, sometimes feel more comfortable confirming it through this screening tool.

If clients are on medication to address severe anxiety and/or depressive symptoms, the BAI and/or BDI-II can also provide helpful pre- and post-medication intervention information. Sometimes my clients report that after several months their medication doesn't feel like it's working. I will ask them to complete a screening. If they score in the moderate to severe range of symptoms, we can then provide this information to their physician so that he or she can conduct a medication review. These measures can also be used at the end of therapy to assess gains in treatment. This is often one of the things we review, along with an updated trauma symptom screening, when we are terminating therapy, to provide us with concrete information on how the client has progressed and improved over time.

### Anger

Anger has a purpose. It is a normal and healthy response when one's safety or personal boundaries are threatened. It alerts us that something feels amiss, and can energize us to defend others and ourselves. If we find ourselves, however, unable to utilize that anger to successfully defend, or if expressing that anger is likely to increase danger, the energy of this important emotion can become "stuck", resulting in either disconnection or unabated rage. Neither is healthy in the long term. Thus, anger is one of the most common issues we are likely to confront as we journey with our clients through the valley.

Acknowledging and expressing anger regarding others who have caused you significant harm requires a level of self-esteem that says, "I don't deserve this. This is wrong." In my practice I have noticed that anger or rage is more often observed at the outset with individuals who have experienced single-incident trauma in comparison to those who have survived chronic or complex trauma. I expect this is the case because complex trauma can impact a person's core identity and, particularly in those who have survived chronic early life trauma, can leave behind an internal sense of having somehow deserved or contributed to what happened to them. This is not to say that survivors of single-incident trauma don't also at times experience guilt or self-doubt related to a traumatic event, but it tends to be more pronounced in those who have experienced prolonged trauma. Also, survivors of complex trauma are more likely to have learned that expressing anger, and even allowing themselves to feel it, can be unsafe. In many cases they've come to expect their expression of anger to be met with responses of minimization, denial, and/or further violence and abuse.

With survivors of complex trauma it can take a lot of work to get to a point where they begin to experience anger, which is a healthy and normal response to what they were subjected. Some will have learned to disconnect from anger as part of their survival strategy. In many cases anger will have been inextricably linked, in their minds and bodies, to violence and other forms of trauma—and, hence, might be repressed and/or avoided at all costs. In order to reconnect with this natural and healthy emotion, they must first connect with compassion for themselves, and recognize that *no one* deserves abuse, neglect, or to be subjected to other forms of trauma—*and this includes them.* This last part can be the hardest part for clients to truly believe, because of the double standard they've internalized that has led them to believe that they are the exception, and thus, are not worthy of love and respect. As therapists we will need to work with these clients to show them how anger is an important signal in their lives to let them know when a boundary is being crossed. We will also need to help them to understand, often through role playing, that anger can be expressed in caring and respectful ways, and in fact can be a constructive force rather than a destructive one. When a client, who previously couldn't feel any anger towards a perpetrator who victimized them, finally gets to this point, I commend them on their progress—pointing out that it demonstrates they have found compassion for themselves and recognized their right to be treated with respect and dignity.

Meg[1] expressed concern that she was beginning to feel anger toward a parent who was physically and emotionally abusive to her throughout her childhood and adolescence. As an adult she continued to have a relationship with this parent who would, at times, behave in manipulative ways and try to exert control over his grown adult daughter. Over time she found herself bristling at this manipulative behavior and feeling angry. She confessed that she was worried this meant she was regressing. She was a bit taken aback, but relieved when I responded, "No this is wonderful! This is about you establishing healthy personal boundaries and trusting your mind and body, which through anger is telling you when someone is violating those boundaries and needs to back off." We discussed how her anger was providing her with a warning that something important was being threatened, and ways she might start to set limits in her relationship with this parent.

In the aftermath of trauma, one is often left with anger at the self. Anger for choices made or not made. There might be anger and shame regarding how one responded during or immediately following the traumatic event. Or there might be anger at oneself for ignoring a feeling that something wasn't right. There might also be anger for not knowing or sensing what was to come, even though in many cases the outcome could not have been predicted. People forget that the knowledge they have in the present was not accessible to them at the time of the trauma. Hindsight is a double-edged sword. It can provide us with valuable learning that we can use to protect ourselves in the future, but sometimes we can also use it to heap blame upon ourselves when we forget that this knowledge wasn't available to us when the trauma was occurring. Anger at the self needs to be met head on with education and compassion—education regarding normal reactions during and after traumatic events—viewed through a lens of compassion. We need to help our clients to understand that if they had known for certain what was going to occur, they might have been able to make decisions to protect themselves or others—or possibly even then, it might not have made a difference. Forgiveness and acceptance of the parts of the self one has been trying to distance from, abandon, deny, or ignore can be a very difficult—but is essential if one is to truly heal.

There may also be anger at others—whether they are individuals, groups, or systems—who perpetrated the trauma, did nothing to stop it even when they had the power to do so, protected the perpetrator(s), blamed the victim(s), and/or minimized, dismissed, or denied that the trauma even happened. Such painful experiences will need to be validated and processed with our clients. These can be difficult pathways for our clients to travel, because there is often no opportunity for resolution with the "others" towards which one feels anger. Nonetheless, our focus is on our clients and helping them to work through their righteous anger, and to direct it in ways that will not continue to cause them pain.

As mentioned previously, the energy of anger can mobilize us to defend that which is being threatened. It can move us into posturing, to try to ward off threats, and then potentially fighting in defense, if that is a feasible option. However, in situations where for our own safety, anger needs to be tamped down—those situations in which posturing and fighting back carry too much risk—the energy of anger is left repressed and unspent. In such situations, submitting or freezing are usually the only options left. Or in situations where anger comes after the fact, there is often nowhere to usefully direct it. What is one to do with all of the pent-up energy that still vibrates in the body and ricochets around the mind whenever one is reminded of the trauma?

When anger is thwarted, energy becomes stuck. It finds a home in parts of the body. We need to work with our clients to help them to identify where the anger is physically located in their bodies. When my clients share parts of their trauma story and express anger, I will ask them to do a body scan from head to toe, and to describe where they feel the anger. Common locations are the jaw, the back of the neck, the chest/heart area, hands, feet, and stomach. It is important that we locate these areas so that conscious efforts can be made to release the physical anger, which if left unchecked, can wreak havoc on the body. To explain, I tell the story of how when I was working on my graduate degree I worked part-time in a group home for girls run by a child protection agency. The things I saw there, the things that parents did to their daughters, left me dealing with a huge amount of rage. Yet, there was nowhere to direct it. I couldn't very well take it out on the abusive parents of these children. The rage sat in my stomach, and caused stomach pain and nausea. I realized that the cruelty that I was witnessing was having a toxic effect on me and made a decision to transform that rage into strength instead. Thus, I decided to do abdominal crunches while tapping into my rage. I did this over several months. As a result, I ended up with very strong abs, and the physical energy of my rage was eventually exhausted. In this way, I challenge my clients to take control of their anger and rage by taking actions to defend against the trauma hurting them further, and to release if from their bodies. Once we identify where the anger sits in their body, we can brainstorm ways to start to transform and release that energy in a healthy, non-destructive way. Working out, in situations where clients are physically able to do so, is a popular strategy. I'll often ask, "When you are feeling angry, is there an impulse to either hit/punch something, or to kick something?" This can help us to find strategies clients can use to release energy through action in the arms (e.g., tennis, hitting a baseball, push-ups) or legs (e.g., kicking a ball, swimming, running, squats). I remind them that releasing this energy has to be conscious, so while engaging in their chosen actions they have to bring up the emotions of anger or rage, so that they will have access to the associated energy. Doing abdominal crunches as part of one's workout is one thing. But getting to a point of exhaustion and then tapping into anger or rage to use that energy to do a few more crunches is different. The energy is different and so is the release. Other popular ways to externalize the anger/rage that have worked for my clients include such things as: singing; painting; mindful breathing; energy work; writing; tearing paper; cutting wood; and walking/running.

## Loss and Grief

One of the pathways that seems to be a mandatory part of the journey out of the valley is the one that deals with loss and grief. Losses experienced as consequences of trauma are varied and life changing. The losses experienced might involve death, significant injury, or disability. It might also, or alternatively, involve loss of one's sense of safety within the world. There can be loss of community or sense of belonging, loss of home or livelihood, or loss of a childhood. Trauma can desecrate one's sense of autonomy, adequacy, and worthiness. One's sense of purpose and meaning in life can be lost. Whatever the type of losses experienced, grief will naturally follow.

There will be times when a person is dealing with traumatic grief as a result of the violent and/or unexpected death of a loved one. In these cases it is important that we listen to the client to figure out whether we need to focus on the grief or the trauma first. How do we tell when a client is currently dealing with grief versus trauma? When our clients are grieving, they will talk about the past and what the person meant to them and/or how they are struggling to face the future without this person. If, however, the client is focused on events surrounding the death, and reliving traumatic events related to the death, our focus will need to be on the traumatic stress reaction.

Grief work will be influenced by what clients believe or don't believe happens after death. When a client believes in God and an afterlife, within whatever faith to which they belong, there are potentially a number of supports open to them. Their faith might be a source of comfort, as might their religious community and faith leader. I've noticed that my clients who believe their loved ones are still watching over them, and in contact with them, though in a different way than before, seem to get through their grief more quickly. This is likely because they do not believe they have lost the person for good, but rather have experienced a change in their relationship. It is also possible to encourage closure with a deceased loved one, if the client believes he/she can still communicate with them in their hearts. Sometimes there are things the client wishes they had said, and I encourage them to still say these things to their loved one, either in session, or through a letter, or in a private prayer at home. This can be a very powerful tool for our clients for whom this is an option.

With clients who do not believe in an afterlife, it will be important to us to understand what their belief system is and how they make meaning of what has happened. Sometimes for those without belief in an afterlife, it can be a matter of providing another perspective such as what if the tables had been turned and their loved one had lived, and they had died instead. What would the client want their loved one to know if their loved one was struggling with the same regrets or feelings that the client is? Asking the client to verbalize what they would say to their loved one can help to shift their perspective, physiology, and emotional response, because in speaking the words out loud, they are speaking to themselves.

In doing this work there will likely be multiple layers of grief that will arise over time. This is normal and to be expected. It can take time for people to realize and come to terms with the depths of their losses and to understand how these have changed them individually, in their relationships with others, and their understanding of life and the world. Learning how to live with and integrate the losses will be a challenge. Many emotions will accompany grief. Anger, denial, guilt, shame, fear, depression, and worry can show up individually and in concert.

Grief is a difficult path to travel. The sadness is exhausting and can make it feel like this path will never end. When my clients doubt that they've made any progress, I remind them of the first tidal waves of grief they experienced on the morning they awoke after the trauma (if it was a single event trauma). On that day after, they might have had a few seconds of reprieve where their mind did not immediately recall what happened, but when they did remember, they were likely "knocked over" be the realization of loss. I ask them to compare that to more recent mornings, where although they might still wake up feeling sad and overwrought with grief, it is likely different than that first morning. Generally, as time passes, the waves of grief are not quite as high, and probably have more space between them. It is through this comparison, and a review of observed progress, that they are often able to realize that they have in fact been moving forward. In cases of complex trauma, I will remind them of specific areas where they have made progress and we will still likely be able to notice the change in their experience of the waves of grief over time, even though there wasn't a specific "morning after" the trauma. Also, when we talk about the waves of grief, I remind them that it isn't uncommon for these waves to become more intense and frequent around trauma anniversaries, trauma-related legal proceedings, special occasions that magnify the loss, etc., but to know that once again, over time, these waves will calm.

*Forgiveness of the Self*

There are all kinds of perceived wrongs that traumatized people will hold against themselves. It may involve how they acted before, during, or after a trauma, last words to someone, not being able to foresee the trauma, etc. These self-incriminations and judgments were often formed through a lens of fear, pain, and hindsight—none of which contribute to a rational and compassionate understanding of their context and resources at the time.

Withholding forgiveness of the self can be a source of major distress, impairment, and pain, at all levels of the person. Likely this is so due to the fragmentation of the self that it causes and maintains. How can a person experience peace and healing if they are in a constant state of self-recrimination, shame, and guilt? How can they heal if so much energy is being invested in compartmentalizing and dividing the self in an attempt to exile the parts of the self that have been most deeply injured? This pathway, and the injury it represents, must be approached with the utmost gentleness and compassion on the part of the therapist. This is a living, festering injury, and if the client desires to escape the valley, at some point they will likely need to uncover and face these parts of themselves.

I explain to my clients that the parts of ourselves we are resistant to forgive are like open wounds. We try to cover them up and ignore them, but in doing so they become infected, and the infection and pain begin to spread to all areas of our person. If we truly want to heal, we need to gather the courage to face these wounded parts of ourselves and hear their truths. It might take time and work before clients are able to approach this pathway. They have likely spent a tremendous amount of effort trying to avoid and forget about these parts of themselves, so this is likely to be a frightening prospect. This is one of the pathways during which I use the Warrior Spirit metaphor, and/or the compassion-focused CBT intervention that I will describe later in this chapter.

## The Question of Forgiveness of Others

For some clients this will not be a question at all. Some will have decided already that they have neither the interest nor inclination to forgive others who in some ways failed them, directly or indirectly, during or after the traumatic experience—and they are at peace with this. For other clients, due to their value system or religious beliefs, they have already made a decision to forgive and are at peace with that. In either of these cases, it would appear that the client and therapist might not have to go down this pathway since the issue has already been resolved. There will be other cases, however, where resolution has not been achieved and more attention is needed.

There are a few presentations that can signal to us that clients might need to do some work in the area of forgiveness of others. The first is when clients state they will never forgive a person or persons, and seem to be experiencing an all-consuming rage and preoccupation with the person(s) and perceived wrong that does not appear to be receding in intensity over a prolonged period of time (e.g., months or years). The second is when clients have a genuine desire to forgive but are distressed because they can't feel it or find it within themselves to do so. The third is when clients continually forgive quickly in highly abusive or violent relationships, and thus by forgiving, place themselves back in dangerous situations with the unrealistic expectation that things will be magically improved.

With clients who are dealing with all-consuming rage toward a perpetrator, it is important to first validate the rage. We need to be patient with these clients in helping them process their rage and other reactions. Forgiveness does not have to be the goal here, but rather our primary goal is to help to free clients from the toxicity of a growing and all-consuming bitterness and anger within their hearts. This might be done through talk therapy, externalizing the anger, and/or imaginal confrontation with the perpetrator. We might work with clients to find ways to use the energy and passion of their rage to fuel efforts of advocacy, systemic change, or some other endeavor that will provide meaning and a sense of purpose. At some point we might need to talk with clients about going down this pathway to find ways that they can transform the toxicity of prolonged rage, so that they do not have to bear this additional injury for the rest of their lives. With these clients, it can be helpful to have them focus on predominant cognitions such as, "I hate (this person)", or "I will never forgive" and notice the physical, emotional, and behavioral correlates of this thought for themselves in the moment. We can then try, if they are willing, to shift the focus to something like, "I am choosing to use the energy of my rage to (insert their desired action or purpose)." Asking them to identify how this shifts their physical sensations, emotional reactions, and will influence future behaviors, will allow them the immediacy of noticing the difference that a change in cognition can have on their well-being and distress level.

We will also work with some clients who express a desire to forgive, but are distressed by the fact that they feel unable to do so. For some of these clients they might feel obliged to forgive due to religious tenets. For others it might be part of their personal value system. For still others it might be about wanting to release themselves from the expenditure of energy and time that is being directed toward anger and resentment toward a specific person or persons. These are just some of the most common reasons I have heard from clients about why they wish to move forward with forgiveness of those involved in their trauma. This too is a complicated pathway. The internal conflict of wishing to forgive and yet not being able to do so, will need to be explored and processed. There will be valid reasons for both. I've found that it is helpful in such times of internal incongruity to suggest to clients that they consider giving themselves permission to be in limbo. It is okay to be conflicted and unable to move forward for a time. It is a natural part of life. If we fight against it, we will likely be stuck longer.

I encourage clients to give themselves permission to breathe and know that for the moment it's okay not to be able to forgive. Changing their belief from "I can't forgive", to "I am open to finding a way to forgive and expect it will come in time" (or something like this), can provide a measure of relief. Once we find a belief that works for them, I will ask them to notice how it feels physically and emotionally. Typical responses to this shift include feeling more relaxed, and noticing a reduction in pain, tension, or heaviness in the shoulders, chest, or stomach. Clients usually report a sense of emotional relief and calm.

The third area that will require our notice is when our clients are in abusive or violent relationships, forgive the perpetrator on an ongoing basis, and by virtue of this, continually place themselves in high-risk situations. With these clients, it can be helpful to get a better understanding of their concept of what "forgiveness" means—and does not mean. If appropriate, we might begin to gently challenge their concept of forgiveness if they believe it means to "forget and act like nothing happened"—when something very important (i.e., abuse/violence) has happened and is likely to continue to happen. This is a complex situation that will require gentleness, patience, and some restraint on our part. While it is okay to express our fear for client safety, it is not okay to become parental and directive. It can be a challenging situation for us as therapists, when we are more invested in the safety of our clients than our clients are themselves.

### Addressing Spiritual Injuries

I've not come across many trauma-related professional learning activities that address the spiritual injuries that can be sustained as a result of trauma, and yet these existential injuries can cause a tremendous amount of distress for our clients. Whether we are talking about emergency workers, soldiers, adults who survived childhood abuse, or those who survived a recent sexual assault, the questions are often the same. "Where was God? Why didn't God do something to stop these terrible things from happening?" For those for whom faith has been an important part of their lives, there is often a feeling of betrayal and abandonment by God. This belief can add another layer to the trauma. With it can come the collapse of the schema one has used to make sense of the world, which can lead to an existential crisis and a profound sense of despair. In these cases, regardless of what name the client calls their Higher Power, this will at some point need to be explored. If you, as the therapist, are not comfortable dealing with this, then referring the client to an appropriate spiritual leader is an option.

Some of our clients might be distressed by feelings of anger or rage against God (by whichever name and in whichever form the client perceives their Higher Power). This anger might be due to feeling betrayed or abandoned by God during the worst parts of the trauma. It might also be more generalized in terms of being angry that God allows "such things" to happen in the world and does nothing to stop them. These feelings of anger might be complicated if accompanied by a belief that it is wrong or sinful to be angry with, or question, God. This needs to be processed as well.

My clients have sometimes struggled with prayer after experiencing or witnessing trauma. Even those who have been very devout in their faith sometimes struggle with how to approach God after the fact—when their hearts, minds, and bodies are so filled with pain, anger, and despair. Some believe it is wrong to approach God with these emotions: "Who am I to question God's will or ask why?" And yet if they can't express their thoughts and feelings, they stay within their minds and bodies where they will fester and possibly alienate them from their source of strength and comfort. It is at times like this when I ask my clients if they believe God already knows what it is in their hearts and minds. All have agreed that they believe this is the case. I suggest then, that since God already understands how they are feeling and why, that maybe it is time that they have an honest and respectful talk with God about their thoughts and feelings so that *they* can come to terms with what is going on inside them. Our clients might wish to handle this through a private prayer. Some may prefer to write it down. Others might wish to speak or pray with a religious faith leader, or to participate in rituals or sacraments within their faith. If a client wishes to use a private prayer but says they can't find the words, I share with them my preferred strategy of praying when witnessing atrocity and feeling anger. I close my eyes and open my heart to God. I allow the intense emotions I have been holding back, to come to the fore. I don't judge or fight them. My prayer is something along the lines of, "God here I am. You know me better than I know myself. Please show me if there is anything I can do to try to make this right. Please lead me to pathways of healing. Your will be done." I trust that God sees the pain and hears the words I can't find—that my heart will say what needs to be said and that God understands. I remind clients that these days God's responses don't usually come accompanied by a burning bush or an angelic visit. I propose that it's more likely they will receive a response through synchronistic happenings in the lives, nature, or the kindness and insights of others. Many find comfort in this idea as we work together to find ways to integrate their trauma experience into their faith and relationship with God.

Some clients will ask if the trauma was part of God's plan for them. Loved ones and/or members of their faith communities might have told them that this is the case. If your client believes this and is at peace with this idea, it's okay to move on from here. If, however, as I've found is often the case, this premise places a client in conflict with their faith and their perception of God, then we will likely need to explore this further. How does one come to terms with the idea that God has approved the horrendous things that have happened to you and/or others, and in effect, sacrificed you or others, for the sake of "a plan"? A child dies a violent death at the hands of an abusive parent. A woman watches her family drown as she tries desperately to save them. A terrorist attack kills and seriously injures hundreds. A medical doctor is tortured and held captive in a South American rebel camp. If one is told this is part of God's plan, then how does one come to terms with the lack of compassion by God? When my clients choose to go down this path, and allow me to accompany them, I will tentatively share how I make sense of these types of things and will often refer them to the timeless book, *When Bad Things Happen to Good People* (Kushner, 1983). I find that Kushner's conclusions work for me personally:

> God does not cause our misfortunes. Some are caused by bad luck, some are caused by bad people, and some are simply an inevitable consequence of our being human and being mortal, living in a world of inflexible natural laws.
>
> (p. 134)

I might share that personally I have come to believe that trauma occurs as a result of cause and effect, whether it be connected to human choice/free will or natural law, and that generally God has chosen not to interfere with either. (I don't understand the exceptions to these rules of God's non-interference but am grateful for them when they happen). I further believe that each of us can use our free will to allow God's grace and compassion to flow through us to others—and if we do so, God is able to use us as instruments of comfort and healing. I suggest to my clients that it will take time, but that they too will find a way to come to terms with what has happened in a way that fits for them.

When lecturing students who are entering careers in emergency services or in counseling, I ask them to think about how the senseless atrocities that they will inevitably bear witness to in their careers, will fit into their belief system. How will these events fit with, or cause disruptions, in their faith (if they believe in a God)? How will they make meaning of these experiences and their role in all of this? I suggest that being proactive and starting to think and talk about this prior to experiencing a crisis of faith might be advantageous. As therapists who bear witness to these atrocities on a daily basis, this will be a challenge that we will need to address personally as well. Not to do so can, over time, lead to burnout and despair on our part, too.

### Changing Relationship Boundaries

Changing relationship boundaries is another potential pathway that some traverse on their journey out of the valley. Following trauma, some clients will immediately decide to change the boundaries of, or to end, certain relationships in their lives. For other clients, this is a consideration that will arise during trauma processing. The exploration of key relationships directly and indirectly related to their trauma is a common theme, especially in cases where trauma occurred as a result of human intention and/or choices.

In cases of complex trauma such as domestic violence or childhood abuse, clients may have unconsciously come to believe that significant relationships in their lives will inevitably involve disrespect, violence, and other boundary violations. To bring client beliefs into consciousness where we can then evaluate them, and begin to shift them according to the client's wishes, I being by picking up a handful of different colored pipe cleaners. I explain that our families are where we first develop a concept or schema about what "love" means and what to expect in the important relationships in our lives. I choose a colored pipe cleaner and say, "Let's say this is love. It comes with different things in different families. If in your family, love came with a sense of humor, then that will be entwined with love". I will take a different colored pipe cleaner to represent a sense of humor, and will twist it lengthwise with the one representing love. "*And if in your family, love came with anger and violence, too, then these will be associated with love as well*". I will then tie in two more different colored pipe cleaners. "*If special holiday times were part of this, then we will add this in too*". Et cetera. I will then continue with, "*What we end up with is a representation of our concept of love—that probably developed without our conscious awareness, based on early experiences. We then carry this with us as our blueprint for the important relationships in our lives. So what I was thinking, if it is okay with you, is that we figure out which other "pieces" are entwined within your concept of love. This will help us to understand your relationships better, and allow you to think about whether you would like to make some conscious decisions about what you want to continue to include, change or add.*"

To complete this exercise I will then provide clients with a sheet of paper and colored markers so that they can write a list about what they learned came with love, as well as any messages they received directly or indirectly about love and relationships. What follows is an example of the type of list my clients will create:

*What I Learned about Love*

- *You can't trust it*
- *It hurts*
- *Sometimes people who say they love me are nice and sometimes they are mean*
- *Love comes with anger and secrets*
- *People who love you will hit you and call you names*
- *"Men only want one thing from women"*
- *I have to be perfect or I'm not good enough*

We then talk about what they have written. I ask my clients to notice what emotions come up as they look at their list, and their physical reaction to the list. What is interesting is how this helps clients to make sense of their behaviors in past significant relationships. I will empathize with what a heavy and limiting schema this has been for them to carry—and how it fit for a time when they felt like they had little power to defend themselves and few choices, but that currently, they can make a conscious decision to rework this schema if they choose to do so. We then work on a second list, in which clients write down what they would like their new schema to look like regarding love and relationships. They might choose to keep parts of their list or to rewrite it totally. When we are finished, we talk about it. I ask clients to notice their emotional and physical reactions to the list, and to imagine how this new schema would impact their behaviors when it comes to important relationships in their lives. This can be a very empowering exercise.

Individuals who have been victimized, and are in an ongoing abusive relationship, become very adept at compartmentalizing their views of the perpetrator, and can become defensive if we, as therapists, are perceived as judging these relationships. It is important that we understand that there is a bond with the perpetrator, and an underlying belief that the perpetrator will change for the better. We will need to gently and respectfully work with the client to understand the dynamics of the abusive relationship—including the parts of the abusive person and relationship that they value, and those they wish were different. I will often share with clients that I've observed that most relationships are as is, unless the people involved are making an active and conscious effort to change. I might point out, if appropriate, that they seem to be surprised and deeply hurt when the relationship doesn't change over time, and this seems to be causing them ongoing distress. I will often remind them that we have no way of knowing if this person in their life will ever change, but until there are signs that this person wants to change and is making efforts to do so, they might want to consider placing their hope "on a shelf"—for now. This would then allow them to prevent ongoing hurt due to expectations that don't fit the situation at this time. If the client is willing, we will begin to discuss how the relationship is impacting them—physically, emotionally, financially, socially, and in terms of their self-concept. At some point, I might gently ask the client that, given there has been no indication from their partner that he/she wants to change or is trying to change, would they want to be in this same relationship a year or 5 years from now.

Clients in abusive relationships often misperceive their options as either being totally immersed in the relationship or abandoning it so that they have no contact with the perpetrator. This can be an obstacle to change, because of the extremity of these options. Initiating a cognitive shift in terms of this misperception can be important in moving forward. I will often draw a horizontal line on a piece of paper. At one end I write "no contact" and at the other end "the way the relationship is now". I will then explain that there are a million options in between and if the client wants to, we can try to identify the right balance for them. I explain that people, for a time, will sometimes choose the "no contact" option for safety reasons, but that is totally up to the client. I explain that it is not my place to pressure them into what option to choose, but rather to help them to identify where on the line they want to be and what that would look like. Then we can work on how to get there. This approach seems to help the client to feel relieved, safer, and less defensive, as we work to help them to assess where they are at and where they would like to be.

Another exercise I use with clients who are involved in abusive or violent relationships is to draw four concentric circles on a sheet of paper. The center circle represents the client. The second circle represents their most emotionally intimate relationships (i.e., their closest relationships), in the third circle are people with whom they are moderately involved, and the fourth circle, represents acquaintances and people with whom they have minimum involvement. I ask them to locate family, partners, and friends on this diagram in terms of where things stand at the present. I will also ask them to locate themselves, in terms of the relationship they have to themselves. This can help us to understand if clients feels centered, disconnected, or somewhere in between. Then I will provide them with a different colored pen or pencil and ask them to use arrows to indicate where they would like the important people in their lives (including themselves) to be in relationship to their center. This can be a helpful tool for client awareness. It can also be a catalyst for discussions regarding what aspects are within the client's control to change, and specifically, how to set practical boundaries with people from whom they would like more distance.

### Accepting It Might Never Make Sense

Trauma survivors often struggle to make sense of the atrocities they have endured. There are many reasons for this. If we understand why and how a traumatic event happened, we might have a better chance of preventing, or responding more effectively, should something similar occur in the future. We might strategize ways that we could have avoided the situation, or activated resources and supports, to protect others and ourselves. If someone intentionally caused the trauma, survivors will often focus on trying to understand and unravel the mindset and reasoning that the perpetrator would have used to justify their behaviors. This might be a fruitful effort, or it might lead to greater distress and an unproductive use of time and energy.

It is not always possible to make sense of trauma. It is not always possible to understand the mindsets of those who intentionally commit atrocities. If clients need to go through the process of trying to understand, then this is a pathway we need to accompany them on. If however, they seem to be stuck or going around in non-progressing circles, we might need to gently remind them that when it comes to trauma, it might never make sense. If trying to make sense of the trauma is taking days, weeks, months, and years of our clients' lives—with no resolution in sight—we might need to gently reflect back to the client that the trauma has already taken much from them, and they deserve to heal. We may need to let them know that unfortunately, it might never make sense, and offer to work with them on healing despite this. It can be both freeing, and a source of grief, for our clients to let go of this endeavor and accept this reality.

## Trauma Processing With the Warrior Spirit

When clients are talking about their trauma experiences and begin to be drawn into reliving, it can be helpful to ask them to step into their Warrior Spirit to keep them anchored in the present moment, while they remember an incident from the past. In this way they can step into their strength and rational mind, and not be overwhelmed by the sensory and affective trauma memory. This strategy can provide a safe distance from the memory, and a time context (i.e., it's in the past and not happening now), while allowing clients to begin to integrate their traumatic emotional and sensory experiences within the history of their lives.

Additionally, when my clients are experiencing traumatic stress flashbacks, for which they are struggling to identify a specific trauma, I ask them how old they feel at the moment. After taking a few moments to think about this question they have, without fail, been able to answer with an age or age range. I then follow up with asking what was going on in their lives at this age. It is in the exploration of these memories that we inevitably find an abandoned part of the self. It is this abandoned part of the self which continues to relive the trauma, whenever triggered, as though stuck in time.

In order to stop the reliving, I ask my client to step into their Warrior Spirit. I then suggest they approach the newly found part of the self within their imagination and provide the type of comfort (in words or actions) that he/she needs—reassuring him/her that the trauma is over and they are safe now. This can be a very powerful experience, and typically brings grounding and a sense of calm.

### A Compassion-Focused CBT Trauma Processing Intervention

Before I explain this new Compassion-Focused CBT trauma processing intervention (CFCBT), I need to explain my professional context. I work in a college counseling setting, with students from diverse backgrounds and experiences that range in age from 17 to 70+ years. This academic setting is often very intense for our students, as the semesters are, on average, only 15 weeks in length. Thus, if significant distress is not reduced quickly, a student can fail not only a course or two, but in some cases, can lose their entire semester and will have to reapply to their program the following academic year. This can lead to negative emotional, social, and financial consequences for the student and/or their families. Thus, when a client is experiencing distress due to PTSD symptoms, I have to consider the implications of any therapeutic intervention in light of the individual's resources, supports, stressors, and the potential impact on their academics.

For the past 15 years, EMDR has been a therapeutic intervention that I have employed very successfully with some clients. I have found that in cases of a single event trauma, where clients already have an established support system and effective distress management strategies, and no history of additional trauma, it typically takes one to three EMDR sessions to process their trauma experience and significantly reduce or eliminate trauma symptoms. In my experience, most of these cases have involved sexual assault, physical violence, or witnessing severe injury/death of another. With clients who have experienced more chronic forms of trauma (e.g., history of ongoing childhood abuse/neglect, domestic violence, kidnapping, war, etc.), I have found that for those clients who are able to tolerate the increased distress that often occurs during and between sessions, EMDR has also been very effective. While some clients will have mild reactions (e.g., exhaustion for a day or two following the session), some might experience severe dissociation and/or flashbacks. Thus, consideration of this form of treatment requires that clients have a substantial distress tolerance and management capacity.

As noted by Shapiro (2001), when scheduling EMDR, given the variety of potential distress reactions, we need to take into account what is going on in clients' lives. Therefore, given the possibility of increased distress following EMDR, I have to work with clients to ensure we are not scheduling these sessions in the week prior to exams or other major academic evaluation components of their program. Unfortunately, having to work around academic schedules doesn't always leave many options—and can mean that, without intervention, clients would have to continue to suffer with PTSD symptoms for a prolonged period of time. In addition to this group of clients, there is also the subset of clients who have tried EMDR, but did not like it and did not want to continue with it. For both of these groups of clients, EMDR was unfortunately not a fit, and we needed another option.

I have also tried traditional CBT with my clients as a means to shift trauma-related cognitive distortions and accompanying distress. The approach I took involved explaining to clients how CBT worked and briefly sharing evidence supporting its effectiveness. We would focus on recent distressing trauma-related reactions, work to identify the thought distortions involved, and try to challenge and change the distortions to more accurately represent reality—noticing the reduction in distress that accompanied this change. I would then provide clients with booklets containing Thought Records for them to fill out during the time between our sessions, as well as information on common cognitive distortions and ways to challenge and change these distortions into more adaptive thoughts. Unfortunately, my experience with this approach was that although clients initially expressed what appeared to be genuine interest in doing this work, 90% of them admitted (usually after not showing for the next appointment), that given how much homework they had already for their academic courses, they didn't have the time or energy to do this additional homework. I quickly realized that though this approach has been shown to be effective for many, it too was not going to fit as an intervention for most of my clients. I didn't want to give up on the value of CBT, however, and have consequently found ways to use it in session (as discussed in different ways throughout this book).

In light of some of the practical challenges of both the traditional CBT and EMDR trauma-processing interventions for some of my clients, I was compelled to try to find another approach that would better fit their needs. Given the evidence for the effectiveness of CBT and EMDR, I wanted to find a way to include pieces of both. What I came up with was a compassion-focused CBT trauma processing intervention that employs a combination of components from CBT and EMDR. I'm not proposing that this approach will fit all clients or therapists, but I have found it to be very effective with many of my clients and offer it as a tool for your toolkit as a trauma therapist.

The CFCBT intervention I use is strengths-based, and client-centered. Compassion is the transformative tool or lens that is used, to bring about a shift in negative cognitions and reduce distress. I've found that this approach is a better fit for my clients who can't make the commitment to ongoing homework, find the distress triggered by EMDR to be too disruptive to their lives, and/or generally don't find traditional CBT or EMDR to be a fit for them personally. Doing the work in session and requesting that clients practice implementing the cognitive shift, as needed in their daily lives, seems to be more manageable for my clients. One of the advantages of this approach is that we are able to contain the distress within session, and clients are also typically able to experience an immediate reduction in distress within one session. The experiential nature of this approach provides immediate positive reinforcement, which can encourage clients as they work through additional cognitive restructuring. This approach still requires that clients have developed a tolerance for short-term, but intense, distress in session. It requires a lot of emotional energy on their part. Regarding scheduling, we don't typically have to worry about fallout during the week following the session, so aren't as limited in our options. However, clients will usually feel very tired, so it is preferable to choose a day where, following the session, clients are able to go home to sleep or engage in other self-care activities.

Even if clients have previously agreed to CFCBT, I will always check-in prior to starting this intervention, to find out if they are up to the work in a particular session. I encourage my clients to listen to their bodies and minds and let me know if it is a fit for them at that time. This connection to, and respect for, the body and mind, are also an important part of healing from trauma. It is an essential component of this approach. Encouraging and supporting this inner listening in session is an opportunity for clients to practice reflecting and making conscious decisions based on what they need at a particular moment in time. Sometimes my clients will have other pressing matters (e.g., a crisis that has arisen, further work on distress tolerance or coping strategies) on which they will want to focus. Sometimes they are not feeling well and don't have the energy required to do the work. It will be important, in this approach, to be respectful of client wisdom regarding the timing of their process.

In this approach, we rely on the basic premise of CBT. Our goal is the restructuring of maladaptive cognitive beliefs in order to directly reduce emotional and physical distress, and indirectly influence behaviors in a more adaptive direction. The EMDR protocol (Shapiro, 2001) to identify key memories associated with both the trauma and the targeted negative cognition has been adapted and incorporated into this model. Imagined exposure is also utilized, as well as dual awareness, which are both components of EMDR.

The basis of this approach is the premise that if one's perception occurs through a lens of fear, pain, shame, or other overwhelming emotions that typify the context of trauma, interpretations can be distorted, leading to inaccurate and distressing (unchallenged) core beliefs about the self. (See Appendix 9: Compassion-Focused CBT—Summary). In order to challenge these distortions, we need to change the lens of perception. Compassion can provide an ideal lens through which to better understand the trauma experience and reconnect with the fragmented parts of the self. It shifts perception and thus can drastically change interpretation of events—providing a narrative that allows for gentler and more adaptive core beliefs about the self.

When clients are willing and ready to start trauma processing, I begin by explaining this approach in detail and answering any questions.

## Identifying and Targeting Negative Cognitions

If clients agree that they would like to try CFCBT, then we start by working with them to identify negative cognitions about the self. These are core beliefs about the self that they feel are true at an emotional level (even if they know in their minds that these statements are not objectively true). I use the Negative Cognition Questionnaire—Initial Form (NCQ-IF), found in Appendix 8 (Sine & Vogelmann-Sine, 1995) for this purpose because I've found it helps clients to more easily find the words to describe negative beliefs about the self, that in many cases have been unconscious and difficult to express up to this point. Clients rate how true each statement feels—"at a gut level". Upon completing the NCQ-IF, they are asked to choose the negative cognition they would like to work on changing.

## Trauma Processing

Once the client has identified the targeted negative cognition, they are asked to say the belief either out loud or silently to themselves, and then to describe: 1) the emotions they experience; 2) what they notice in their bodies in terms of physical reactions to the statement; and 3) how this belief affects their behaviors. These responses are noted for comparison purposes at the end of the intervention.

Beginning with the targeted negative cognition, clients are asked to describe three key memories associated with this belief. The first memory clients are asked to share is the first time in their life that they recall feeling that this belief was true. The second is the most recent time they felt this belief was true. The third is the memory of the most distressing time they felt this belief was true. (Sometimes these will overlap).

During client descriptions of these memories, the therapist provides empathy, validation, and reflection of client strengths while quietly noticing themes, patterns, and the factors underlying the creation of the cognitive distortions. Once clients have described the associated memories, the therapist shares his/her observations, highlighting themes amongst the memories, and emotional and other factors that influenced the development of the core belief that is being targeted. In this way, we begin to understand the context and emotional lens through which clients viewed their experiences, which will help us to make sense of how these negative beliefs were created and maintained.

Next, clients are asked to reconsider the identified memories through a lens of compassion, and to notice how the memories appear differently through this lens. Clients are asked what it would look like and/or sound like, if they were to respond compassionately to the frightened, hurting, dissociated, etc., parts of themselves in the trauma-related memories. The concept of the Warrior Spirit can also be used here—asking the client to imagine what their Warrior Spirit would say to the injured parts of themselves. If the client struggles with how their compassionate self would respond, the therapist can model compassionate responses.

### Rewriting the Distressing Cognition

Therapist and client then work together to rewrite the distressing belief about the self into one that is both more accurate and adaptive. The rewritten statement has to be one that clients can accept at both the rational and emotional levels or it will be rejected straight away. It won't usually be a prescriptive belief that reflects the opposite of the targeted cognition, because for many clients such statements would just not be acceptable at an emotional level. I've found that the statements that clients are ready to embrace are more reflective of a process. For example, clients who target the belief, "I am unlovable", might be open to rewriting it to reflect the truth, "I am learning to love myself," (as opposed to believing at that moment "I am loveable"—which is a statement that they might not yet be able to embrace). Clients who wish to change the belief, "I am damaged", might be comfortable with something like, "I have been injured but am healing". The important thing is that the words reflect what the client finds true at an emotional and gut level, while being more positive. It might take some time to get the words to feel like a fit, but this is important.

Once an appropriate rewritten cognition is identified, clients are asked to say it to themselves either out loud or quietly within their own minds, and describe: 1) how it feels emotionally; 2) what they notice about their physical reactions to the statement; and 3) how they expect that accepting this rewritten belief might affect their behavior. One of the most common reactions I've found from clients emotionally is an uncertainty regarding how they are feeling. It seems to take some time to process this new belief. Clients will often say it feels "strange", but "hopeful". (I take this as a positive indication that the brain is working on some rewiring). Physically, clients usually express a reduction in sensations of pain, pressure, heaviness, and/or a sensation of feeling more relaxed. Behaviorally, they tend to express an expectation that they will be more open to more varied people and/or experiences in their lives as related to this adjusted belief.

### Post-Session Client Homework and Self-Care

Clients need to be reminded that it will take time for this new belief to take over from the old one. I explain that it helps if we think of the brain as a forest containing some well-worn pathways. It is easiest and quickest to take the pathway that already exists. Thus, when a situation arises with which the brain is familiar, it will automatically opt for the easiest pathway or response. However, we are now asking the brain to use a pathway that has only been used once. At first the brain reacts in surprise, "What? Why?" it asks. The brain might resist, "But I've already got a path for this. You want me to make a new one?" And we are answering, "Yes!" Creating this new path will take lots of repetition. When the brain is on autopilot and a situation arises that would typically trigger the old belief, even if clients have been practicing focusing on creating a new way, there will be times when the brain will revert to the old path. That's okay. It will happen. Clients are encouraged, however, as soon as they realize they are going down the old path, to stop and redirect the brain down the chosen path to establish the new belief. It is important for clients to know that this will take time and effort. There will be times when the brain reverts to old ways of thinking. This is not failure. This is to be expected. It will take time, but eventually, with effort, their brain will create a new pathway that becomes dominant and leads to the new preferred belief. To make this easy to understand, I will compare it to the client's experience of learning to ride a bicycle, becoming skilled in a sport, or learning to play an instrument. I remind them how in the beginning they had to focus so much attention on the details of learning these skills, but after a time, they became automatic, as the brain utilized the repetition of their learning to create new neural pathways. This makes sense to clients and demonstrates that they have already been successful at similar endeavors in the past.

Clients will likely feel exhausted following this trauma processing session since re-experiencing the details and distress associated with traumatic memories, as well as engaging in cognitive restructuring, takes a tremendous amount of energy. Thus, it can be helpful to end these sessions with asking clients what they are going to do for themselves in terms of self-care. This provides clients with a gentle reminder of how important self-care is in the healing process.

### An Example of a CFCBT Session Incorporating the Warrior Spirit

Note: This is not an actual session but rather is an example that provides an accurate representation of the complexity and intensity of these sessions.

THERAPIST:   Now that you've completed the Negative Cognitions Questionnaire, I'm going to ask you to look through the statements that you have rated and to decide which one you would like us to work on changing this session. It can be one of the highest rated statements, but it doesn't have to be. We can start with whatever you are comfortable with.

CLIENT:   Okay. Since this is new for me, I think I'll pick one that's around a 6 to start. We can keep the 7's for later. . . . Um, let's see. Okay. I think I want to go with this one.

THERAPIST:   (looks at the NCQ-IF and reads the statement the client is pointing to) "I am permanently damaged".

CLIENT:   Yeah. That's the one.

THERAPIST:   Ok. Before we get into the memories connected to this belief, I'm going to ask you to say the statement "I am permanently damaged" to yourself—either out loud or inside your mind and notice what emotions come with it.

CLIENT:   (closes her eyes for a few moments and then opens them). I feel sad . . . and hurt . . . lonely . . . ashamed.

THERAPIST:   (nods). And what are you noticing in your body, if you scan it from head to toe? Any tension, heaviness, or pain . . . or anything else?

CLIENT:   (quiet for a moment). I feel pressure here. (Hand indicating chest area). I feel like there are tears behind my eyes and my stomach hurts.

THERAPIST:   (Nodding). Okay. So it sounds like this belief is causing you a lot of emotional and physical distress. It hurts in your heart and in your body.

CLIENT:   Yeah. It does.

THERAPIST:   So how do you think this belief, "I am permanently damaged", affects your behavior. How does it affect the things you choose to do and choose not to do?

CLIENT:   Well I guess that it's why I don't want to get close to people. . . . I think if they get to know me and find out that I'm broken, they won't want to be around me. . . . I think it's why I keep to myself, and make excuses when people at work invite me to go out.

THERAPIST:   Given how this belief causes you to feel, it's understandable that you would want to withdraw and protect yourself. How about we start to work at understanding where it came from?

CLIENT:   Okay.

THERAPIST:   So this is the part where I ask you to talk about three memories that are connected to this belief. One of these will be the first time you remember feeling like you were permanently damaged. One will be the most recent time you recall feeling that way. And the third one will be the most distressing time you felt the statement "I am permanently damaged" was true. You can talk about these in any order.

CLIENT:   Um. . . . The first time I felt this way was when I was about 5 years old. There were a bunch of girls I played with at recess. One of them, Ashley, was sometimes nice to me and sometimes really mean. She said that only girls with blond hair and blue eyes could play. I was the only one with dark hair and brown eyes. So all the girls played without me. I didn't realize then that I was Black. I thought there was something bad about me because I wasn't like them and there wasn't anything I could do about it.

THERAPIST:   How awful . . .

CLIENT:   Yeah. I cried a lot that year. Ashley was a bully, but I didn't understand it then. I thought the problem was me.

THERAPIST:   I imagine that it would have been really confusing and hurtful for you.

CLIENT:   Yeah. I couldn't understand why some days she was so nice to me and other days so mean. I thought it must be something about me.

THERAPIST:   Did anyone step in to support you or help you with this situation?

CLIENT:   No. I didn't tell anyone. My parents were stressed because my grandfather was dying and I didn't want to bother them.

THERAPIST:   So, you ended up having to deal with this all alone.

CLIENT:   Yeah. I did talk to my dog, Koko, about it though. (laughs)

THERAPIST:   (laughs) I imagine Koko was a good listener.

CLIENT:   Yes, she was. And she stayed with me when I cried.

THERAPIST:   I'm glad she was there with you.

CLIENT:   Me too.

THERAPIST:   Are you able to talk about the most recent time you felt this way?

CLIENT:   Yes. That's an easy one. That was the second week of college. I went to see my professor at the end of class to give her the form that tells her I'm a student with a disability and can write my tests in the Test Center, so that I can have more time. She looked at the form and crumpled it up and threw it in the trashcan. She said that maybe I needed to think seriously about if I really belonged in this program. I was shocked and devastated. I couldn't believe it. I worked hard to get into this program. She knows nothing about me and there she was telling me I didn't deserve to be there. I left the class in tears and had a panic attack. That night I had nightmares and the next day, I started having flashbacks.

THERAPIST:   Oh my goodness! I'm so sorry you had that experience. No one deserves that. It sounds like this experience was a trigger for you.

CLIENT:   It took me a while to realize that. At first it felt like how she treated me was about me. I questioned myself, you know, wondering if I was asking for special treatment that I shouldn't be getting. I started doubting that I belonged at college. I thought maybe because of my PTSD and panic attacks I shouldn't be here. But then I realized that, like my disability counselor said, this is about giving me the time I need in a quieter space to show what I've learned. She said that this is like allowing me to wear glasses to read and write the test. It's an accommodation that helps me to show what I know, but it doesn't change what I know. She was right.

THERAPIST:   Yes, she was. I'm glad you were able to realize that.

CLIENT:   Me too, but it took a little while. During the panic attack, I remembered the breathing we had practiced and that helped. Then I went for a walk outside. I listened to the birds, and looked at the flowers for few minutes. Then I went inside and got a cold drink. I saw my friend Alyssa in the hall and she gave me a hug and was really supportive. That helped me calm down. Still, that night, I had nightmares. Then the next day I had flashbacks about the accident. . . . The accident is probably the other memory we need to talk about.

THERAPIST:   The most distressing memory?

CLIENT:   Yeah.

THERAPIST:   Do you need a moment before we talk about that?

CLIENT:   No, I think I'm good.

THERAPIST:   Okay, but if we need to take a break, you let me know.

CLIENT:   Okay. (Quiet for a few moments). The worst time—when I felt permanently damaged was after the accident. I still remember the accident like it happened yesterday. We were driving to Florida for a vacation and were on the Interstate. We'd celebrated Christmas the day before with all of my relatives. In the car we were singing Christmas songs. We were all being silly and laughing. I was so happy. Since then, I've never been as happy as that. . . . It all happened so fast. All of a sudden there was so much snow that we couldn't see past the front of our car. Then there were these terrible sounds. . . . I can't even describe most of them . . . crashing sounds . . . sounds that I now know meant people were dying . . . and the screams . . . maybe it was me screaming. . . . I don't know. I was confused at first. I didn't understand what happened. Then there was pain like I'd never felt before. I couldn't see my sister or brother in the car, even though I was sitting between them. All I saw was twisted metal and snow. I was terrified. I couldn't move and couldn't see my family. Then I guess I passed out.

(*Client crying. Therapist is leaning in. Silence.*)

THERAPIST:   (Softly spoken). Sarah, are you still here with me? In this office . . . and knowing that this is a memory that, as terrible as it was, is over?

CLIENT:   (Whispers and looks up at the therapist). Yeah. I'm here.

THERAPIST:   I know this is difficult. Would it help to take a few deep breaths or maybe a sip of water?

CLIENT:   Yes, I think so.

*(Therapist and client do some deep breaths together. Client has a drink of water).*

CLIENT:   Okay. I'm better now. . . . When I woke up in a hospital bed, I was frantic. I was asking for my family. No one would answer my questions. I started crying. I couldn't understand why no one would tell me they were okay. . . . Then my auntie came in. She was crying. She sat beside my bed and held my hand. She told me that I had been in a bad car accident. She told me that she thanked God that I survived. I asked about my parents, and Caleb, and Maya. I had a hard time understanding her at first. She told me that my mom and brother didn't make it. . . . Only my dad, Maya and me survived. . . . And Maya was in surgery. My family went from five people to three—just like that. . . . I later heard that 36 people died in the 21-car pileup we were in. Two of those people were some of the most important people in my life. I felt permanently damaged then. . . . I felt like who I was broke into a million pieces that could never be whole again. For a while I wished we had all died together. It hurt so much.

THERAPIST:   So many traumatic losses in such a short time. It sounds like these losses broke your heart and turned your life upside down.

CLIENT:   Yes. It hurt so much. I didn't think I would live through it. And I felt like, if I did, I would always be broken.

THERAPIST:   I imagine it was unbearable.

CLIENT:   Yeah. It was . . .

THERAPIST:   And yet . . . somehow . . . you did survive. You were stronger than you knew. . . . How were you able to get through this?

CLIENT:   I'm not sure. . . . I guess . . . at first, I knew my dad and sister would need me and I had to be there for them. . . . And I thought about my mom. . . . It was like I could hear her telling me that she still had my back and she wanted me to live my life and go after my dreams. . . . Some days it was so hard to get out of bed. . . . And, of course I had to learn to walk again. . . . People were very kind . . . my nurses and doctors were so nice . . . and some of the kids and teachers from my high school would come to see me even though they didn't know what to say. . . . My aunties and uncles and cousins kept telling me they would help me to get through it. And there was part of me that knew I had to keep going even when the best I could do was just to wake up in the morning.

THERAPIST:   It sounds like you were stronger than you knew . . . and that the support of other people was a source of hope and motivation for you.

CLIENT:   Yeah, I guess so. I'm still surprised I was able to get to a point where I was ready to go to college. I'm proud of that, but there are days I still feel broken . . . damaged.

THERAPIST:   There has been a lot of loss for you . . . a lot of pain. . . . The words "broken" and "damaged" sound pretty final though don't they? I imagine these kinds of experiences can really leave a person thinking they are "damaged"—and yet, I tend to think of it in terms of being injured or wounded instead . . . because then healing is possible.

All three of the memories you mentioned were very painful experiences that you were powerless to stop. In each, you experienced injuries to your sense of self and specifically how you perceived your place in the world. After the accident, it must have been hard to find your place, when it felt like your world . . . your family . . . had been totally devastated. . . . The fact that you kept going, despite all of this . . . speaks to your extraordinary resilience and spirit . . . and the strength you drew from the love around you.

CLIENT:   I didn't feel very strong at the time.

THERAPIST:   I've found that the strongest people are often very tired. . . . They are so busy concentrating on taking the next breath and the next step to think about the strength that it takes to keep going.

CLIENT:   I guess so . . .

THERAPIST:   Can we go back to considering the first time you remember feeling permanently damaged . . . to the memory of when you were 5 years old and being targeted and excluded by a bully in school. That's likely where this belief slipped in without being challenged. After a belief like that slips in, it takes root and grows—usually without our permission or awareness. Can you remember how that 5 year-old part of you felt when she was being bullied? What were the emotions?

CLIENT:   I remember feeling sad and lonely . . . and like something was wrong with me—so I wanted to hide away from everyone. I felt confused. I didn't know why she was treating me differently from everyone. I wondered why I was different and was sad about it.

THERAPIST:   So when the bullying happened. . . . You were this 5 year-old little girl who was feeling confused, sad, hurt, and alone. It was through this lens that you tried to make sense of what was happening. It was through this lens of sadness, hurt, confusion and loneliness that you saw what was happening to you, and concluded that there was something wrong with you . . . and came to the belief that you were permanently damaged.

CLIENT:   Yes.

THERAPIST:   And when you step into your wisest self, your strongest and most compassionate self . . . your Warrior Spirit . . . how might you see this situation differently—looking instead through a lens of compassion? What did that 5-year old part of you need to hear instead? What would your Warrior Spirit say to her?

CLIENT:   I would say to her that it's not her fault. That Ashley is mean and a bully but that there is nothing wrong with her. I would tell her that her dark eyes and hair are beautiful and she looks like her mom. I would tell her I'm proud of her. (Tears).

THERAPIST: That is lovely. . . . It's probably what she has needed to hear for a long time. It sounds like she can count on you and doesn't need to feel alone anymore. . . . Would you be willing to take her out of this memory, using your imagination, so that she doesn't need to relive this anymore?

CLIENT: Yes. I can do that. I can take her home with me.

THERAPIST: I imagine that would make her very happy. She would never have to be alone again. . . . Could we take a moment to allow you to do that in your mind?

Client nods and closes her eyes for a few minutes, then opens them.

THERAPIST: How was that?

CLIENT: It was good. She was happy. (Straightens up in her chair and gives a small smile).

THERAPIST: Could we now go back to the memory of what happened with your professor? It sounds like you've worked through a lot of that already, but let's look at it through the lens of compassion. How does it look?

CLIENT: I can see that I was hurt and felt disrespected. At first I thought it was about me, but then I realized it wasn't. This professor doesn't know anything about me so it can't be about me. I know how hard I worked to get into college and I deserve to be there, like everyone else. I'm not broken because I need to write my tests in a quieter room. It just helps me to concentrate and there's nothing wrong with that.

THERAPIST: That all sounds about right, doesn't it. . . . (Smiles).

CLIENT: Yeah . . . I guess it does. (Smiles).

THERAPIST: Now how about we go back to the time after the accident. . . . When you were lying in the hospital bed and heard the news that you had lost your mom and brother. You said you felt "permanently damaged" and broken into a million pieces. You didn't know how you were going to survive this loss. What if your Warrior Spirit or most compassionate and wise self could speak to you at that moment in time. What would she say?

CLIENT: I'm not sure . . .

THERAPIST: Do you think she would tell you that she understands that you are overwhelmed with grief right now . . . that she knows, like no one else can . . . the depths of your pain . . . and that she also knows, without a doubt, that you will find your way through this?

CLIENT: Yeah . . . I think she would say those things . . .

THERAPIST: Anything else?

CLIENT: . . . maybe she would tell me that my relatives, and the doctors and nurses, and lots of other people would help me through this . . . and that even though I couldn't imagine it at the time, I would some day learn to live life again . . . and I would be coming to college . . .

THERAPIST:   It sounds like your compassionate, Warrior Spirit, would want to provide you with hope at your darkest hour. She knows how strong you really are . . .

CLIENT:   Yeah . . .

THERAPIST:   Okay. So let's go back to the belief, "I am permanently damaged". Does it still feel like it fits for you?

CLIENT:   No. I guess it doesn't anymore . . .

THERAPIST:   So let's try to find a belief that is a better fit. . . . One that is more accurate, hopeful and supportive. If the belief, "I'm permanently damaged", no longer feels true, then we need help you find a belief that feels true, at a gut level, to replace it. What might that be?

CLIENT:   I'm not sure . . .

THERAPIST:   Might it be something along the lines of . . . "I've suffered injuries but am healing". . . . Whatever it is, the words have to feel right for you. . . .

CLIENT:   Something like that . . . maybe . . . "I've been injured but I'm healing" . . .

THERAPIST:   "I've been injured but I'm healing". . . . When you say that to yourself does it feel like it fits?

CLIENT:   Yeah.. . . It fits.

THERAPIST:   Okay. . . . So when you say that to yourself . . . "I've been injured but I'm healing", what emotions do you feel?

CLIENT:   Um. . . . It feels different . . . a little strange . . . but, I feel hopeful . . . a little sad but mostly hopeful. Still sad because of the losses but I think that's normal.

THERAPIST:   Yes, I believe that it is.. . . . How does your body feel when you say to yourself, "I've been injured but I'm healing"?

CLIENT:   I feel like the pressure in my chest is gone. I feel more relaxed . . . not afraid . . . like I'm gonna be okay.

THERAPIST:   And how might accepting this belief affect how you behave?

CLIENT:   I feel like I have hope. I don't feel like I have to hide from people. I know that I've been through a lot and I'm strong. Not everyone will understand, but what's most important is that I understand. I'm not broken. I'm healing.

THERAPIST:   That's wonderful! You've done a really important piece of work here today. I know it wasn't easy. Now you've got two pieces of homework. The first is that whenever the thought comes up that you are broken or damaged, you need to replace it with the new belief you've chosen . . . "I've been injured but I'm healing". . . . It will likely take a lot of practice until your brain rewires itself to go there automatically. Relapses are normal so don't worry about them. This is going to take a lot of repetitions, but I think the fact that the belief is a better fit and helps you to feel better physically and emotionally, will help. Do you think you could work on that?

CLIENT:   Yeah, I can work on that.

THERAPIST:  Now the second homework assignment is for tonight. . . . You will likely be more tired than usual this evening so it will be important to be sensitive to that and give yourself what you need. What is one kind thing you can do for yourself today?

CLIENT:  I don't know. . . . Um. . . . I guess I could take time to read a book I've wanted to read . . . and I could go to bed early.

THERAPIST:  That sounds like good self-care. Part of doing trauma work is taking good care of yourself afterwards—treating yourself with the same depth of compassion and kindness that you would give to your loved ones if they were going through a challenging time.

CLIENT:  I'll try to do that.

At the next session, the therapist will check in with the client to see if the new belief still feels like it fits and how she has been adjusting to this new belief. If willing, the client will choose another cognition to work on from the NCQ-IF form, and this will continue in following sessions until the client wants to stop, or until the ratings have all moved to 1s and 2s. Sometimes clients will want a break from this intervention, because it is emotionally, cognitively, and physically tiring work. Alternatively, the client might wish to talk more about the targeted memories and process these further through discussion, or he/she might wish to talk about a recent happening, new crisis, focus further on self-care and stabilization, etc. In this work we always allow the client to lead the process.

## Note

1  This example does not refer to a specific individual case, but rather is a variation of one that has occurred over the years with several clients.

# 11 Preparing Clients for Counseling Termination

## Living With the Scars

> The scar meant that I was stronger than whatever it was that tried to hurt me.
> —Jeannette Walls (2005, p. 286)

Recovery from PTSD does not mean that one will be able to resume life as though nothing has happened. There will be scars—visible and/or invisible. Hopefully, our clients will have learned to appreciate the strength and resiliency that those scars represent. Part of our task as we near the end of the counseling relationship is to prepare our clients regarding how they will live with the scars. The other task is to celebrate their successes and progress, and to encourage them as they work to reclaim their lives and their sense of self.

## Preparing Clients for the End of the Counseling Relationship

The impending end of the counseling relationship can be a source of distress for some of our clients, particularly those who have experienced complex trauma. For these clients, the counseling relationship might represent the first (and sometimes only) time in their lives where they have felt heard, seen, and valued. It might be the first time they experienced unconditional caring and support. It might also be the first time they allowed themselves to be emotionally vulnerable and did not suffer interpersonal boundary violations. Within this context, it is easy to understand why the loss of this relationship might be deeply felt. It is thus essential that we are sensitive to, and respectful of, what our clients need as we approach the end of the counseling relationship.

I've often heard it said that, as therapists, we need to start to prepare our clients for the inevitable termination of the counseling relationship, beginning in the very first session. This might sound a bit harsh at first, until you consider that when we work from a client-centered approach, it is during that introductory session that we set up the expectation that therapy is a time-limited process and our goal is to assist clients to develop the knowledge, skills, and abilities to manage their distress, process their trauma (if that is their goal), and reclaim their lives. We work with clients to support them as they relearn to trust their own bodies and minds, their instincts, and to recognize their resiliency. Our work is ultimately successful when our clients are able to move forward without our ongoing involvement in their lives. In presenting this goal and expectation at the outset, we are conveying the message that we believe that our clients will achieve their goals, and also that they have the capacity and wisdom to manage their own lives. This might be a new message for some of them. Accepting the truth of this message might require some cognitive restructuring.

Furthermore, in client-centered practice, we are very cognizant of not wanting to encourage our clients to develop an unhealthy dependency on us as therapists. Adult clients are viewed as having rights and abilities to make their own choices and decisions. Our role is not to take over making these choices and decisions for our clients, but rather to help them to develop understanding and skills around what information, processes, supports, and/ or resources they require to make the best decisions for themselves. By setting these expectations at the outset, clients are aware that when the work is finished, or in some cases a "piece" of the work is finished, they will move on with their lives without us—and know that this is healthy, and as it should be.

When termination of the therapeutic relationship is approaching and a date has been set, there are things we can do to help the relationship to wind down in a respectful manner, and to assist clients with this important transition. For clients who have suffered through interpersonal trauma, the ending of significant relationships in their lives might have been intertwined with violence, abandonment, terror, blaming, and manipulation, etc. Thus, this is an important opportunity for cognitive restructuring. It is a chance to let them experience the ending of a relationship in a new way—one that will likely involve some sadness, but within a context that is respectful, caring, supportive, and in many ways positive and celebratory of all that they have accomplished.

During this phase of the therapeutic process, it may be helpful to focus on some key areas including: how clients might deal with possible setbacks or challenges; the importance of ongoing self-care; processing feelings and thoughts about the ending of the counseling relationship; and asking what they would like the focus to be on during the last session.

Through the course of doing trauma work with specific clients, you will likely get a sense of the types of challenges they might continue to face in the future. Clients might also have their own particular concerns about the potential challenges they might have to deal with once they are no longer in counseling. Exploring potential challenges that might arise, particularly those that are causing concern for our clients, can allow for proactive discussions and strategizing around how they might effectively address such challenges. This work can help to alleviate some of the stress clients might be experiencing about handling such challenges on their own. These conversations present opportunities to remind clients of their competency and successes in having dealt with similar challenges during the course of your work together, and to emphasize the resources and supports that will continue to be available to them even after the counseling relationship has ended.

One of the most emotional conversations we might have with our clients is how they are feeling about the end of the therapeutic relationship. These endings do not always occur at preferred places in the therapeutic process. Sometimes they are a result of external circumstances rather than client choice. These types of circumstances can contribute to making the ending of the therapeutic relationship particularly emotional for our clients. Clients might experience a sense of loss and grief as the impending end date approaches. Some might experience relief and joy that they have finished the work they wanted to do and are moving forward in our lives. Feelings might be clear or mixed. For some, issues of abandonment might surface and require processing. Some will wish to discuss how they are feeling at great length. Some will want to keep it brief. Some might not want to discuss how they are feeling at all. It is important that we not enforce our agenda in this area either. We need to respect and trust that clients know what they need. If we don't, we will undermine one of the core messages of our work, that being that clients are the experts on themselves and have the right to make their own decisions about what is best for them.

Ongoing self-care is critical if our clients are to retain their capacity to manage distress. Thus, we might wish to have a discussion with clients about planning how they will integrate these strategies into their lives on an ongoing basis. In some cases, during the course of therapy, clients will have already established a routine of self-care in their daily lives. Others might still be responding reactively with self-care only when they are experiencing significant distress. In either case, reviewing their progress, helping them identify the strategies they've recognized are most helpful, and congratulating them on their efforts are ways of underscoring the importance of self-care and reminding them that prioritizing and engaging in self-care is neither a luxury nor a self-indulgence, but rather is a necessary means of supporting their ongoing health and well-being.

Another discussion to have with clients will be regarding what they would like to focus on in the last appointment. Sometimes clients will have preferences about this. Other times they might ask for therapist suggestions. If this is the case, I offer that some clients have found it helpful for us to review their progress and accomplishments over the course of therapy.

## Integrating the Trauma Experience: Living With the Scars

Integrating trauma into one's life is part of an ongoing process, as is living with the scars, whether visible or invisible. Trauma processing can be effective in finally locating these experiences in time, i.e., the past, so that they no longer take over one's present. However, in the present there will inevitably be reminders of the consequences of the trauma within our clients' lives. Part of the challenge in reclaiming one's life following trauma is learning how to live with these lifelong reminders.

## Dealing With Disabilities and/or Chronic Pain

Physical/psychological disabilities and/or chronic pain can be ongoing consequences of trauma. Even though clients may have accomplished their therapeutic goals and have finished this piece of work, these ongoing injuries can be a daily, "in one's face", reminder of the trauma experience. Hopefully, by this point, clients have come to realize that it can be beneficial, and there is no shame, in allowing others to assist them with their challenges.

As therapists, part of helping our clients to learn to live with the scars might require us to investigate, and advocate for, appropriate supports. Our clients might require a medical team to address their pain management needs. Some of our clients might benefit from physiotherapy, chiropractic care, massage therapy, etc. If our clients do not have the financial means to pay for these services, we might need to assist them in looking into subsidized services. I've found that many of my clients have benefited from the care provided through university- or college-based health profession training programs which offer clinics to the community at significantly reduced fees, in order to provide supervised students in these programs with hands-on experience in their chosen professions. Also clients might be a fit for research studies in the community that offer treatment. Additionally, I have found that in exceptional circumstances, if clients were willing to allow me to share minimal information regarding their circumstances, there were religious or other groups who were willing to provide the financial support to allow clients to access what they needed.

Learning to live with disabilities or ongoing pain following trauma can be a lifelong process. One has to relearn how to do things within one's new limitations. It can be frustrating and elicit new levels of grief each time one comes face-to-face with new restrictions. I've worked with clients who, as a result of a traumatic event, now live with chronic back pain. I've empathized with their heartbreak when their toddler comes to them asking to be picked up, and mom or dad can't do it. There's the athlete whose life was centered on sports, who now finds he can barely walk. There's the soldier who loved his work, but now finds himself discharged from the military due to injuries sustained on his last tour. While we help these clients to grieve and to try to accept their new realities—while still finding joy in life, compassion for themselves, and meaning, they still have to live with these struggles and losses on a daily basis. We might want to encourage them to join peer support groups in person or on-line. It can help to reduce isolation and despair to have people in their life who really "get it".

## Preparing for Anniversaries

One of the most fascinating things I've observed about the human body is the way it can remember trauma anniversaries, even when the conscious mind appears to have forgotten. Clients who have been symptom-free, might all of a sudden start having nightmares, headaches, flashbacks, or other traumatic stress symptoms in the days leading up to a trauma anniversary. We need to let our clients know that this is a possibility, and to encourage them to be especially gentle with themselves and mindful of what they need around these dates.

There seems to be a heightened possibility of increased frequency and intensity of trauma symptoms around anniversary dates, particularly in the first few years following trauma. Thus, I often encourage clients to try to minimize commitments on important trauma-related dates to allow for additional self-care and rest if needed. If they have supportive and understanding loved ones in their life, I will encourage them to let their loved ones know that this might be a difficult time of year for them. In many cases when clients have done this, their loved ones have offered additional supports such as protecting them from contact with difficult people in their lives, bringing them meals, assisting with household tasks, etc. It can be a wonderful opportunity for our clients to learn to accept the love and support that is offered, and in so doing, giving themselves the message that they, too, are worthy of love and kindness.

Sometimes clients will choose to use these dates to find a reflective way to honor their survival, and/or acknowledge their losses. Having these discussions with our clients can help them to prepare for anniversaries throughout their lives, to know what is normal, and to know that they have the ability to proactively activate supports for themselves both internally and externally.

### Loss of Relationships by Circumstance or Choice

Occasionally, through the course of our work with trauma survivors, clients will decide to end ongoing abusive or toxic relationships. Or alternatively, as a result of speaking out about the reality of their experience of trauma, our clients might be ostracized by family and/or friends. This seems to be particularly true in cases where survivors confront childhood abuse or sexual violence. Speaking their truth can seriously disrupt the shield of denial and minimization that others have been using to avoid the issues, which can sometimes result in loved ones turning on survivors rather than perpetrators. If our clients have experienced these losses, this might be another scar that they will have to continue to carry.

Losing one's family can be a devastating loss, even if our clients know that these relationships were harmful to them. The sense of isolation can be hard to bear. Clients may dread holidays, and specifically being asked by others in their lives, even casually, what they will be doing for these holidays. They often worry what other people will think if they admit that they have no contact with their family. There might be a sense of shame attached to this admission. In these cases it is important to validate our clients' pain while reminding them that the shame doesn't belong to them. Also we might want to suggest that these clients consider "choosing" their families. I tell my clients that we can have families through bloodlines or through heart connections. They seem to like this idea, and it can provide a sense of hope and power, to replace feelings of despair and loneliness.

## Active Termination

The last counseling session is often one about which clients are nervous. Ending relationships is stressful for most of us, and possibly more so when it comes to the type of special attachment that can occur within the therapeutic alliance.

A small percentage of clients will find this last session too distressing and will choose to cancel without rebooking, or will just not show up. Some will forget about the appointment. In such cases, it is appropriate to follow up with a simple e-mail or phone call to let them know they were missed and to ask if they would like to reschedule. If clients indicate that rescheduling doesn't work for them, I will typically ask if it would be okay for me to send them a letter to summarize their accomplishments.

During the last session, we focus on whatever topic clients have chosen. Prior to this session, I will typically go through all my counseling notes and will make summary notes of their initial presenting issues and symptoms, as well as their progress, key insights, and accomplishments during our work together. I might also pull out copies of their pre- and post-therapy assessments (i.e., BAI, BDI-II, NCQ, and/or TSSSC) to review with them and provide a visual validation of their progress. During the last session, I tell clients that I have prepared this information and ask their permission to review it with them. I've found that clients are open to this, and that the act of reviewing their progress in such a comprehensive way is a very positive and powerful way to end the last session. On a more personal note, I tell them how honored I have been that they have allowed me to walk with them during this part of their journey. I tell them about the qualities that I admire in them and of my belief in their ongoing resiliency and strength to handle whatever comes their way in life. And finally, as they are leaving I hand them a letter I have written. In this letter I have summarized some of the information we reviewed in this last session, in order to provide a concrete reminder of their progress, personal strengths, and resiliency.

## The Question of Follow-up

Depending on the setting in which you work, a follow up appointment with a recently ended client relationship may or may not be an option. In most cases, it is not something that I would typically do in my work. However, there are certain cases where a client is feeling reticent about the ending of the counseling relationship and asks to check-in later in the school term to touch base and evaluate how they have been doing. Likewise, if it is an option in your setting, there might be some situations in which your client would benefit from a follow-up appointment, a month or few months down the road to check-in.

## Therapist Closure

I have found that providing a written letter/summary to my clients regarding their progress and reminding them of their strengths has been a nice way for me, too, to find closure in ending the therapeutic relationship. Discussing these endings in clinical supervision sessions can also provide a time and place for us to work through our own reactions and thoughts regarding these endings. We might be left with mixed emotions at the end of our work with clients. Through this work we will have come to admire them and care for them. While we celebrate their successes and independence, we too might miss being part of their journey and knowing how things work out. Our clients have allowed us a tremendous honor. We too are changed by the therapeutic relationship—hopefully in ways that will make us aware of, and humbled by, the magnificent strength and resiliency of the human spirit.

# Appendices

# Appendix 1

## Traumatic Stress Symptom Screening Checklist (TSSSC)

*Shirley Porter, M.Ed., RP, RSW*

Name: _____     Date: _____

Indicate which of the following symptoms you have been experiencing and how distressing they have been:

| Symptoms | Check if "Yes" | If yes, how distressing have these symptoms been? 1= A Little    5 = Extremely | | | | |
|---|---|---|---|---|---|---|
| **Intrusive** | | 1 | 2 | 3 | 4 | 5 |
| Nightmares | ☐ | ☐ | ☐ | ☐ | ☐ | ☐ |
| Night terrors (awaking terrified but not sure why) | ☐ | ☐ | ☐ | ☐ | ☐ | ☐ |
| Flashbacks to trauma (might be physical, emotional, visual, sounds, and/or smells) | ☐ | ☐ | ☐ | ☐ | ☐ | ☐ |
| "Zoning out" or "spacing out" | ☐ | ☐ | ☐ | ☐ | ☐ | ☐ |
| Feeling *physical* distress when reminded of the trauma | ☐ | ☐ | ☐ | ☐ | ☐ | ☐ |
| Feeling *emotional* distress when reminded of the trauma | ☐ | ☐ | ☐ | ☐ | ☐ | ☐ |
| **Avoidant** | | 1 | 2 | 3 | 4 | 5 |
| Avoiding reminders of a traumatic/ painful event or events: | | | | | | |
| • Places | ☐ | ☐ | ☐ | ☐ | ☐ | ☐ |
| • People or types of people | ☐ | ☐ | ☐ | ☐ | ☐ | ☐ |
| • Objects | ☐ | ☐ | ☐ | ☐ | ☐ | ☐ |
| • Discussions, activities, or events | ☐ | ☐ | ☐ | ☐ | ☐ | ☐ |
| • Memories | ☐ | ☐ | ☐ | ☐ | ☐ | ☐ |
| • Thoughts | ☐ | ☐ | ☐ | ☐ | ☐ | ☐ |
| • Feelings | ☐ | ☐ | ☐ | ☐ | ☐ | ☐ |

| Symptoms | Check if "Yes" | If yes, how distressing have these symptoms been? 1= A Little    5 = Extremely | | | | |
|---|---|---|---|---|---|---|
| **Mood and Thoughts** | | 1 | 2 | 3 | 4 | 5 |
| Forgetting important parts of a traumatic/painful event or events | ☐ | ☐ | ☐ | ☐ | ☐ | ☐ |
| Negative beliefs about yourself, others, and/or the world | ☐ | ☐ | ☐ | ☐ | ☐ | ☐ |
| Feeling disconnected from other people | ☐ | ☐ | ☐ | ☐ | ☐ | ☐ |
| Socially withdrawn | ☐ | ☐ | ☐ | ☐ | ☐ | ☐ |
| Unable to feel positive emotions (e.g., happiness, hope, excitement) | ☐ | ☐ | ☐ | ☐ | ☐ | ☐ |
| Sadness/Grief | ☐ | ☐ | ☐ | ☐ | ☐ | ☐ |
| Fear/Terror | ☐ | ☐ | ☐ | ☐ | ☐ | ☐ |
| Shame | ☐ | ☐ | ☐ | ☐ | ☐ | ☐ |
| Horror | ☐ | ☐ | ☐ | ☐ | ☐ | ☐ |
| Despair | ☐ | ☐ | ☐ | ☐ | ☐ | ☐ |
| Guilt/Regret | ☐ | ☐ | ☐ | ☐ | ☐ | ☐ |
| Anger/Rage | ☐ | ☐ | ☐ | ☐ | ☐ | ☐ |
| **Arousal** | | 1 | 2 | 3 | 4 | 5 |
| Irritability | ☐ | ☐ | ☐ | ☐ | ☐ | ☐ |
| Emotional Outbursts or "over-reacting" | ☐ | ☐ | ☐ | ☐ | ☐ | ☐ |
| Alcohol, medication, and/or substance abuse | ☐ | ☐ | ☐ | ☐ | ☐ | ☐ |
| Always looking for threats | ☐ | ☐ | ☐ | ☐ | ☐ | ☐ |
| Reckless or dangerous behaviors (e.g., driving while intoxicated, high-risk sex, starting fights) | ☐ | ☐ | ☐ | ☐ | ☐ | ☐ |
| Never able to relax or take your guard down | ☐ | ☐ | ☐ | ☐ | ☐ | ☐ |
| Startle easily | ☐ | ☐ | ☐ | ☐ | ☐ | ☐ |
| Concentration difficulties | ☐ | ☐ | ☐ | ☐ | ☐ | ☐ |
| Insomnia or other sleep difficulties | ☐ | ☐ | ☐ | ☐ | ☐ | ☐ |

| Symptoms | Check if "Yes" | If yes, how distressing have these symptoms been? 1= A Little  5 = Extremely | | | | |
|---|---|---|---|---|---|---|
| *Complex* | | 1 | 2 | 3 | 4 | 5 |
| Self-injury or harming behavior | ☐ | ☐ | ☐ | ☐ | ☐ | ☐ |
| Feeling physically numb and/or like you are disconnected from your body | ☐ | ☐ | ☐ | ☐ | ☐ | ☐ |
| Negative beliefs about yourself (e.g., "I am unlovable" . . . "permanently damaged" . . . "not good enough") | ☐ | ☐ | ☐ | ☐ | ☐ | ☐ |
| Ongoing physical pain without an obvious cause: | | | | | | |
| • Stomach or intestinal pain | ☐ | ☐ | ☐ | ☐ | ☐ | ☐ |
| • Headaches | ☐ | ☐ | ☐ | ☐ | ☐ | ☐ |
| • Back or neck pain | ☐ | ☐ | ☐ | ☐ | ☐ | ☐ |
| • Muscle aches | ☐ | ☐ | ☐ | ☐ | ☐ | ☐ |
| • Nausea and/or vomiting | ☐ | ☐ | ☐ | ☐ | ☐ | ☐ |
| • Other: | ☐ | ☐ | ☐ | ☐ | ☐ | ☐ |
| Difficulty managing emotions and calming yourself down | ☐ | ☐ | ☐ | ☐ | ☐ | ☐ |
| Inability to trust of feel close to others | ☐ | ☐ | ☐ | ☐ | ☐ | ☐ |
| Lack of purpose or meaning in life | ☐ | ☐ | ☐ | ☐ | ☐ | ☐ |

# Appendix 2
## Suicide Risk Assessment

Client Name: _____ D.O.B. _____
Current Address: _____ Phone Number: _____
Date and Time of Risk Assessment: _____
Emergency Contact: _____ Relationship: _____
Emergency Contact Phone Numbers: _____
Physician Name: _____ Phone: _____
Current Diagnoses: _____
Current Medication(s): _____

*Intensity of suicidal ideation now?* _____ (out of 10)
*Intention of acting now?* _____ (out of 10)
*How intense does it get at its worst?* _____ (out of 10)
*Intention of acting at its worst?* _____ (out of 10)

*Past Suicidal Ideation: Yes or No*        *Past Attempt: Yes or No*
If yes, details:
_____
_____

*Current Plan: Yes or No*     *Means available to Complete Plan: Yes or No*
If yes, details:
_____
_____

*Access to Weapons: Yes or No*
If yes, details (i.e., types, how many, where located)
_____
_____

*Current Physical Pain: Yes or No*      *If yes, rating out of 10:* _____
If yes, details:
_____
_____

*Current Traumatic Stress Symptom Screening Checklist Attached: Yes or No*
*If yes, areas that require immediate attention:*

_____

_____

*Recent triggering event, trauma, or other losses: Yes or No*
If yes, details:

_____

_____

_____

_____

*Current supportive people: Yes or No*
If yes, details:

_____

_____

*Current living situation:*

_____

_____

*Current deterrents to suicide: Yes or No*
If yes, details:

_____

_____

| *At-risk Behaviors* | Yes | No | If yes, details: |
|---|---|---|---|
| *Self-Injury* | ☐ | ☐ | |
| *Illicit or Prescription Drug Abuse* | ☐ | ☐ | |
| *Alcohol Abuse* | ☐ | ☐ | |
| Other: | ☐ | ☐ | |

*Mobilizing Supports and Resources:*

| Resource | Contact Info | Contacted with Client | Counselor will Contact | Client will Contact as Needed |
|---|---|---|---|---|
| Crisis Line or Center | | ☐ | ☐ | ☐ |
| Hospital Emergency Department | | ☐ | ☐ | ☐ |
| Police | | ☐ | ☐ | ☐ |

| Resource | Contact Info | Contacted with Client | Counselor will Contact | Client will Contact as Needed |
|---|---|---|---|---|
| EMS | | ☐ | ☐ | ☐ |
| Family/Friends | | ☐ | ☐ | ☐ |
| Physician/ Psychiatrist | | ☐ | ☐ | ☐ |
| Other Professional - Specify: | | ☐ | ☐ | ☐ |
| Other Community Services—Specify: <br> • <br> • | | ☐ | ☐ | ☐ |

*Safety Plan Completed: Yes or No*          *Safety Plan Attached: Yes or No*
*Follow-Up Counseling Appointment: Yes or No*
*If Yes, with:* _____ *Time and Date:* _____
*Counselor perception of immediate risk (out of 10):* _____
*Counselor observations, interventions, and recommendations:*

_____

_____

_____

_____

_____

_____

_____

_____        _____        _____

Counselor Name (Print)        Counselor Signature        Date

_____        _____        _____

Consulted with (Print)        Signature        Date

I, (*Client Name*)_____, (*Date of Birth*: _____), do voluntarily consent to allow (*Therapist/Agency*) _____ to receive and release information regarding this *Suicide Risk Assessment* and accompanying documents (e.g., *Safety Plan, Traumatic Stress Symptom Screening Checklist*) to the following individuals, agencies, or institutions for the specified purpose(s):

| Name: | Contact Information: | Purpose: |
|---|---|---|
| • _____ | _____ | _____ |
| • _____ | _____ | _____ |
| _____ | _____ | _____ |


_____          _____
(Client Signature)                         (Date)

_____          _____
(Witness Signature)                       (Date)

# Appendix 3
## Safety Plan

Client: _____     Date: _____

Completed with Counselor (Name): _____

Things I can do to reduce my distress—to calm, soothe, or distract:
- _____
- _____
- _____
- _____
- _____
- _____

People or organizations I can contact (including contact information):
- _____
- _____
- _____
- _____

Places I can go where I feel safe:
- _____
- _____
- _____
- _____

People, places, or things I need to avoid—because they tend to make things worse:
- _____
- _____
- _____
- _____

What I need to remember:
- _____
- _____
- _____
- _____

My motivation to get through this:
- _____

# Appendix 4

## Understanding Your Window of Tolerance[1]

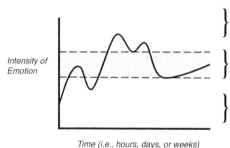

} Emotions that exceed this window can cause unbearable pain (e.g., hurt, sadness, despair, anger, grief, shame).

} *Window of Tolerance*—i.e., emotions that fall within this window are tolerable and can be managed with existing coping strategies.

} Feelings of unbearable numbness and disconnection describe the emotions that fall below this window.

*Intensity of Emotion*

*Time (i.e., hours, days, or weeks)*

*Figure A.1* Window of Tolerance

If you are under more stress than usual due to PTSD symptoms, and/or other physical, emotional, financial, or relationship challenges, your window of tolerance will likely become narrower. Things that didn't bother you before might all of a sudden feel overwhelming.

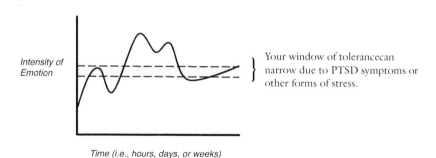

*Intensity of Emotion*

} Your window of tolerance can narrow due to PTSD symptoms or other forms of stress.

*Time (i.e., hours, days, or weeks)*

*Figure A.2* Window of Tolerance Narrows with Distress

When this happens you will be naturally motivated to try to find ways to move back into your window of tolerance. It is at these moments, if your usual coping strategies and supports don't seem to be effective, that you might be tempted to engage in riskier behaviors (e.g., alcohol or substance use, high risk sex, self-harm, gambling) to try to find relief from unbearable pain. Unfortunately, some of these higher risk-coping strategies can bring along more complications to add to your already heavy burden.

In terms of your window of tolerance, our goals in counseling are to help you find the combination of healthy coping strategies and supports that will: 1) give you control so that you will know what you need to do to move yourself back within your window of tolerance when you feel like you are being pushed out of it; and 2) stretch or widen your window of tolerance for distress.

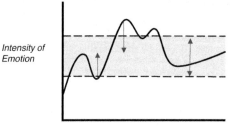

*Intensity of Emotion*

*Goals:* To help you to learn how to more effectively

- move back into your window of tolerance when you start to feel overwhelmed; and

- widen your window of tolerance for distress.

*Time (i.e., hours, days, or weeks)*

*Figure A.3* Goals of Counseling

## Note

1 This phrase is first used by Daniel J. Siegel in *The Developing Mind: How Relationships and the Brain Interact to Shape Who We Are*. New York: Guilford Press, 1999, p. 253. The application of the concept of window of tolerance to trauma was developed by Pat Ogden, Kekuni Minton and Clare Pain, (2006) in *Trauma and the Body: A Sensorimotor Approach to Psychotherapy*. New York: Norton.

# Appendix 5
## Individual Distress Tolerance Plan

### How to Increase Your Window of Tolerance and Add to Your Toolkit for Effective Coping

There are interventions that can help to both widen your window of tolerance and assist you to more effectively move back within your window of tolerance when you are feeling distressed. Some of these are:

- **Counseling** with a qualified professional.
- **Medical Support and/or Medication** prescribed by your doctor to treat illness/pain—if appropriate.
- **Distraction** strategies can give you a break from distorted negative thought spirals or behaviors by directing your attention to something neutral or more positive.
- **Self-soothing** strategies using your senses (i.e., taste, touch, smell, sight, and sound) can help to calm and/or energize you.
- **Mindfulness** strategies redirect your focus back to the present moment, because too often our minds and bodies are caught up in either a past we can't change or a future we fear. There are three types of mindfulness strategies that you may find helpful: 1) mindful, non-judging observations of your thoughts, emotions, and physical sensations; 2) mindful attention, using your senses, to what is happening around you, in your environment, in the present moment; and 3) mindful attention to what is really being asked of you in *this moment.*
- **Accepting Support from Others**. These strategies involve accepting offers of support from loved ones. This might mean sharing your challenges with them. It might mean accepting their offers of help with things you need to get done in your daily life.
- **Education**. Understanding the effects of trauma on the mind and body, normal responses to trauma including the range of PTSD symptoms, and what to expect in the healing process can help to reduce unnecessary distress caused by fear and confusion.

*Your Distress Tolerance Toolkit*

You can add to your toolkit by finding the specific distraction, self-soothing, and mindfulness strategies that work for you. Going through the lists below, check off those strategies that:

- *worked for you in the past;*
- *you use now; or*
- *you are willing to try.*

---

- ○ Exercise
- ○ Go for a walk or run
- ○ Draw or color a picture
- ○ Clean
- ○ Text a friend
- ○ Play a video game
- ○ Play a board game with friends
- ○ Attend a community event
- ○ Make yourself a hot drink
- ○ Chew gum
- ○ Write in a journal
- ○ Listen to music
- ○ Light a scented candle
- ○ Paint or sculpt
- ○ Play an instrument
- ○ Watch a movie or TV show
- ○ Pet or play with an animal
- ○ Look around the room and find your favorite colors
- ○ Take a hot shower or bath
- ○ Dress in comfortable clothes
- ○ Read
- ○ Make your favorite meal
- ○ Bake (e.g., cookies, cake, bread)
- ○ Put on your favorite lotion or fragrance
- ○ Carry a picture of a loved one
- ○ Take a nap
- ○ Visit your favorite websites
- ○ Cry
- ○ Call or visit a friend
- ○ Play sports
- ○ Do chores
- ○ Put clean sheets on the bed
- ○ Count to 10
- ○ Accept help from others

- Attend a support group
- Just breathe
- Listen to the sound of waves
- Watch fish in an aquarium
- Build something
- People watch
- Watch a sunrise or sunset
- Squeeze a rubber ball
- Get a massage
- Go for a drive or ride on a bus or subway
- Plan a trip
- Go to the library
- Go shopping
- Meditate or pray
- Do yoga
- Take pictures or videos
- Sing
- Daydream about your hopes or goals
- Do a craft
- Write a poem or story
- Watch a funny video
- Look at flowers and breathe in their scents
- Look at artwork
- Watch snowflakes fall
- Go outside and breathe in the smells of nature
- Enjoy dessert
- Suck on a piece of candy
- Take a bubble bath
- Organize your room or desk
- Give yourself a manicure or pedicure
- Catch up on your e-mails
- Participate in hobbies
- Go out to eat
- Do a puzzle, crossword, or word search
- Look at the clouds
- Gaze at the stars and moon
- Do laundry
- Look at nature around you
- Write a letter
- Hug someone
- Talk to a friend or loved one
- Do something nice for someone
- Tend to a garden or plants

- Other: _____

# Appendix 6
## Sample Referral Letter to Physician

(Date)
*Re: Jane Doe (D.O.B. January 1, 1995)*

Dear Dr. Smith:

I am writing to you with the written and informed consent of Jane Doe, who is my counseling client, to share the following confidential information with you.

Jane informed me that she will be meeting with you this coming week, and we thought it would be helpful if you had the following background information.

Jane has experienced a number of traumatic incidents during her lifetime including:

- At 7 years old surviving a car accident in which her mother and brother were killed;
- At 18 years old, being sexually assaulted; and
- At 20 years old, witnessing the prolonged painful death of her grandmother (who she lived with) as a result of bone cancer.

Recently, her grandfather has been diagnosed with stage IV cancer.

Jane reports debilitating symptoms including: nausea and vomiting; muscle pain and tremors; chills; insomnia and nightmares; flashbacks; dissociation; difficulty concentrating; as well as overwhelming grief and terror—all of which she said have been ongoing since the sexual assault, but have worsened in the past two months. Consequently, she reports she has been missing work for 2–3 days/week during the past three weeks.

I have encouraged Jane to meet with you for a medical assessment. I will be continuing to provide her with therapy.

I hope this information is helpful to you. Please contact me directly if I can be of further assistance.

Kind regards,
(Therapist Name, Credentials) (Agency Name)

# Appendix 7
## Sample Therapist Letter to Client

(Date)

Dear (Client Name),

I realize this is a difficult time for you and that sometimes in the darkness it can be hard to remember who you are and how far you have come. I wanted to take a moment to write some of my observations from our work together.

Life has not been easy for you. You have faced more challenges in the first 20 years of your life than some people will face in a lifetime. However, you have persisted in trying to find ways to heal. I have come to know you as a person who is intelligent and insightful, strong, courageous, and resilient. It has been my honor and privilege to work with you. You have survived the impossible already, and have come through it as a good person. You have so much to be proud of.

Don't forget to lean into your Warrior Spirit in moments of darkness—these are memories of a time you have already survived. They are a reliving, but they are not happening now. Step into your Warrior Spirit—into the awareness that even though your body and mind is reliving trauma—you are safe in the present moment. You are in the process of reclaiming yourself and your life. You are starting to recognize and embrace your power.

What do you need in this moment? Sometimes we need to ask this several times a day—because the answer might be different at different times. The answers to this question are within you, and will help you to get through this.

Remember too, that you are not alone. You are cared for. You are "good enough" exactly as you are. Rest in this truth.

—(Therapist Name)

# Appendix 8

## Negative Cognition Questionnaire—
## Initial Form (NCQ-IF)

*Larry F. Sine, Ph.D.*
*Silke Vogelmann-Sine, Ph.D.*

Name: _____     Date_____

Please circle the number below to indicate how true each of the following statements **feels** about you at a gut level. The scale goes from 1 being "Untrue" to 7 being "Totally True".

**NOTE: If you begin to experience very distressing/unpleasant feelings or sensations while completing this questionnaire, discontinue immediately and discuss this situation with your therapist at the next session.**

|  | Untrue | | | | | | Totally True |
|---|---|---|---|---|---|---|---|
| 1. I don't deserve love | 1 | 2 | 3 | 4 | 5 | 6 | 7 |
| 2. I am a bad person | 1 | 2 | 3 | 4 | 5 | 6 | 7 |
| 3. I am terrible | 1 | 2 | 3 | 4 | 5 | 6 | 7 |
| 4. I am worthless (inadequate) | 1 | 2 | 3 | 4 | 5 | 6 | 7 |
| 5. I am shameful | 1 | 2 | 3 | 4 | 5 | 6 | 7 |
| 6. I am not lovable | 1 | 2 | 3 | 4 | 5 | 6 | 7 |
| 7. I am not good enough | 1 | 2 | 3 | 4 | 5 | 6 | 7 |
| 8. I deserve only bad things | 1 | 2 | 3 | 4 | 5 | 6 | 7 |
| 9. I cannot be trusted | 1 | 2 | 3 | 4 | 5 | 6 | 7 |
| 10. I cannot trust myself | 1 | 2 | 3 | 4 | 5 | 6 | 7 |
| 11. I cannot trust my judgment | 1 | 2 | 3 | 4 | 5 | 6 | 7 |
| 12. I cannot succeed | 1 | 2 | 3 | 4 | 5 | 6 | 7 |
| 13. I am not in control | 1 | 2 | 3 | 4 | 5 | 6 | 7 |
| 14. I am powerless (helpless) | 1 | 2 | 3 | 4 | 5 | 6 | 7 |
| 15. I am weak | 1 | 2 | 3 | 4 | 5 | 6 | 7 |
| 16. I cannot protect myself | 1 | 2 | 3 | 4 | 5 | 6 | 7 |
| 17. I am stupid (not smart enough) | 1 | 2 | 3 | 4 | 5 | 6 | 7 |

| | | | | | | | |
|---|---|---|---|---|---|---|---|
| 18. I am insignificant (unimportant) | 1 | 2 | 3 | 4 | 5 | 6 | 7 |
| 19. I am a disappointment | 1 | 2 | 3 | 4 | 5 | 6 | 7 |
| 20. I deserve to die | 1 | 2 | 3 | 4 | 5 | 6 | 7 |
| 21. I deserve to be miserable | 1 | 2 | 3 | 4 | 5 | 6 | 7 |
| 22. I cannot get what I want | 1 | 2 | 3 | 4 | 5 | 6 | 7 |
| 23. I am a failure (will fail) | 1 | 2 | 3 | 4 | 5 | 6 | 7 |
| 24. I have to be perfect (please everyone) | 1 | 2 | 3 | 4 | 5 | 6 | 7 |
| 25. I am permanently damaged | 1 | 2 | 3 | 4 | 5 | 6 | 7 |
| 26. I am ugly (my body is hateful) | 1 | 2 | 3 | 4 | 5 | 6 | 7 |
| 27. I should have done something | 1 | 2 | 3 | 4 | 5 | 6 | 7 |
| 28. I did something wrong | 1 | 2 | 3 | 4 | 5 | 6 | 7 |
| 29. I am in danger | 1 | 2 | 3 | 4 | 5 | 6 | 7 |
| 30. I cannot stand it | 1 | 2 | 3 | 4 | 5 | 6 | 7 |
| 31. I cannot trust anyone | 1 | 2 | 3 | 4 | 5 | 6 | 7 |
| 32. I cannot let it out | 1 | 2 | 3 | 4 | 5 | 6 | 7 |
| 33. I do not deserve | 1 | 2 | 3 | 4 | 5 | 6 | 7 |
| 34. It's not okay to feel (show) my emotions | 1 | 2 | 3 | 4 | 5 | 6 | 7 |
| 35. I cannot stand up for myself | 1 | 2 | 3 | 4 | 5 | 6 | 7 |
| 36. I am different (don't belong) | 1 | 2 | 3 | 4 | 5 | 6 | 7 |
| 37. I should have known better | 1 | 2 | 3 | 4 | 5 | 6 | 7 |
| 38. I am inadequate | 1 | 2 | 3 | 4 | 5 | 6 | 7 |

Please insert below any negative statements about yourself not covered above. Then rate them in the same manner.

| | Untrue | | | | | Totally True | |
|---|---|---|---|---|---|---|---|
| | 1 | 2 | 3 | 4 | 5 | 6 | 7 |
| | 1 | 2 | 3 | 4 | 5 | 6 | 7 |
| | 1 | 2 | 3 | 4 | 5 | 6 | 7 |
| | 1 | 2 | 3 | 4 | 5 | 6 | 7 |

# Appendix 9
## Compassion-Focused CBT—Summary

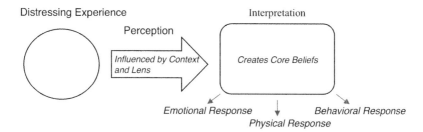

*Figure A.4* Basic Premise of CFCBT

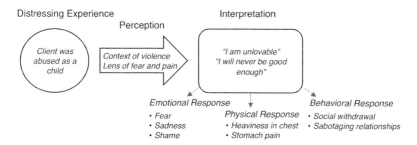

*Figure A.5* Example

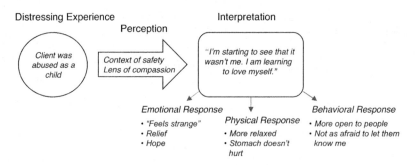

Figure A.6 Example of Rewriting Beliefs using CFCBT


## Therapist Notes

*Do not use if this intervention if client is in crisis or unable to tolerate and manage distress.*

- Explain to client the basic premise regarding how inaccurate core beliefs can be a source of continuing distress in daily life (use diagrams above).
- Ask client to complete the NCQ-IF, Appendix 8.
- Next ask client to choose the negative cognition you will work on together. Have the client say the belief to him/herself and identify their emotional, physical, and behavioral reactions to it. Make note of these.
- Ask client to identify and describe three instances in their lives where they felt this belief was true:
  - Earliest memory
  - Most distressing memory
  - Most recent memory
- Note themes across these memories and summarize.
- After reviewing the three memories, ask the client to "step out of" each of the memories and instead to view them through a present-day lens of safety and compassion. If client is unable to make this shift, then the counselor should model compassionate reframing. Work with client to identify a new, more adaptive and accurate belief. Tentative beliefs such as "I'm starting to realize" or "I'm learning to" are fine. Ensure the client is comfortable with the new belief—at a gut level.
- Ask the client to say the new belief to him/herself and to identify his/her emotional, physical, and behavioral reactions to it. (It will likely feel strange at first). Encourage the client to substitute this new belief whenever the old one arises. Explain that it will take practice and many repetitions while the brain works on creating a new pathway to this more helpful belief.

# References

Afifi, T. O., Taillieu, T., Zamorski, M. A., Turner, S., Cheung, K., & Sareen, J. (2016). Association of child abuse exposure with suicidal ideation, suicide plans, and suicide attempts in military personnel and the general population in Canada. *Psychiatry, 73*(3), 229–238.

Ahman, S., & Stalnacke, B. M. (2008). Post-traumatic stress, depression, and anxiety in patients with injury-related chronic pain: A pilot study. *Neuropsychiatric Disease and Treatment, 4*(6), 1245–1249.

American Psychiatric Association. (1980). *Diagnostic and statistical manual of mental disorders* (3rd ed.). Washington, DC: American Psychiatric Association.

American Psychiatric Association. (2013). *Diagnostic and statistical manual of mental disorders: DSM-5*. Washington, DC: American Psychiatric Association.

American Psychological Association. (2017). *Clinical practice guideline for the treatment of Post-Traumatic Stress Disorder (PTSD) in adults*. Retrieved from www.apa.org/ptsd-guideline/ptsd.pdf

Andrews, B., Brewin, C. R., Philpott, R., & Stewart, L. (2007). Delayed-onset post-traumatic stress disorder: A systematic review of the evidence. *American Journal of Psychiatry, 164*, 1319–1326.

Ashwell, K. (2012). *The brain book: Development, function, disorder, health*. Richmond Hill, Canada: Firefly Books.

Babington, A. (1997). *Shell shock: The history of the changing attitudes to war neurosis*. London: Leo Cooper.

Beck, A. T. (1976). *Cognitive therapy and the emotional disorders*. New York: International Universities Press, Inc.

Beck, A. T., & Steer, R. A. (1993). *Beck anxiety inventory manual*. San Antonio, TX: Psychological Corporation.

Beck, A. T., Steer, R. A., & Brown, G. K. (1996). *Manual for the Beck depression inventory-II*. San Antonio, TX: Psychological Corporation.

Beck, J. S. (2011). *Cognitive behavior therapy: Basics and beyond* (2nd ed.). New York: Guilford Press.

Bercier, M. L., & Maynard, B. R. (2015). Interventions for secondary traumatic stress with mental health workers: A systematic review. *Research on Social Work Practice, 25*(1), 81–89.

Bisson, J. I., Roberts, N. P., Andrew, M., Cooper, R., & Lewis, C. (2013). Psychological therapies for chronic Post-Traumatic Stress Disorder (PTSD) in adults. *Cochrane Database of Systematic Reviews, 12*, Art. No. CD003388.

Black, C. (1982). *It will never happen to me*. Denver: M.A.C. Printing.

Bober, T., & Regehr, C. (2006). Strategies for reducing secondary or vicarious trauma: Do they work? *Brief Treatment and Crisis Intervention, 6*(1), 1–9.

Bogousslavsky, J., & Tatu, L. (2013). French neuropsychiatry in the Great War: Between moral support and electricity. *Journal of the History of the Neurosciences, 22*(2), 144–154.

Brady, J. L., Guy, J. D., Poelstra, P. L., & Brokaw, B. F. (1999). Vicarious traumatization, spirituality, and the treatment of sexual abuse survivors: A national survey of women psychotherapists. *Professional Psychology: Research and Practice, 30*(4), 386–393.

Breuer, J., & Freud, S. (1957). *Studies on hysteria.* New York: Basic Books.

Brewin, C. R., Andrews, B., & Valentine, J. D. (2000). Meta-analysis of risk factors for posttraumatic stress disorder in trauma-exposed adults. *Journal of Consulting and Clinical Psychology, 68*(5), 748–766.

Bride, B. E. (2007). Prevalence of secondary traumatic stress among social workers. *Social Work, 25,* 63–70.

Briere, J. N. (1992). *Child abuse trauma: Theory and treatment of the lasting effects.* Newbury Park, CA: Sage Publications.

Brownlow, J. A., Harb, G. C., & Ross, R. J. (2015). Treatment of sleep disturbances in post-traumatic stress disorder: A review of the literature. *Current Psychiatry Reports, 17*(6), 1–10.

Bruner, V. E., & Woll, P. (2011). The battle within: Understanding the physiology of war-zone stress exposure. *Social Work in Health Care, 50*(1), 19–33.

Burgess, A. W. (1983). Rape trauma syndrome. *Behavioral Sciences and the Law, 1*(3), 97–113.

Burgess, A. W., & Holmstrom, L. L. (1974). Rape trauma syndrome. *American Journal of Psychiatry, 131,* 981–986.

Butler, S. (1992). *Healing skills and gender issues: Unlocking traumatic memories—Keynote address.* Lecture conducted from Western University. London, Canada.

Catherall, D. R. (1995). Coping with secondary traumatic stress: The importance of the therapist's professional peer group. In B. H. Stamm (Ed.), *Secondary traumatic stress: Self-care issues for clinicians, researchers, and educators* (pp. 80–92). Baltimore: The Sidran Press.

Chappell, D., Geis, G., & Fogarty, F. (1974). Forcible rape: Bibliography. *Journal of Criminal Law and Criminology, 65,* 248–263.

Charcot, J. M. (1889). *Lectures on the diseases of the nervous system.* London: New Sydenham Society.

Choi, G. (2011). Secondary traumatic stress of service providers who practice with survivors of family or sexual violence: A national survey of social workers. *Smith College Studies in Social Work, 81,* 101–119.

Collins, S., & Long, A. (2003). Working with the psychological effects of trauma: Consequences for mental health-care workers—A literature review. *Journal of Psychiatric and Mental Health Nursing, 10,* 417–424.

Corneil, W., Beaton, R., Murphy, S., Johnson, C., & Pike, K. (1999). Exposure to traumatic incidents and prevalence of posttraumatic stress symptomatology in urban firefighter in two countries. *Journal of Occupational Health Psychology, 4*(2), 131–141.

Courtois, C. C. (2004). Complex trauma, complex reactions: Assessment and treatment. *Psychotherapy Theory, Research, Practice, Training, 41*(4).

Crocq, M. A., & Crocq, L. (2000). From shell shock and war neurosis to post-traumatic stress disorder: A history of psychotraumatology. *Dialogues in Clinical Neuroscience*, *2*(1), 47–55.

Dansky, B. S., Brewerton, T. D., Kilpatrick, D. G., & O'Neil, P. M. (1997). The National Women's Study: Relationship of victimization and posttraumatic stress disorder to bulimia nervosa. *International Journal of Eating Disorders*, *21*(3), 213–218.

Darensburg, T., Andrew, M. E., Hartley, T. A., Burchfiel, C. M., Fekedulegn, D., & Violanti, J. M. (2006). Gender and age differences in posttraumatic stress disorder and depression among Buffalo police officers. *Traumatology*, *12*(3), 220–228.

Davis, D. M., & Hayes, J. A. (2011). What are the benefits of mindfulness? A practice review of psychotherapy-related research. *Psychotherapy*, *48*(2), 198–208.

De Bellis, M. D. (2010). The neurobiology of childhood neglect. In R. A. Lanius, E. Vermetten, & C. Pain (Eds.), *The impact of early life trauma on health and disease: The hidden epidemic* (pp. 123–132). Cambridge: Cambridge University Press.

DiViva, J., & Zayfert, C. (2010). Treating post-traumatic sleep problems: Applying CBT for insomnia to traumatized populations. *International Society for Traumatic Stress Studies (Producer): Webinar*. Retrieved from http://www.istss.org/education-research/online-learning/recordings.aspx?pid=AMREC10-01

Dobson, K. S., & Dozois, D. J. A. (2010). Historical and philosophical bases of the cognitive-behavioral therapies. In K. S. Dobson (Ed.), *Handbook of cognitive behavioral therapies* (pp. 3–38). New York: Guilford Press.

Felitti, V. J., Anda, R. F., Nordenberg, D., Williamson, D. F., Spitz, A. M., Edwards, V., Koss, M. P., & Marks, J. S. (1998). Relationship of childhood abuse and household dysfunction to many of the leading causes of death in adults. *America Journal of Preventative Medicine*, *14*(4), 245–258.

Figley, C. R. (1995). *Compassion fatigue: Coping with secondary traumatic stress disorder in those who treat the traumatized*. New York: Brunner/Mazel.

Figley, C. R. (2002). Compassion fatigue: Psychotherapists' chronic lack of self care. *Journal of Clinical Psychology*, *58*(11), 1433–1441.

Foa, E. B., & Rothbaum, B. O. (1998). *Treating the trauma of rape*. New York: The Guilford Press.

Ford, J. D. (2010). Complex adult sequelae of early life exposure to psychological trauma. In R. A. Lanius, E. Vermetten, & C. Pain (Eds.), *The impact of early life trauma on health and disease: The hidden epidemic* (pp. 69–76). Cambridge: Cambridge University Press.

Ford, J. D., Courtois, C. A., Steele, K., van der Hart, O., & Nijenhuis, E. R. S. (2005). Treatment of complex posttraumatic self dysregulation. *Journal of Traumatic Stress*, *18*(5), 437–447.

Freud, S. (1954). *The origins of psycho-analysis: Letters to Wilhelm Fliess, drafts and notes: 1887–1902*. New York: Basic Books, Inc.

Freud, S. (1962). The aetiology of hysteria. In *The standard edition of the complete psychological works of Sigmund Freud, volume III (1893–1899): Early psycho-analytic publications* (pp. 187–221). London: Hogarth Press and the Institute of Psycho-Analysis.

Freud, S. (2015). *Beyond the pleasure principle*. New York: Dover Publications.

Galovski, T. E., Wachen, J. S., Chard, K. M., Monson, C. M., & Resick, P. A. (2015). Cognitive processing therapy. In Cloitre, M., & Schnyder, U. (Eds). *Evidence based treatments for trauma-related psychological disorders: A practical guide for clinicians.* Zurich, Switzerland: Springer International Publishing.

Gersons, B. P. R., & Schnyder, U. (2013). Learning from traumatic experiences with brief eclectic psychotherapy for PTSD. *European Journal of Psychotraumatology, 4.* doi:10.3402/ejpt.v4i0.21369

Glenn, R. W. (1987). *Men against fire in Vietnam.* Fort Leavenworth, KS: School of Advanced Military Studies—Army Command and General Staff College.

Goldsmith, R. E., Barlow, M. R., & Freyd, J. J. (2004). Knowing and not knowing about trauma: Implications for therapy. *Psychotherapy: Theory, Research, Practice, Training, 41*(4), 448–463.

Grossman, D. (2009). *On killing: The psychological cost of learning to kill in war and society.* New York: Back Bay Books.

Gupta, M. M. (2013). Review of somatic symptoms in post-traumatic stress disorder. *International Review of Psychiatry, 25*(1), 86–99.

Herman, J. L. (1992). Complex PTSD: A syndrome in survivors of prolonged and repeated trauma. *Journal of Traumatic Stress, 5*(3), 377–391.

Herman, J. L. (1997). *Trauma and recovery: The aftermath of violence—From domestic abuse to political terror.* New York: Basic Books.

Hofmann, S. G., Sawyer, A. T., Witt, A. A., & Oh, D. (2010). The effect of mindfulness-based therapy on anxiety and depression: A meta-analytic review. *Journal of Consulting and Clinical Psychology, 78*(2), 169–183.

Hoge, C. W., Riviere, L. A., Wilk, J. E., Herrell, R. K., & Weathers, F. W. (2014). The prevalence of Post-Traumatic Stress Disorder (PTSD) in US combat soldiers: A head-to-head comparison of DSM-5 versus DSM-IV-TR criteria the with the PTSD checklist. *Psychiatry, 1*(4), 269–277.

Jacobson, C. M., & Gould, M. (2007). The epidemiology and phenomenology of non-suicidal self-injurious behavior among adolescents: A critical review of the literature. *Archives of Suicide Research, 11*(2), 129–147.

Janet, P. (1920). *The major symptoms of hysteria.* New York: The MacMillan Company.

Jones, E., & Wessely, S. (2003). 'Forward psychiatry' in the military: Its origins and effectiveness. *Journal of Traumatic Stress, 16*(4), 411–419.

Jones, L., Hughes, M., & Unterstaller, U. (2001). Post-Traumatic Stress Disorder (PTSD) in victims of domestic violence: A review of the research. *Trauma, Violence, & Abuse, 2*(2), 99–119.

Kadambi, M. A., & Truscott, D. (2004). Vicarious trauma among therapists working with sexual violence, cancer, and general practice. *Canadian Journal of Counselling, 38,* 260–276.

Kang, H. K., Natelson, B. H., Mahan, C. M., Lee, K. Y., & Murphy, F. M. (2003). Post-Traumatic Stress Disorder and Chronic Fatigue Syndrome-like illness among Gulf War veterans: A population-based survey of 30,000 veterans. *American Journal of Epidemiology, 157*(2), 141–148.

Katz, J., & Melzack, R. (2011). The McGill Pain Questionnaire. In D. C. Turk, & R. Melzack (Eds.), *Handbook of pain assessment* (pp. 45–66). New York: Guilford Press.

Kessler, R. C. (2006). Post-traumatic stress disorder: The burden to the individual and society. *Journal of Clinical Psychiatry, 61*(Suppl. 5), 4–12.

Kessler, R. C., Berglund, P., Demler, O., Jin, R., Merikangas, K. R., & Walters, E. E. (2005). Lifetime prevalence and age-of-onset distributions of DSM-IV disorders in the National Comorbidity Survey Replication. *Archives of General Psychiatry*, 62(6), 593–602.

Kessler, R. C., Sonnega, A., Bromet, E., Hughes, M., & Nelson, C. B. (1995). Post-traumatic stress disorder in the National Comorbidity Survey. *Archives of General Psychiatry*, 52, 1048–1060.

Killian, K. D. (2008). Helping till it hurts? A multimethod study of compassion fatigue, burnout, and self-care in clinicians working with trauma survivors. *Traumatology*, 14(2), 32–44.

Klonsky, E. D. (2011). Non-suicidal self-injury in United States adults: Prevalence, sociodemographics, topography, and functions. *Psychological Medicine*, 41(9), 1981–1986.

Koenen, K. C., Roberts, A. L., Stone, D. M., & Dunn, E. C. (2010). The epidemiology of early childhood trauma. In R. A. Lanius, E. Vermetten, & C. Pain (Eds.), *The impact of early life trauma on health and disease: The hidden epidemic* (pp. 13–24). Cambridge: Cambridge University Press.

Kulka, R. A., Schlenger, W. E., Fairbank, J. A., Hough, R. L., Jordan, B. K., Marmar, C. R., Weiss, D. S., & Grady, D. A. (1990). *Trauma and the Vietnam War generation: Report of findings from the National Vietnam Veterans Readjustment Study*. New York: Brunner/Mazel.

Kushner, H. (1983). *When bad things happen to good people*. New York: Avon Books.

Lanius, R. A. (2011, October). Self-reflections, mindfulness, and the traumatized self: Clinical and neurobiological perspectives. Paper presented at *the Brain, mind & body: Trauma, neurobiology and the healing relationship conference*. The University of Western Ontario, London, Canada.

Lanius, R. A., Williamson, P. C., Densmore, M., Boksman, K., Gupta, M. A., Neufeld, R. W. J., Gati, J. S., & Menon, R. S. (2001). Neural correlates of traumatic memories in posttraumatic stress disorder: A functional MRI investigation. *American Journal of Psychiatry*, 158(1), 1920–1922.

Lanius, R. A., Williamson, P. C., Hopper, J., Densmore, M., Boksman, K., Gupta, M. A., Neufeld, R. W. J., Gati, J. S., & Menon, R. S. (2003). Recall of emotional states in posttraumatic stress disorder: An fMRI investigation. *Biological Psychiatry*, 53(3), 204–210.

Leach, M. M., Aten, J. D., Boyer, M. C., Strain, J. D., & Bradshaw, A. K. (2010). Developing therapist self-awareness and knowledge. In M. M. Leach, & J. D. Aten (Eds.), *Culture and the therapeutic process: A guide for mental health professionals* (pp. 13–36). New York: Routledge.

Ledoux, J. (1996). *The emotional brain: The mysterious underpinnings of emotional life*. New York: Simon & Schuster.

Leskin, G. A., Woodward, S. H., Young, H. E., & Sheikh, J. I. (2002). Effects of comorbid diagnoses on sleep disturbance in PTSD. *Journal of Psychiatric Research*, 36(6), 449–452.

Levy-Gigi, E., Szabo, C., Kelemen, O., & Keri, S. (2013). Association among clinical response, hippocampal volume, and *FKBP5* gene expression in individuals with posttraumatic stress disorder receiving Cognitive Behavioral Therapy. *Biological Psychiatry*, 74, 793–800.

Linehan, M. M. (1993). *Cognitive-behavioral treatment of borderline personality disorder*. New York: Guildford Press.

Marshall, S. L. A. (1947). *Men against fire: The problem of battle command in future war.* New York: William Morrow and Co.

Martin, D. J., Garske, J. P., & Davis, M. K. (2000). Relation of the therapeutic alliance with outcome and other variables: A meta-analytic review. *Journal of Consulting and Clinical Psychology, 68*(3), 438–450.

McCann, L., & Pearlman, L. A. (1990). Vicarious traumatization: A framework for understanding the psychological effects of working with victims. *Journal of Traumatic Stress, 3*(1), 131–149.

Melzack, R. (1975). The McGill Pain Questionnaire: Major properties and scoring methods. *Pain, 1*, 277–299.

Melzack, R., Taenzer, P., Feldman, P., & Kinch, R. A. (1981). Labour is still painful after prepared childbirth training. *Canadian Medical Association Journal, 125*(4), 357–363.

Myers, C. (1915). A contribution to the study of shell shock: Being an account of three cases of loss of memory, vision, smell and taste, admitted into the Duchess of Westminster's War Hospital, Le Touquet. *The Lancet, 185*(4772), 316–320.

Nadorff, M. R., Nazem, S., & Fiske, A. (2011). Insomnia symptoms, nightmares, and suicidal ideation in a college student sample. *Sleep, 34*(1), 93–98.

Neylan, T. C., Marmar, C. R., Metzler, T. J., Weiss, D. S., Zatzick, D. F., Delucchi, K. L., Wu, R. M., & Schoenfeld, F. B. (1998). Sleep disturbances in the Vietnam generation: Findings from a nationally representative sample of male Vietnam veterans. *The American Journal of Psychiatry, 155*(7), 929–933.

Nolan, C. R. (2016). Bending without breaking: A narrative review of trauma sensitive yoga for women with PTSD. *Complimentary Therapies in Clinical Practice, 24*, 32–40.

Ogden, P., Minton, K., & Pain, C. (2006). *Trauma and the body: A sensorimotor approach in psychotherapy.* New York: Norton.

Ohayon, M. M., & Shapiro, C. M. (2000). Sleep disturbances and psychiatric disorders associated with posttraumatic stress disorder in the general population. *Comprehensive Psychiatry, 41*(6), 469–478.

Ozer, E. J., Best, S. R., Lipsey, T. I., & Weiss, D. S. (2003). Predictors of posttraumatic stress disorder and symptoms in adults: A meta-analysis. *Psychological Bulletin, 129*(1), 52–73.

Pearlman, L. A., & Mac Ian, P. S. (1993). Vicarious traumatization among trauma therapists: Empirical findings on self-care. *Traumatic Stress Points: News for the International Society for Traumatic Stress Studies, 7*(3), 5.

Pearlman, L. A., & Mac Ian, P. S. (1995). Vicarious traumatization: An empirical study of the effects of trauma work on trauma therapists. *Professional Psychology: Research and Practice, 26*(6), 558–565.

Pearlman, L. A., & Saakvitne, K. W. (1995). Treating therapists with vicarious traumatization and secondary traumatic stress disorders. In C. R. Figley (Ed.), *Compassion fatigue: Coping with secondary traumatic stress disorder in those who treat the traumatized* (pp. 150–177). New York: Brunner/Matzel.

Pietrzak, R. H., Goldstein, R. B., Southwick, S. M., & Grant, B. F. (2011). Prevalence and axis I comorbidity of full and partial posttraumatic stress disorder in the United States: Results from wave 2 of National Epidemiologic Survey on alcohol and related conditions. *Journal of Anxiety Disorders, 25*, 456–465.

Pols, H., & Oak, S. (2007). War and military mental health: The US Psychiatric response in the 20th century. *American Journal of Public Health, 97*(12), 2132–2142.

Porter, S. (2010). Counselling, suicide risk assessment, and retention in a community college (2004–2009). *College Quarterly, 13*(3). Retrieved from http://files.eric.ed.gov/fulltext/EJ930395.pdf

Porter, S. (2011). Personal counselling at an Ontario community college: Client groups, service usage, and retention. *Canadian Journal of Counselling and Psychotherapy, 45*(3), 208–219.

Porter, S. (2016). *Surviving the Valley: Trauma and beyond.* London, Canada: Althouse Press—Western University.

Resnick, H. S., Kilpatrick, D. G., Dansky, B. S., Saunders, B. E., & Best, C. L. (1993). Prevalence of civilian trauma and posttraumatic stress disorder in a representative national sample of women. *Journal of Consulting and Clinical Psychology, 61*(6), 984–991.

Richards, K. C., Campenni, C. E., & Muse-Burke, J. L. (2010). Self-care and well-being in mental health professionals: The mediating effects of self-awareness and mindfulness. *Journal of Mental Health Counseling, 32*(3), 247–264.

Robinson, H. M., Sigman, M. R., & Wilson, J. P. (1997). Duty-related stressors and PTSD symptoms in suburban police officers. *Psychological Reports, 81*(3), 835–845.

Rogers, C. (1961). *On becoming a person.* Boston: Houghton Mifflin Company.

Rothschild, B. (2000). *The body remembers: The psychophysiology of trauma and trauma treatment.* New York: W. W. Norton and Company.

Rothschild, B. (2011). *Trauma essentials: The go-to guide.* New York: W. W. Norton and Company.

Rytwinski, N. K., Scur, M. D., Feeny, N. C., & Youngstrom, E. A. (2013). The co-occurrence of major depressive disorder among individuals with posttraumatic stress disorder: A meta-analysis. *Journal of Traumatic Stress, 26*, 299–309.

Salloum, A., Kondrat, D. C., Johnco, C., & Olson, K. R. (2015). The role of self-care on compassion satisfaction, burnout and secondary trauma among child welfare workers. *Children and Youth Services Review, 49*, 54–61.

Salmon, T. (1917). *The care and treatment of mental diseases and war neuroses ("shell shock") in the British Army.* New York: War Work Committee of the National Committee for Mental Hygiene.

Schauben, L. J., & Frazier, P. A. (1995). Vicarious trauma: The effects on female counselors of working with sexual violence survivors. *Psychology of Women Quarterly, 19*, 49–64.

Schauer, M., Neuner, F., & Elbert, T. (2005). *Narrative exposure therapy: A short term intervention for traumatic stress disorders after war, terror, or torture.* Ashland, OH, US: Hogrefe & Huber.

Scheflin, A. W., & Brown, D. (1996). Repressed memory or amnesia: What the science says. *The Journal of Psychiatry & Law, 24*, 143–188.

Schore, A. N. (2016). *Affect regulation and the origin of the self.* New York: Routledge.

Seigel, D. J. (1999). *The developing mind: How relationships and the brain interact to shape who we are.* New York: Guildford Press.

Shapiro, F. (2001). *Eye Movement Desensitization and Reprocessing (EMDR).* New York: Guilford Press.

Shapiro, S. L., Brown, K. W., & Biegel, G. M. (2007). Teaching self-care to caregivers: Effects of mindfulness-based stress reduction on the mental health of therapists in training. *Training and Education in Professional Psychology, 1*(2), 105–115.

Sheline, Y., Shou, H., Yang, Z., Oathes, D., Satterthwaite, T., Cook, P., Satchell, E., & Shinohara, R. (2017). Cognitive behavioral therapy improves fronto-parietal network neuroplasticity across major depression and PTSD: Evidence from longitudinal fMRI studies of functional connectivity. *Biological Psychiatry*, *81*(Suppl. 10), S143–S144.

Sine, L., & Vogelmann-Sine, S. (1995). Appendix A. In F. Shapiro (Ed.), *Eye movement desensitization and reprocessing: Basic principles, protocols, and procedures*. New York: Guilford Press.

Sjostrom, N., Waern, M., & Hetta, J. (2007). Nightmares and sleep disturbances in relation to suicidality in suicide attempters. *Sleep*, *30*(1), 91–95.

Smid, G. E., Mooren, T. T. M., van der Mast, R. C., Gersons, B. P. R., & Kleber, R. J. (2009). Delayed posttraumatic stress disorder: Systematic review, meta-analysis, and meta-regression analysis of prospective studies. *Journal of Clinical Psychiatry*, *70*(11), 1572–1582. doi:10.4088/JCP.08r04484. Epub 2009, July 14.

Spoormaker, V. I., & Montgomery, P. (2008). Disturbed sleep in post-traumatic stress disorder: Secondary symptom or core feature? *Sleep Medicine Reviews*, *12*, 169–184.

Stalnacke, B. M., & Ostman, A. (2010). Post-traumatic stress in patients with injury-related chronic pain participating in a multimodal pain rehabilitation program. *Neuropsychiatric Disease and Treatment*, *6*, 59–66.

Stein, D. J., Ipser, J. C., Seedat, S., Sager, C., & Amos, T. (2006). Pharmacotherapy for Post-traumatic Stress Disorder (PTSD). *Cochrane Database of Systematic Reviews*, *1*, Art. No. CD002795.

Sterud, T., Ekeberg, Ø., & Hem, E. (2006). Health status in the ambulance services: A systematic review. *BMC Health Services Research*, *6*, 82.

Sue, D. W. (2001). Multidimensional facets of cultural competence. *The Counseling Psychologist*, *29*(6), 790–821.

Sue, D. W., & Sue, D. (1999). *Counseling the culturally different: Theory and practice*. New York: John Wiley & Sons.

Sue, D. W., & Sue, D. (2016). *Counseling the culturally diverse: Theory and practice*. Hoboken, NJ: John Wiley & Sons.

Swank, R. L., & Marchand, W. E. (1946). Combat neuroses: Development of combat exhaustion. *Archives of Neurology and Psychiatry*, *55*, 236–247.

Swinbourne, J., Hunt, C., Abbott, M., Russell, J., St. Clare, T., & Touyz, S. (2012). The comorbidity between eating disorders and anxiety disorders: Prevalence in an eating disorder sample and anxiety disorder sample. *Australian & New Zealand Journal of Psychiatry*, *46*(2), 118–131.

Teicher, M. H., Rabi, K., Sheu, Y., Seraphin, S. B., Andersen, S. L., Anderson, C. M., Choi, J., & Tomoda, A. (2010). Neurobiology of childhood trauma and adversity. In R. A. Lanius, E. Vermetten, & C. Pain (Eds.), *The impact of early life trauma on health and disease: The hidden epidemic* (pp. 112–122). Cambridge: Cambridge University Press.

Tjaden, P. G., & Thoennes, N. (2006). *Extent, nature, and consequences of rape victimization: Findings from the National Violence Against Women Survey*. Retrieved from https://stacks.cdc.gov/view/cdc/21858

Trippany, R. L., Kress, V. E. K., & Wilcoxon, S. A. (2004). Preventing vicarious trauma: What counselors should know when working with trauma survivors. *Journal of Counseling and Development*, *82*, 31–37.

Trippany, R. L., Wilcoxon, S. A., & Satcher, J. F. (2003). Factors influencing vicarious traumatization for therapists of survivors of sexual victimization. *Journal of Traumatic Practice, 2*(1), 47–60.

U.S. Department of Veterans Affairs. (2017, May 31). *History of PTSD in veterans: Civil War to DSM-5.* Retrieved from www.ptsd.va.gov/public/ptsd-overview/basics/history-of-ptsd-vets.asp

van der Kolk, B. A. (1994). The body keeps the score: Memory and the evolving psychobiology of posttraumatic stress. *Harvard Review of Psychiatry, 1*(5), 253–265.

van der Kolk, B. A. (2002). The assessment and treatment of complex PTSD. In R. Yehuda (Ed.), *Treating trauma survivors with PTSD.* (pp. 127-156). Washington, DC: American Psychiatric Press.

van der Kolk, B. A. (2014). *The body keeps the score:Brain, mind, and body in the healing of trauma.* New York, NY: Viking Penguin.

van der Kolk, B. A., & Fisler, R. (1995). Dissociation and the fragmentary nature of traumatic neurosis: Overview and exploratory study. *Journal of Traumatic Stress, 8*(4), 505–525.

van der Kolk, B. A., Spinazzola, J., Blaustein, M. E., Hopper, J. W., Hopper, E. K., Korn, D. L., & Simpson, W. B. (2007). A randomized clinical trial of Eye Movement Desensitization and Reprocessing (EMDR), fluoxetine, and pill placebo in the treatment of posttraumatic stress disorder: Treatment effects and long-term maintenance. *Journal of Clinical Psychiatry, 68*(1), 37.

Walls, J. (2005). *The glass castle: A memoir.* New York: Scribner.

Weierich, M. R., & Nock, M. K. (2008). Post-traumatic stress symptoms mediate the relation between childhood sexual abuse and nonsuicidal self-injury. *Journal of Consulting and Clinical Psychology, 76*(1), 39–44.

Yealland, L. R. (1918). *Hysterical disorders of warfare.* London: MacMillan and Co.

# Index

Note: Page numbers in *italic* indicate a figure on the corresponding page

Printed in Great Britain
by Amazon

39674404R00126